MW00399216

"A brave and searching book for the inte........ ......... ...... .... .. ... ... ... reflection, understanding, and validation."

—Rachel Morris, counselor, sex psychotherapist to *Cosmopolitan* U.K.

"*After His Affair* isn't about him; it's about her—her journey from infidelity to wholeness. The women's stories are a powerful testimony to the anguish women experience in the wake of infidelity, but also to the inner strength and the growth that can result. The stories and exercises provide tools for women to use through a dark period and offer hope that there truly is light at the end of the journey."

—Marilyn Milos, Founder and Director of *NOCIRC*

"A practical and liberating spiritual perspective that sees through the subtle cultural and psychological justifications for infidelity. Callander reframes the experience of infidelity as a critical, even if unwelcome, turning point in a woman's life through which she can awaken to her own strength and wholeness."

—Shoshana Alexander, co-author of *Awakening Joy: Ten Steps to Happiness*

"*After His Affair* gives voice to the trauma of women struggling to survive infidelity. This brave book will help validate and support a woman on this terribly challenging journey."

—Janis Abrahms Spring, Ph.D., author of *After the Affair: Healing the Pain and Rebuilding Trust When a Partner Has Been Unfaithful*

"Meryn Callander, like a wise and compassionate friend, is a respectful guide through the ordeal of personal and collective betrayal. The women's stories are varied and compelling. Even as an experienced relationship counselor, I found this book eye-opening and provocative. I am recommending this to my clients—women and men."

—Joy J. Holloway, Ph.D., Transpersonal Psychological Counselor

"When met with the trauma of an affair, it is important to surround oneself with good, wise company. This book offers that company—not only from its author, but also from a wise, honest and vulnerable circle of women within its pages... providing the validation, truthfulness and practical advice necessary for healing and transformation."

—Kelly Peta Wendorf, CEO, The Institute of the Southwest, author, teacher

"*After His Affair* gives sorely needed direction, hope, and support for the hard work of recovery. The author takes you by the hand, sits next to you and tells you how it is—with understanding, support, and validation. She lays a foundation for readers—those recently betrayed and those who may, years later, carry remnants of the betrayal—to rebuild themselves and then their lives. There is potential for wholeness and healing after an affair. This book facilitates that."

—Elly Taylor, relationship counselor and author of *Becoming Us*

"*After His Affair* addresses an extremely important and often neglected issue—the legacy left the children in the wake of infidelity. The majority of adults involved in unfaithful relationships had unfaithful parents. Traumatized as children, they buried the pain. Forming healthy adult relationships requires addressing this childhood trauma. And, better still, not passing it on to the children."

—Dennis Ortman, Ph.D., author of *Cheating Parents: Recovering from Parental Infidelity*

"In this courageously written book, Callander exposes the cultural, patriarchal ignorance that legitimizes, even romanticizes, infidelity—while inspiring women who have been betrayed to heal, emerging stronger and more whole than ever before."

—Kristi Cowles, *Singing Wolf Productions*

"Callander offers an authentic voice and refreshing take on this taboo subject. She is a shining example of how speaking one's truth is not only good for a woman's soul, but also so very needed for us all."

—Beth Martens, Archetype and Business Coach, *Authentic Voice*

"Knowledge and understanding are important facets of any recovery, and this book brings so much information to the women who hold this book in their hands. A truly difficult time becomes more manageable."

—E. Fuhr, www.allbooksreviewint.com

"Callander is a superb communicator and a tireless advocate for authentic relationships. This is a profound and inspiring work that took courage to tell the whole story."

—Meg Jordan, Ph.D., RN, Integrative Health Studies, California Institute of Integral Studies

"There are many books on how to find your ideal mate and how to help a marriage in trouble, but few address the devastation to women and children when a man is unfaithful. This is an exceptional book that I highly recommend for both women and men. Callander combines in-depth stories with good science to give readers tools to prevent an affair as well as deal with its aftermath. Psychotherapists, marriage and family counselors, and other health-care professionals will also find *After His Affair* an extremely valuable resource."

—Jed Diamond, PhD, author of *Stress Relief for Men* and *Surviving Male Menopause*

ISBN: 978-0-9625882-4-2

Cover design and layout: Siena Ariel Callander
Cover photo: Shira Tamir
Typesetting, interior design and layout: Siena Ariel Callander

Akasha Publications
PO Box 8422
Asheville, NC 28814
United States

www.afterhisaffairbook.com

Library of Congress Control Number: 2014919148

## DEDICATION

To my daughter, Siena Tierra Ariel

And to you, the reader.

*May all beings be well,*

*May all beings be happy,*

*May all beings be at peace with themselves and their world.*

"You can search throughout the entire universe for someone who is more deserving of your love and affection than you are yourself, and that person is not to be found anywhere. You yourself, as much as anybody in the entire universe deserve your love and affection."

—Buddha

# Contents

# Chapter Synopsis

## Chapter 1: *Healing a Broken Heart*

This book is written for the woman who senses, intuits, in some way instinctively knows that she will not only survive this nightmare, she will emerge to shine. And for the woman who, reading this now, resonates with this as the truth that she, too, will claim for herself. However fleeting that impulse, it is there. She says, from the very depths of her being, in face of the anguish that threatens to consume her, *"Yes, I will."* The intention is set ... but first, how does a woman even *survive* a broken heart? It's difficult to value and to allow our grieving, our anger, our rage, the time and space to move us into a deeper life. How can we make good of these experiences of infidelity, in our individual lives?

## Chapter 2: *The Nature of Infidelity*

A window into the depth and breadth of the devastation and trauma left in the wake of infidelity, that reaches far beyond the woman who has been betrayed, and her family.

Love and marriage alone do not protect anyone against temptation. The workplace and internet are the fastest growing danger zones of attraction *and* opportunity for affairs. After an affair, couples who choose to may rebuild a relationship that grows in depth, honesty, and intimacy. Regardless, there is always the unwanted, uninvited potential for reclaiming a more authentic self.

## Chapter 3: *Coming Home to Ourselves*

This book is not *just* about how women are betrayed—it's about how we betray ourselves. A woman betrays herself every time she denies the wisdom of her instincts and intuitions, says *"yes"* when she really wants to say *"no."* In doing so, she forfeits her inner authority and personal power. The losses, shame, and anger reach an all-time high at infidelity, carrying many a woman to acclaim *Enough, no more.* Becoming aware of the inner voices that perpetuate a reality that says she is "not enough," fundamentally flawed, unworthy of love, a woman sows the seeds for the journey home to herself.

## Chapter 4: *In the Aftermath of Infidelity—The First Year*

While every woman's experience will differ according to a whole *range* of factors, there is always the shock, the grief, the shame, the anger ... the disbelief, the shattered heart. There are the friends avoiding her, fantasies of wishing her partner dead and the other woman in hell, suicidal thoughts—all normal responses to his infidelity. Knowing this does not diminish the raw intensity of the emotions, but it may relieve a woman of the fear she is going crazy.

## Chapter 5: *The Early Years and the Adults We Become*

Many of us, often unconsciously, carry from childhood the belief that we are in some way unworthy of love. We learned as children that betrayal is the name of the game. By succumbing to the demands of others as to who we "should" be and what we "should" do, we betray ourselves. However, we are not victims of the past, and we are not irreparably damaged.

## Chapter 6: *Women Betrayed—The Beliefs and Illusions that Blind Us*

The stories of women who have been betrayed reveal the myriad ways that the absence of self-love and the subsequent self-betraying patterns appear in a woman's life. They blind her, placing her in a position to be betrayed. Her ruthless self-judgment, not knowing what she wants or needs, her inability to set boundaries, and her looking to a man for security and fulfillment are epidemic among women.

## Chapter 7: *Unraveling the Patterns of Self-Betrayal*

This chapter is replete with practices and processes that are designed to engage a woman in the process of identifying and changing any self-betraying patterns, healing her broken heart, and reclaiming her inner authority and personal power. Grounding, self-inquiry, and self-compassion are essential elements in retrieving those lost instincts and intuitions that are hers to guide, inform, and protect her.

## Chapter 8: *Choosing to Stay*

These stories of couples that chose to renew their marriages have their wisdom to share with each of us, regardless of whether we left, stayed, or are uncertain. The first step is restoring trust. This requires establishing safety and cultivating goodwill. Rebuilding a relationship demands huge reserves of courage, resolve, and patience—and can culminate in a marriage that is richer, deeper, and more mature than before.

## Chapter 9: *The Other Woman—Sluts, Bitches, Whores!*

A woman who is betrayed feels deeply violated—firstly by her husband, but also by the Other Woman. Her shock at the depth of venom she feels towards the Other Woman intensifies her feelings of shame and bewilderment. Anger itself is not good or bad—the body needs to eliminate it, not suppress it. Initially, a woman may use it to empower herself. She must be careful, though, or it can hurt her—badly.

## Chapter 10: *Projections—What We Resist, Persists*

As long as a woman projects her anger onto *him* or onto the Other Woman, she disempowers herself. While the intensity of her hostility and desire for retaliation is understandable, as long as she carries these feelings and remains at the effect of these emotions, she perpetuates her own suffering. Recognizing how and why these same feelings live in her, she can choose to use them wisely.

## Chapter 11: *Forgiveness—As the Wound of Infidelity Heals*

To forgive may seem an impossible ideal as a woman grapples with her anguish, fear, rage … Allowing herself to be admonished or judged by others for not forgiving exacerbates her sense of betrayal and alienation. Encouraging forgiveness is to be out of touch with the reality of the depth of her hurt and pain. In time, a woman may discover a need to forgive, for her own sake.

## Chapter 12: *Bad Girls—Looking for Love In All the Wrong Places*

Of course, there are *many* bad girls, and here we see they are not *all* bad. To a degree, rising from the ashes requires an understanding of the "Other Woman"—who she is, why she did what she did. The journey, for these women, is not unlike that of the women they betrayed. Although understanding is one thing, forgiveness another—entirely.

## Chapter 13: *The Drug that Masquerades as Love*

Once tasted, the passion of forbidden love—like any powerful drug—is difficult to resist. Sexual impulse is the animal drive in humankind, the deep primal longing that serves to perpetuate the species. But in a committed relationship, satisfying that longing with someone outside of the relationship equals infidelity.

## Chapter 14: *Once Friends—Colluding in Our Silence*

A woman may be deeply saddened, conflicted, and confounded to find friends avoiding her; wanting to remain "neutral," and stay friends with both; actively siding with or colluding with the unfaithful partner; not speaking out in the face of his unfaithfulness. She may feel abandoned not only by her partner, but also by others she thought to be her friends.

## Chapter 15: *Weathering the Tsunami*

Having, somehow, survived that initial shock, the reverberations of the devastation of infidelity continue to pour and ripple through a woman's life. Will it never end? She does what she needs to do to get through each day—and to cultivate a sense of hope and possibility for the future. Women share how they supported themselves in weathering these years.

## Chapter 16: *Reaching Out for Help—The Gift of Empathy*

The tendency can be to isolate yourself ... to believe you are a terrible person, an embarrassment, a wrathful bitch, a failure—a disaster, really—as a human being. Here, we see the importance of reaching out for support, and the strength found in the company of women who accept you as you are and communicate through their empathy, *"I see you, I love you, and you are not alone."*

## Chapter 17: *Children of Infidelity—How They Hurt, and How They Heal*

Children feel betrayed when a parent cheats on their spouse. Regardless of age, they react with intense feelings of anger, anxiety, guilt, shame, sadness and confusion. They are left with a host of psychological issues that—unresolved—can plague them throughout their life. Understanding the emotional impact of their parent's betrayal is an important part of the healing process.

## Chapter 18: *Fidelity—A Lie, a Bear Trap, or Whole-Hearted Commitment?*

Fidelity is a bear trap when a woman naïvely, unconsciously, accepts the collective assumptions and understanding of what it means. Even people in happy marriages have affairs. The assumption that love alone will protect a marriage has led to many an infidelity. What are the danger signs? How can a woman protect her marriage, and why bother?

## Chapter 19: *Coming Apart, with Care and Compassion*

Here we learn from the stories of couples that having chosen to end their relationship, cleanly and caringly negotiate a coming apart. Knowing that *"someone had done that, and it could be done,"* carries the potential to open doors—and hearts—to kinder ways of ending a relationship that has run its course.

## Chapter 20: *It All Starts Right Now*

Surely respect, empathy, and compassion for others are not only fundamental principles that make a society work, but also the expression of an awareness of our interdependence? At what cost do we trivialize, dismiss, or deny the repercussions of betrayal? Are we, through this unrelenting epidemic of infidelity, being invited to choose a higher ground—not simply as a moral stand but an immanently practical one?

# Why I Wrote This Book

I was one of the many women who didn't have a clue. Then, one day, it seemed my world turned upside down. Now, having spoken with many women who have been betrayed—and women who have, themselves, betrayed—the devastation is driven home to me.

I write as a woman who has both betrayed, and been betrayed. I write through the voices of other women, and my reflections on their experiences. I write as the stories are told—in an intimate and conversational, rather than clinical or psychological, way.

I am deeply concerned that infidelity has become an accepted way to exit or to challenge a committed relationship, or simply to *"get a bit on the side."* I am concerned at the level of denial about the trauma that is induced. I am concerned that every act of infidelity normalizes and legitimizes another. The repercussions of infidelity don't "go away" with the ending of the affair or the breaking up of the marriage, and extend way, way beyond the family itself.

Polls show that around 85% of people say infidelity is wrong. More than 90% of married individuals do not approve of extramarital sex, and yet almost half admit to having had an affair. What drives this dichotomy between what we say we should do and what we do?

Virtually every one of us has been, or will be, in some way touched by this epidemic. I began to wonder, as supposedly aware, passionate, and compassionate women, how can we make good of these experiences of infidelity in our individual lives? How might we avoid—or heal from—the trauma of infidelity? These questions pressed in on me, and this book was born.

# CHAPTER 1

## *Healing a Broken Heart*

This book is written for the woman who senses, intuits, or in some way instinctively knows, often in the near immediate aftermath of the discovery of her partner's infidelity, that she will not only survive this nightmare—she will emerge to shine. And for the woman who, reading this now, resonates with this as the truth that she, too, will claim for herself. However fleeting that intuition, that instinct, it is there. She says, from the very depths of her being, in face of the anguish that threatens to consume her, *Yes, I will.* The intention is set, the seeds are planted.

Over the coming months and even years, this moment of certainty will disappear, be buried under mountains of tears—tears of grief, of rage, of shame, of disappointment, of despair. The life-force of this certainty that *"I will"* will on occasion emerge as a glimmer of hope or possibility on the horizon of her awareness, only to disappear again. If a woman even recalls those early moments of her *knowing* and *willing* this, she will find herself alone at sea for days, weeks, and months at a time, unable to retrieve any access to that possibility.

Is this a negative perspective? The stance of a victim? An affirming of the horrors of infidelity? No. It is a statement of truth. The way it is for a woman who refuses to just "forgive and forget." Who refuses to be betrayed or cast aside without protest. Who has the courage to bare her face and her heart to the reality of her partner's infidelity. Who will now accept and tolerate nothing but the truth.

No more disrespect. No more justifications and rationalizations. No more lies. No more deceit. *Enough. No more.*

Will she falter? Will she hide? Will she feel she can't go on? Of course she will. She is human. That is what is so real about her and what is so beautiful about her, even in her grief, and in her rage.

Being able to say one is a survivor of infidelity is an accomplishment. Yet there comes a time to move from simply surviving, to healing her broken heart. There is a danger in calling herself by names she has assigned herself or been assigned by others, names taken on during this terrible time of her life—victim, poor thing, frigid wife, wrathful bitch. There comes a time when these names and mindsets have run their course. A time when it dawns on her that the worst is over; she has survived.

Slowly, gradually, and on occasion with a rush, windows to a new life begin to open, here and there. More and more often, she is surprised to find gratitude seeping into her body. More and more she glimpses, she is touched by, she is gifted with spontaneous moments of expansive possibility, of happiness, even of joy.

However, let's look first at how a woman can even survive a broken heart.

## Surviving a Broken Heart

Some women will build a protective wall around their heart to ensure they will never be vulnerable to that much pain again. However, when the heart is armored, it is difficult if not impossible for love to get in *or* out. Sadly, we can see these women everywhere. They may appear strong and always in command, or stoic—seemingly untouched by their own or another's feelings or emotions. Shut off to the experience of their feelings and emotions, they numb not only their receptivity to pain, but also to pleasure. Others are more obviously bitter; cold; isolated behind that wall. These women are usually incapable of forming intimate relationships.

Many women, having learned that good girls don't do it and nice girls don't even think about it, find themselves unable to express their anger—or even to feel it. Many fear losing their attractiveness, believing anger "isn't pretty." Others believe it is not "spiritual" to be angry—to be incensed—and so don't allow themselves to express or experience the depth of the devastation of the infidelity. Denied this expression, the psyche has no choice but to relegate it to the shadows. Unseen, unacknowledged, it does not go away—it festers, eating away at a woman's life-force.

Other women, heart broken, ripped apart, somehow emerge from this nightmare more awake and aware than ever before. Staying present to the fullness of the unwanted and uninvited emotions coursing through them, befriending the depths of their human experience, they emerge with hearts more tender, wise, and compassionate—more open to the world around them. These are the women who return to life with a new knowing.

It's difficult, in this culture, to value and to allow our grieving, our anger, and our rage the time and space and to move us into a deeper relationship with our authentic self. We're supposed to just "get over it," get back to work—work supposedly being the antidote to those emotions that are screaming to be heard and tended to. We have learned the anger is "not nice," causes trouble, and that grieving is a bummer: *"What, you're not over that yet?"*

## An Unwanted, Uninvited Entreaty

If a woman is not yet "over it," she begins to think that perhaps there is something wrong with her. Often—as we will see—her friends may be uncomfortable with the rawness and intensity of her heartbreak and anguish. They may simply not know how to respond, or they may feel confronted by their own unresolved feelings from past infidelities. Yet, it is natural and healthy for a woman to feel anger when violated, and to grieve the loss of what she cares deeply about.

In every feeling that arises in a woman in the aftermath of infidelity, there are the seeds of insight and of new knowledge. What would it mean if each of these feelings was to be welcomed as a messenger, a teacher, a gift—not as something to be suppressed or controlled, but something to learn from, something to be experienced so that a woman may return to life with a new knowing?

What if a woman was to recognize this experience as an unwanted, uninvited entreaty to reclaim her inner authority, authentic presence, and personal power?

## Grasping the Reality of Infidelity

In the shock and bewilderment of her partner's unfaithfulness, a woman will feel her whole world has been turned upside down. It is as if she has found herself stranded on a desolate island wondering, *How did I get here?* The shock, disorientation, confusion, self-judgment and fear diminish any clarity of mind. The healing of her heart, the reclaiming of her life, and her not falling prey to the same nightmare again requires an understanding of the nature of the territory she stands on, and what happened to leave her stranded here.

My hope is that as a woman turns the pages of this book she will find herself grasping not only the reality of the circumstances in which she finds herself, but also what brought her to this place, and what will bring her home to herself.

Ultimately, this is the journey through infidelity, and to the extent a woman lives into and grasps the fullness of her predicament, she will emerge from the ashes stronger, wiser, and with a new knowing. How each woman will come to that, is her own story. There is no map. Every woman's path is her own to walk. However, as we will see, the threads of the same fabric weave in and out of every woman's journey.

In the stories told here, women will recognize the threads, the markers, and the wake up calls. They will recognize that while each of us must walk this path alone, we need not do so without the empathy, the encouragement, and the love of others who are travelling, or have travelled, this terrain—or those who having lived life long and deep and can meet us there, with wisdom and compassion.

As with a plant, a seed that becomes a sprout that becomes a magnificent blossoming rose bush that we gaze on in wonder to exclaim, *What a magnificent rose* ... the rose that we see in all its fullness today began its life in the depths of the underworld, in the dark, as a seed. The magnificence of the rose we see today is dependent on the soil in which it grew and the life-giving energies of the rains and the sun that nourished and tended it.

Too often, too many a woman has poured those life giving energies onto others—at the expense of denying herself that which will allow her to blossom, to flourish and to prosper. Why? This is for every woman to answer, herself. The answer to this question is one that every woman who does not merely survive but who emerges from the depths of infidelity to stand in her own authentic presence, will discover in her own way, and at her own pace.

Is this call to attend to her own needs another level of narcissism—that very quality that is central to some degree in every act of infidelity? No, for as a woman she will always, when being true to herself, recognize her place in the larger web of life, and so her choices will be made in the light of this awareness. *Do as you will, and harm none.*

The stories shared in this book are in some way every woman's stories. Hard earned stories of women pulling themselves up from the depths of their shame, their grief, their bewilderment, their rage; to step up and out to meet the call to be true to their own inner authority. In doing so, at some point every woman on this journey will be required to cultivate the *Warrior Woman* or *Sacred Warrior*.

> *"The 'Sacred Warrior' is the personification of Courage within a [person] that allows them to keep their heart open in hell; the hell of their own frustration, confusion, fear, discouragement, anger, resentment ..."*
>
> —Chogyam Trungpa, *The Sacred Path of the Warrior*

# The Warrior Woman

As a Warrior, a woman is strong, grounded, centered. Her heart is open—for hers is the heart of a woman who knows and recognizes her interdependence with all creation in the great web of life. She stands in a place of wisdom, strength, and equanimity. She knows in every fiber of her being when enough is enough. She knows how to say *Enough, no more* in a way that no one questions it. When needed, she summons the fierceness of the Warrior, rather than collapsing into grief or projecting her rage onto another. Standing as a Warrior is not about overriding and dismissing the grief, nor is it about lashing out or in some way reacting destructively to the rage. The anguish, the broken heart, even the rage can still be there, but she directs her will and wields her sword from a strong, central self—balanced and whole.

It's only when a woman hits the point of *Enough, no more* that she accesses the fierceness, the strength, and the determination to begin to cultivate the Warrior. Whatever it is that gets a woman to that place—be it rage, disgust, frustration—she needs to use it. Whenever she feels herself falling into disempowering and debilitating thoughts or feelings, she calls herself back to the stance of the Warrior: *I will not do this to myself.* When she feels she cannot access that Warrior energy, she calls in compassion for herself. Even bringing herself to a place of compassion requires an element of fierceness—the fierceness not to give in to the disempowering patterns: *STOP. I will not go there.*

When a woman can catch herself on the precipice, before she collapses into the grip of debilitating and disempowering emotions, she can take a full and deep breath from the depths of her being, and call *STOP. No more.* She calls herself back and drawing on her breath, her will and her imagination, she feels the earth under her feet and centers her attention in her body. She breathes, further activating that quality of fierceness, and in that moment names where she is: *Look where I am, look where I went again, look what I'm doing to myself.* She thanks herself for seeing the dynamic so clearly, and from that point of clarity and compassion she is able to discern what is the right action, in this moment.

To catch herself on the precipice or to pull herself back can be very difficult when in the depths of the aftermath of infidelity. It's such a horrible, horrendous time. The storyline that carries all her greatest fears is activated, in all likelihood like never before. The depth and intensity of the emotions streaming through her can be overwhelming. It's not easy. It can feel as if she is diffusing a nuclear power plant in her body. Cultivating the Warrior Woman requires she remind herself again and again to take one breath at a time, one moment at a time, one step at a time. It requires her being present to the now, rather than to whether or not there is "progress." She sets her heart and mind on the magnetism of her intention and does what she needs to do moment-to-moment, day-to-day, until it is accomplished. She may need to call herself back one thousand times a day. But each time that she calls herself back, each time that she stands in that place of Warrior, the cracks in her story that run on disempowerment deepen, and the newer, empowering stories and possibilities find their way in.

Each time she calls herself back into the body, into the Warrior stance, she ignites a different vibrational frequency that will carry her from the insights and understanding of the conceptual mind, and the fleeting experiences of empowerment, into a cellular change at the level of being as she steps into her own inner authority and personal power.

The triumphant Warrior Woman stands in the independent thought and action of the virgin archetype, a woman who is complete in herself. She is not a virgin to be alone but to be with others without entanglement. She represents a "being with" that fosters intimacy and mutual creativity that is sourced in soul and spirit rather than in instinct and passions—not that the latter do not have a place. When in a relationship with another, she relates from a position of strength and independence while recognizing her interdependence with all within the circle of life. *Do what you will and harm none.*


## A World Turned Upside Down

I had lived, in my head, in a world where virtually no one I knew had had an affair. Then, one day, it seemed my world turned upside down and inside out. I found myself hearing stories from women who had been betrayed—or had betrayed another! I found that virtually all of my dearest women friends had, at some time in their adult life, been on either side—or both sides—of infidelity. While years, even decades, stretched between many of them and that experience, every one of them spoke of the betrayal with an intensity and passion that belied the passage of time.

Now, having spoken with many women in the immediate aftermath of the discovery of infidelity, the devastation is driven home to me. The shock strikes, even shatters, the very core of one's being. We have sympathy for women who have lost their partner in a fatal accident, or in war—at least there can be some honor found in this. At least the loved one can live on as the loved one in the heart and memories of the woman who is left alone, but in infidelity—there is no honor.

Most women find themselves astounded that this is happening *"to me!"* Astounded at how devastating it is that their partner has betrayed them.

*"The anguish was beyond words. I don't think this battered heart could endure it again." "I didn't know it was possible to be alive and to feel so much pain."* How can it hurt so much, when it happens every day?

Women find themselves dreading going to work, going shopping, or to school to pick up their children—they hear, or imagine they hear, everyone talking about them. They find friends avoiding them, "unfriending" them on Facebook, actively siding with or colluding with the unfaithful partner. They are confounded as they find themselves wishing the unfaithful partner and his lover dead, rotting in hell. They may be bewildered or consumed by wrath as to how the "other woman" could do this. And they wonder—what do I say to the children? What does this mean for the children?

## A Wake Up Call

I am deeply concerned that infidelity has become, to many, an accepted way to exit or to challenge a committed relationship, or simply to *"get a bit on the side."* I am concerned at the level of denial about the trauma that is induced and the consequences of the suppression of that trauma. I am concerned that every act of infidelity normalizes and legitimizes another. I am concerned about the reverberations of these betrayals on our children, our families, our communities—and the greater feminine collective. I now understand how a partner's having an affair is like their *"dropping a nuclear bomb on the family."* The repercussions run deep, don't go away with the ending of the affair or the dissolution of the marriage, and spread way beyond the immediate family.

### LINDA:

*Recently, I asked my sister and cousin about their affairs, both had had them. And both said it was insanity born of unhappy marriages. I told them I felt left out, that I am in a minority of people who haven't had an affair. In fact, I feel weird about it, like there is something wrong with me that I am not out having a torrid love affair with hot sex that is all so great it would be worth the piles of bodies I leave in my wake, including my child's, right? That's the definition of affair, right? You have a blast while the bodies pile up.*

I was one of the many women who don't have a clue about "what's wrong" or "what's the big deal" about women betraying other women, and taking license consciously or unconsciously to extend their sexual energy out in the seduction of another woman's partner. I got my first hint of this, my first wake up call, from a colleague speaking of the stand she had taken with a man, Mark, who had recently betrayed his partner.

**GRACE:**

*I regret that my relationship with Mark must change if I am to walk my talk. No malice—but that's the way it is. He is no longer welcome here as a houseguest. As for the Sisterhood's loyalty for their kind—the other woman scenario—I think there is a lot of work to be done on conscious action and consequences.*

I began to wonder, as supposedly aware, awake, passionate and compassionate women, what are we being called to wake up to, to reclaim? And where and how do we begin? I recalled the slogan of my early days in feminist spirituality, that *"the personal is the political."*

> *"We do not realize that we suffer history in our individual lives, and that culture change does not just happen outside, in the streets or to other people, but takes place in our own experience and at considerable personal cost."*
>
> —David Tacey

And I wondered how can we, as women, make good of these experiences of infidelity in our individual lives?

## Women Betrayed

There are many books and a growing number of online websites supporting couples in healing from the experience of infidelity. This book is not focused on addressing the couple or on a man's experience of infidelity. It is focused on the woman, her experiences, and the healing and empowering potentials inherent in those experiences. While primarily written for the woman who has been betrayed, an element of her healing her broken heart and coming home to herself will be her having some understanding of the "other woman," and also of those women who colluded in the infidelity—actively or through their silence. I also look at the wider repercussions of infidelity on our families, our children, our communities, and the Sisterhood.

This book is not steeped in research or in clinical experience. It is suffused with the lived experiences of women, and reflections on their experiences. Of course, absolutely, it is not only men who are unfaithful to their wives or partners; and of course men too are the recipients of infidelity, as are partners in homosexual relationships—the pendulum swings both ways. Here, however, I focus exclusively on women in heterosexual relationships. My hope is that in these stories and reflections, a woman will recognize aspects of her own patterns—her own story. That she will recognize where she might be caught, where she may fall by the way, and how she might avoid—or heal from—the trauma of infidelity. My hope is that she may, through it all, come into a deeper, richer, and more rewarding relationship with herself—and so inevitably with those around her.

Whether as a woman who has been betrayed, as sister or friend to a woman betrayed, as daughter or mother of a woman betrayed, or as a woman who herself has betrayed a sister through an illicit sexually partnering, virtually every one of us has been, or will be, in some way touched by this epidemic.

Modern science verifies what the ancient traditions have always known: that in both tangible and mysterious ways, we are all interconnected. Our every word, thought, action, reverberates throughout the web of life.

It is not my intention in writing to place blame or guilt; for neither will serve us. However, as long as we do not allow ourselves to see and acknowledge our own role and responsibility, whether we are the harmed, the harmer, or an observer, we will remain not only victims but perpetrators of the trauma of infidelity.

Coming home to ourselves is in many ways a call to those who choose, those who dare, to recognize and honor the implications and reverberations of these connections with respect, most directly, to those we purport to love—or have loved. To recognize that we are not alone in this, and that we need each other. To search for the gifts, the gold, the wisdom to be found in all that has been uninvited, unwanted …

And to love, again.

> *"I am not what happened to me. I am what I choose to become."*
> —Carl Jung

# CHAPTER 2

## *The Nature of Infidelity*

*"If there were a Richter scale for emotional earthquakes, the discovery of an affair would register at the outermost end of the dial. Some people manage to recover quickly; the majority however, feel as if they have been hit by a seismic event in a part of the country where there has never been one before. They are not prepared for the tremor that knocks them off their feet and destroys their home life."*

—Shirley P. Glass, Ph.D., *Not "Just Friends:" Protecting Your Relationship from Infidelity and Healing from the Trauma of Betrayal*

In emerging from the ashes of infidelity stronger, wiser, and with a new knowing, I believe it is important a woman have some understanding of the depth and breadth of the impact of infidelity on women and their families today, as revealed through the psychological literature and statistics. This is the emphasis of this chapter, and to a degree the next, which set a larger context in which you can hold the voices of the women in the chapters that follow.

Many people today contend that monogamy or marital fidelity is a thing of the past. It is true that there are a number of seemingly reasonable justifications for infidelity: People live longer, and it can be unrealistic to expect married couples to remain faithful throughout their lives. Both men and women today engage in an incredible range of varied experiences outside the home, and have more opportunity to interact with new people—making infidelity more inevitable. Some people will claim that our culture's liberalized sexual mores make marriage anachronistic. Today's workplace and the internet are the fastest growing danger zones of attraction *and* opportunity for affairs. Anyone can anonymously access sexual chat rooms, online dating, and porn websites. The list of intimate and sexual activities on the borderline of infidelity is endless.

Is monogamy, then, a thing of past? A 2013 Gallup Poll highlighted America's steady, overwhelming, and growing disapproval of married men and women having an affair, with more than 90% saying they believe infidelity to be morally unacceptable. This percentage has steadily grown over the last four decades.

Clearly, despite all of their exposure to infidelity, Americans are becoming increasingly conservative about marital transgressions. Surveys indicate that children still expect fidelity and loyalty between their parents, and adult children whose parents cheated still want monogamous relationships themselves. Like 93% of the American public, they believe marital fidelity is the most important element in a successful marriage.

Yet many Americans cheat. Although numbers on adultery are notoriously difficult to pin down, primarily because people lie to researchers, conservative estimates indicate that 30 to 60% of all married individuals in the U.S. will be unfaithful at some point in their marriage. The percentage is higher for men than women, although the percentage of women is increasing.

Conflicting messages and values from the media make dealing with infidelity very perplexing. For instance, the reporting of Tiger Woods' multiple affairs lost him contracts with some corporate sponsors, but at the same time, his mistresses appeared on the front cover of almost every celebrity and current affairs magazine.

Different cultures approach infidelity differently. In Russia, for instance, therapists sometimes suggest extramarital relationships as a path to happiness. In Japan, if a man pays for sex, it is usually not considered an affair. As Pamela Druckerman writes in *Lust in Translation*, *"Societies have their own rules on who can cheat, and for what reason. Everyone seems to know the rules, even if they don't follow them."*

While it may be true that everyone seems to know the rules, it is equally true that popular notions about infidelity are clouded by myths.


## Facts and Assumptions About Infidelity

Shirley P. Glass, Ph.D., states that just because infidelity is increasingly common, doesn't mean most people understand it. Much of the conventional wisdom and advice about what causes affairs, how to "affair proof" a marriage and how to repair relationships after infidelity, is misguided and misleading.

Here are a few assumptions and facts gleaned from Glass's research and clinical experience.

**Assumption:** Affairs only happen in unhappy or unloving marriages.

**Fact:** Affairs can happen in good marriages. Affairs are less about love and more about sliding across boundaries.

**Assumption:** Affairs occur mostly because of sexual attraction.

**Fact:** The lure of an affair is how the unfaithful partner is mirrored back through the adoring eyes of the new love. Another appeal is that individuals experience new roles and opportunities for growth in new relationships.

**Assumption:** The person having an affair isn't "getting enough" at home.

**Fact:** The truth is that the unfaithful partner may not be *giving* enough. In fact, the spouse who gives too little is at greater risk than the spouse who gives too much, because he or she is less invested.

**Assumption:** Starting over with a new love leads to a life of eternal bliss.

**Fact:** 75% of all unfaithful partners who marry the affair partner end up divorced.

In addition to the myths above, Glass has found the following:

- You can have an affair without sex. Sometimes the greatest betrayals happen without touching. Infidelity is any emotional or sexual intimacy that violates trust.

- Because child-centered families create conditions that increase the vulnerability for affairs, the children may ultimately be harmed.

- People are more likely to cheat if their friends and family members have cheated.

- When a woman has an affair, it is more often the result of long-term marital dissatisfaction, and the marriage is harder to repair.

- More than 90% of married individuals believe that monogamy is important, but almost half of them admit to having had an affair.

- An affair is not always about the marriage. There are often cultural or contextual factors involved. This is very important information for women, because women too often blame themselves.

- 82% of the unfaithful partners Glass treated had an affair with someone who was initially "just a friend."

- After an affair, people often try to justify it by rewriting unhappiness into the marital history. This is a way to make themselves feel they didn't do such a terrible thing.

## Infidelity: When is it Not?

Some expectations of what constitutes fidelity are explicit—perhaps most commonly, never to have sexual intercourse with another person. Many expectations of fidelity are more implicit—they may be in the mind of one or other partner, but not clearly defined. At what point does a friendship with someone of opposite sex violate the boundaries of a marriage? *How emotionally intimate can I be? How much affection can I show? How revealing can I be of my personal life and especially of my relationship with my spouse?* Complaining to a friend of the opposite sex often leads to an affair of the heart (*You're the only one who understands me*), then to a sexual liaison.

When do playful flirting, affectionate hugging or kissing cross the line? What about flirty text messages? What about online relationships? Only 46% of men queried in one study believed that online affairs are adultery. Many couples are conflicted about outside relationships that are viewed by one partner as being "too close," and by the other as "just friends." It's not always easy to recognize the thresholds that mark the passage from platonic friend to extramarital affair partner, which makes it all too easy to—wittingly or unwittingly—step over that threshold.

> *"Love alone does not protect anyone from temptation."*
>
> —Shirley P. Glass, Ph.D., *Not "Just Friends"*

Glass counsels caution when you hear the words: *"I'm telling you, we're just friends."* Even people in happy marriages who never intended to be unfaithful may form deep, passionate connections before they realize they've crossed the line that separates platonic friendship from romantic love. Many of these friendships are between peers, and develop at the workplace. More and more marriages are being threatened by friendships that have, often unwittingly, slowly and insidiously turn into love affairs.

The unfaithful partner's realization that they are betraying their own beliefs and moral values, may provoke an internal crisis as well as a marital one. While each partner enters the relationship with certain expectations and assumptions about being faithful, few talk openly about what these are.

Each couple must decide together what constitutes a fundamental betrayal.

## Affairs Don't Just Happen

It is always true that both partners had a role in the events that led to the affair. Healing will require that each partner recognize and be accountable for their part in what led to the affair, most especially if there is to be any rebuilding of trust and intimacy. However, both are not equally accountable for the affair. No one can make another stray. Affairs don't just happen. In the words of Glass, affairs *"involve a decision to cross the line and engage in behaviour that almost always had been defined ahead of time by the couple as not acceptable."*

> *"Each person knows, even if one tries to delude the other, that a border has been crossed and a betrayal has occurred."*
>
> —Dennis Ortman, Ph.D., *Transcending Post-Infidelity Stress Disorder*

## The Discovery of Infidelity

The discovery of infidelity is devastating because it shatters our most basic assumptions about the security we expect in committed relationships. Virtually no other marital problems cause as much heartbreak and devastation as infidelity.

In Glass's clinical sample, 24% of betrayed spouses who knew about their partner's infidelity were severely anxious, 18% extremely anxious to point of panic, and 30% clinically depressed. A startling 89% took years to come to terms with the betrayal.

> *The word trauma means wounded, and the offended person has been wounded to the core of her being by her partner's betrayal of trust.*
>
> —Dennis Ortman, Ph.D., *Transcending Post-Infidelity Stress Disorder*

The most severely traumatized are those who had the greatest trust and were the most unsuspecting.

## The Trauma of Infidelity

**SUZANNE:**

*I was twenty-eight years of age and my daughter was three when my husband left me for another woman. I experienced abandonment, horror, and a deep depression that I didn't recover from for three and a half years. My daughter really suffered, because she had an extremely unresponsive mother who cried at times for days and sometimes forgot to feed her.*

*The best thing I did was live with others. I wrapped my daughter up and went and knocked on a friend's door. Friends would nurture us, feed us, be kind to us. I was never shamed. I describe having community as having several people who you can call sobbing in the middle of the night and they will stay on the phone with you. I had friends like that …*

Today we know from neurobiology that as human beings we are so deeply wired for attachment that when we lose it, it's our very survival that feels threatened. Hearing of it can feel, as one woman said, *"like a 747 crashed into my heart."* Emotional pain activates the same area of the brain as is activated when we are physically hurt. The emotional pain becomes a physical pain; a pain felt in the body.

Understanding the experience of infidelity is a traumatic event for the betrayed partner has important implications for healing. On discovering her partner's infidelity, a woman may react as if she has been viciously attacked. Starting over seems to be an overwhelming—if not impossible—undertaking. As therapist Kay Rutherford, Ph.D., writes in her article, *Infidelity: Not a Pretty Picture,* *"Infidelity shatter(s) her assumptions of what her life once held true … the one who was her security is now her source of danger."*

Remember, affairs do not have to be sexual. Some are primarily emotional. Infidelity is any emotional or sexual intimacy that violates trust. Post-traumatic Stress (PTS) symptoms are common. Some psychologists believe that there is no greater trauma than to be betrayed by the very person we count on the most to care for, support, and protect us.

A growing number of therapists are recognizing betrayed partners as victims of PTS and treating them in ways that parallel programs recommended for any person exposed to life threatening events such as war, criminal attacks, or natural disasters. People experiencing PTS are very emotional. They cry easily, and their emotions run rampant. They may hear a song or see a photo that can send them into an abrupt outpouring of tears or angry accusations. They may obsess over the details of the affair. They may have flashbacks; they may be compulsive in avoiding potential reminders of the event. Emotional reactions sweep from intense fear, helplessness, and emotional numbing to heightened anxiety, irritability, and intense rage. Although all are common reactions to infidelity, these behaviors are very erratic and upsetting to both the betrayed person and their partner.

Coping strategies require a balance between respecting and validating the betrayed partner's reactions, and doing what's possible to contain or manage them. Living with fear and stress day in and day out takes a huge toll not only on our emotional wellbeing, but also physical health. The full impact may not become apparent until years later, when it shows up in the form of physical illness. A woman may need professional support and medication to cope with the overwhelming emotions. In the event of thoughts of homicide or suicide, professional support is crucial.

### EVA:

*What would I want to say to a woman who had been betrayed? Firstly, that I am very sorry for the immense, debilitating emotional anguish that she is feeling, as no one should have to experience this. Then I would say that she will survive this, one day at a time, and she will emerge from it both deeper and wiser. I would tell her to stay still, not to overreact, that all things reveal themselves in time. I would tell her that there is a life afterwards, and that she should not necessarily throw the marriage away without work and deep introspection on both sides.*

## Why Some People are More Traumatized than Others

To someone who has not experienced the trauma of infidelity, it is difficult to appreciate the magnitude of the devastation. It cuts to the very core of a woman's being. Unresolved, the trauma remains in the body for years—often for a lifetime. It may show up many years later in the form of some physical ailment.

Janis Abrahms Spring, Ph.D., in *After the Affair: Healing the Pain and Rebuilding Trust When a Partner Has Been Unfaithful*, writes that the severity of the traumatic reaction is determined by:

1) How the discovery was made.

2) The extent of shattered assumptions. All of us operate from a set of basic assumptions about our relationships, our partners and ourselves. We are traumatized when these are shattered because our safe, predictable world is no longer safe or predictable. Reaction to infidelity is intensified by how much the betrayal deviates from our basic assumptions about our mutual commitment to monogamy. Spouses who had no reason to doubt their mutual commitment to exclusivity are deeply traumatized.

3) Individual vulnerabilities of the betrayed partner. Reactions are also based on personal relationship history, self-worth, and emotional stability. Who we are is also partly a result of past experiences. People with low self-esteem may have greater difficulty recovering because they interpret the betrayal as proof of their own inadequacies. Individuals who didn't develop basic trust during childhood are especially vulnerable to deception by a loved one. Infidelity brings up all those childhood wounds for a person who was lied to or who had parents who didn't keep promises. Those who were physically sexually or emotionally abused may be re-traumatized when someone they have counted on betrays their trust. Those who had a parent who betrayed their partner, may be at greater risk of trauma if they are betrayed by their chosen partner.

## Alive, Sexy and Free

**REBECCA:**

*When my sister heard my husband was going to a weekend retreat at a clothing optional hot springs spa, she asked me whether I was concerned. I told her I trusted him, absolutely. I did. He had been there before. We both had. Well, my sister's instincts were correct ... When I heard he was having an affair with a woman he had met there, I asked him to please, stop. He said that the moment he met this woman, was overwhelmed by the attraction he felt to her, but that there would be no future to it—it was not a threat to our marriage. I asked him to please stop seeing her, so that we could talk about this with someone. He told me he could not pass up a chance to feel this alive. He said what he wanted was to bring to our relationship these "newfound parts" of himself he had experienced in the relationship with this other woman. I asked him again not to do this. He replied, "I can't stop."*

Some people believe that the rising prevalence of infidelity means a woman should expect it, and the anguish will be less because *"it happens to everyone these days."*

### LINDA:

*My own sister had been having an affair for years, and concealed it from everyone. She thought confessing it to me would help me to understand how prevalent they are, and to accept "reality."*

The distress of a mother whose son has been killed in a war is the same whether his is the first or five thousandth death. The anguish of a woman who has been raped is no less because her body and psyche has been violated in a group rape. And the anguish of the woman who has been betrayed by her husband is none the less because her neighbor has similarly been betrayed. Every woman walks through the experience single-file, as does her child.

> *"He might cheat because he thinks he deserves to fulfill all of his needs, no matter who he might hurt."*
>
> —Shirley P. Glass, Ph.D., *Not "Just Friends"*

While it may appear that the unfaithful partner's actions benefit him at least in the short-term, it has disastrous effects on members of their family. Kay Rutherford, Ph.D., writes that the unfaithful partner wants a simple life—to have sex easily and without responsibility—and though this may be viewed as simple for the unfaithful partner, it is far from simple for the others involved.

The one who has been unfaithful has a sense of narcissistic entitlement, a pattern of behaviors that encompass more than just "the incident." The damage inflicted on the partner, children, and the family may never hit home. The unfaithful partner then continues to place blame on the spouse, or something or someone else. He feels his actions are not his fault. He uses phrases that absolve him of responsibility and portray innocence: *"I'm with her but I love you," "She came on to me,"* or, *"I have a right to have my needs met." "In actuality,"* Rutherford writes, *"it's all about him. He can only go to his own hurt, not others'."*

Note: "Partner" refers to committed relationship where the persons involved have taken a spiritual vow, or have an articulated agreement, or mutual understanding that all physical and sexual intimacies remain within the relationship itself.

## The Legacy of Infidelity and Divorce

Infidelity—and the divorce that often follows—is a legacy passed from one generation to the next. As adults, these children of infidelity are more likely to be unfaithful to their own partner, and children of divorced parents have a higher than average divorce rate as adults.

Jennifer Harley Chalmers, Ph.D., *Surviving an Affair*, believes one of the important lessons children learn when a parent is unfaithful is thoughtlessness: *"doing what you please, regardless of how it affects other people."*

Research by Judith Wallerstein, co-author of *The Unexpected Legacy of Divorce*, shows that experiencing parental divorce during childhood has a sleeper effect. The worst symptoms often appear when children of divorce leave home and try to form intimate relationships and families of their own, but do so with much less ability to trust and little idea of what a lasting marriage looks like. Ana Nogales's study, reported in *Parents Who Cheat: How Children and Adults Are Affected When Their Parents Are Unfaithful*, indicates that this sleeper effect applies similarly to children of infidelity.

In 2012, one quarter of adults under forty-five in the U.S. were children of divorce. This means that today, in the U.S. alone, many millions of people are struggling with the residue of divorce in their personal lives. Wallerstein questions what it may mean that a million new children a year are added to our *"march of marital failure."* Now if we add the children of parents who separate, and children of infidelity, to those numbers …

Seeing more and more relationships fail or fall to infidelity reinforces the belief that failure is inevitable. Yes, adults have greater freedom and more opportunity than perhaps ever before, but there are hidden costs—and the costs are escalating. It is for each parent to determine the legacy they will leave for their children.

## Marriage: To Be or Not To Be?

In a culture inundated with disposable items and the relentless production lines of new and improved models, when something doesn't work, or doesn't bring the satisfaction it initially did, people are ever ready to dispose of it. Relationships—like many things—are more easily disposed of than worked on. If a person's car breaks down, what do they do? Do they take it to the junkyard or to the mechanic? What does it say of a person—of a culture—when their relationship is more disposable than their car?

These dilemmas are exacerbated by the increased pressure we put on marriage. The expectations of marriage have grown as other social networks—with friends, extended families, neighborhood groups and so on—have broken down. In marrying, the expectation is that the couple will form a lifelong bond that is safe, nurturing, loving, financially stable, and exciting.

Andrew Cherlin, author of *The Marriage-Go-Round,* believes we have a *"schizophrenic culture about marriage."* He explores the American habit of marriage "churning"—people divorcing and remarrying quickly. *"We value marriage, but we also value thinking about ourselves—what makes us happy, what makes us most fulfilled. We think if we are not happy we have the right to end our relationships."*

On average, marriages end after eleven years. This raises the question: Have the past decades created such levels of narcissism that we will not tolerate a relationship that doesn't give us unabating bliss? Psychotherapist Rachel Morris believes that our modern culture is counter-intuitive to sticking with marriage through the long haul; that to do so is totally at odds with modern messages of choice and freedom and ambition.

Despite the seeming incompatibility between marriage and modern messages of choice and freedom, growing numbers of young adults are saying they want a monogamous marriage, and growing numbers of Americans are disapproving of infidelity. Yet we are more likely to accept infidelity in our own relationships, rather than see it as the automatic deal-breaker we saw it as in the past—and more likely to confront it directly with the help of therapists and counselors.

It's important to help people understand what it means to work on a relationship and to withstand periods of adversity, and to deeply reflect on what they—as individuals, as a couple and a family—lose when they leave.

While not all marriages can—or should—be saved, no therapist can save a marriage if either partner is not committed to working on the issues brought to the fore through the infidelity. Sometimes too much damage has been done, or reconciliation remains elusive, or the unfaithful partner is unwilling to leave the affair in order to work on the relationship.

Couples who have a strong commitment to rebuilding their relationship and have the strength and determination to do so, have a high probability of staying together and renewing a relationship that grows in depth, honesty, and intimacy.

Whether a couple stays together or comes apart, there will always be the unwanted, uninvited potential for a woman's discovering and reclaiming a more authentic self.

## Infidelity: An Unwanted Invitation to Heal

Most women are unaware of the degree of trauma they carry in their body, even years later. This is especially so when the experience has been set aside as quickly as possible, so that they can "get on with their lives." They are often unaware of the magnitude of the infidelity's impact on them, unaware that the imprint remains in their body unless consciously attended to, and unaware that it diminishes a woman's ability to reclaim the fullness of her authentic presence.

### SUZANNE:

*If what gets restimulated in us as a result of betrayal is sidestepped, if the emotions are not addressed, we will bring what has not been resolved into the next relationship. If the focus of a relationship is on the fear of being betrayed, it perpetuates the energy of fear, and will more often than not, attract what we want to avoid. We may become very clingy, or we may be unable to get close to others—or we will feel close then attack because of the possible threat of someone betraying us again.*

*The trauma of infidelity is a wound that carries with it a great deal of potential for healing that we never asked for. This requires that we attend to whatever it is within ourselves that allows us to draw to ourselves—consciously or unconsciously— the kind of relationship that could likely bring about an experience of betrayal.*

*We dare not turn away from the issues that need to be addressed so that we can heal from the trauma of betrayal—we owe that to ourselves if we want to be happy. And who doesn't want to be happy?*

This process of healing takes time—its own time. Ultimately, it is only when the feelings that emerge in the aftermath of infidelity have been allowed due passage that a woman will recognize the experience as a messenger—a wake up call to the truth of who she is beyond and beneath this story that she now finds herself trapped in.

When a woman is able to even consider the possibility that this experience of infidelity is an invitation to become more—not less—of the woman she is born to be, she sets foot on the journey home to herself.

# CHAPTER 3

## *Coming Home to Ourselves*

This book is not just about how women are betrayed or how they betray others. At its heart, it's about how we betray ourselves, and how with awareness, compassion, and courage, we can step onto the path of the Warrior Woman and begin the journey home to ourselves.

This is an inside-out process. It's not about what others say or what is expected of us. It's a process of self-discovery—of shattering long held illusions and accessing our inner knowing, personal truths, and self-worth. This is not something that can be rushed, but we can engage in a process of inquiry and awakening that will set us firmly on the path.

In the coming chapters, we will see that the ground for betrayal is laid well before a partner's infidelity. The seeds are planted every time a woman acts outside of her integrity; every time she does not speak her truth; every time she compromises for the sake of fitting in, saying yes when she wants to say no.

We will come to recognize the patterns of self-betrayal that put a woman in a position to be betrayed, and blind her to the truth of what is happening—sometimes for decades, sometimes for an entire lifetime.

This does not in any way mean that a woman is responsible for her partner's unfaithfulness. He, alone, chose to do what he did. However, it is in recognizing the myriad ways in which she has betrayed herself, that a woman can choose new ground for herself—the ground of her own authentic presence.

## The Grip of Patriarchy

As women, it is helpful to remember that we are enmeshed in a social and political system of patriarchy that for millennia has put women "in their place." It is the very air we breathe. While we have created more freedom and possibility for empowerment than ever before, the effects of patriarchy still reach insidiously into our lives.

The impact of this patriarchy, both personally and collectively, has been devastating for women. We have done exceedingly well in learning and transmitting, generation to generation, what must be held in silence or veiled. These aspects of ourselves that we have learned to deny, dismiss, and invalidate are held captive in the shadows of our fear, shame, mistrust, and ruthless self-judgment.

These issues may sound outdated, but the truth is women still face this reality whenever we find and use our voices. Brené Brown, in *Daring Greatly*, quotes a 2005 U.S. study on conformity to feminine norms, which reported that the most important attributes associated with being feminine are being nice, pursuing a thin body ideal, showing modesty by not calling attention to ones talents or abilities, being domestic, and caring for children.

## Injury to Instinct

Virtually every one of us has been birthed from a lineage of women controlled by fear—whether it be the fear of abuse, abandonment, or of quite literally being burned at the stake. These practices to control women are not archaic; they are very much alive today. It is from this fear, programmed at a cellular level of the body and deeply imprinted in the psyche, that we silence ourselves. The dismissal, ridicule, and invalidation of a woman's instinctual and intuitive knowing has resulted in women losing trust in their ability to access the wisdom of their bodies that exists to guide, inform, nourish, and protect them.

> *"Injury to instinct cannot be underestimated as the root of the issue when women are ... stuck in ... destructive patterns. The repair of injured instincts begins with acknowledging ... that usual boundaries of insight and protection have been disturbed."*
>
> —Clarissa Pinkola Estés, *Women Who Run With the Wolves*

Boundaries are an essential component of any healthy relationship. A boundary articulates the behaviors that are acceptable—and those that are not. Instinct-injured, a woman's innate ability to distinguish what is in fact respectful and healthy and what is not in her relationship to herself or another, is severely compromised.

Most women feel compelled to comply with external demands and expectations—often unspoken—that determine what they may think, feel,

42

and do; and what they may *not* think, feel, and do. Whenever a woman dismisses or disregards her own needs—her inner sense of what is the most nourishing or right action for her to take in that moment—she weakens the capacity of her instincts and intuition to provide her with trustworthy guidance and direction.

Not knowing what she herself needs or wants, feeling "less than or "not enough," a woman is disempowered and prey to betrayal.

## The Never-Ending Pursuit of Love and Approval

Even though a woman may intellectually believe otherwise, most women in actuality think that their self-worth is dependent on their outer appearance and the degree to which men are magnetized to them. Passed, often silently, from mother to daughter through our female lineage, this belief is sourced—as we will see—in a woman's earliest childhood experiences. It is perpetuated, of course, by the advertising industry using women as a vehicle to promote the worth or value of a product.

### LOUISE:

*While I have enjoyed great successes musically and academically, as well as many enduring and meaningful relationships, I have agonized about my weight, my skin color, my complexion, my hair ... I have spent hours and days and weeks and months of my life planning how I might improve these, and fantasizing about how everything will be alright when I look like "that woman in the magazine." And so I have purchased countless numbers of tanning sprays and creams, pursued innumerable diets, fanatical regimes, wardrobe overhauls.*

*It's really hitting home for me, now that I have a daughter. I feel so angry and outraged—it seems virtually impossible to disengage myself, or to protect her from this never-ending pursuit to be—what—good enough, approved of, worthy of love? As if what's on the outside is more important than what's inside?*

As we will see in both the stories of women who have been betrayed and those who have betrayed, this looking toward men to reflect their value and worth and to find acceptance, validation, and fulfillment is endemic in the feminine collective.

Having bought into the cultural programming that her worth, her happiness, and her fulfillment is to be found outside of herself, a woman will try to live up to an image of what she thinks others want her to be.

43

Abandoning her own needs, instincts, and intuitions, she lives a life of self-betrayal and in so doing shapes an environment in which she is highly susceptible to being betrayed by others.

When a woman claims her inherent value, she is no longer held hostage to these illusions. Secure in her own authentic being, she has nothing to prove. She is free.

*"Who looks outside, dreams. Who looks inside, awakens."*

—Carl Jung

## The Key to Freedom: Self-Awareness

Key to a woman's freedom is an *awareness* of the voices, the stories, running relentlessly inside her mind that perpetuate this betrayal of self. Whenever a woman recognizes these voices, and the roles she plays in response to them, they no longer control her. She can begin to make new choices—choices based on new values that affirm her dignity and worth. Calling in the fierceness and determination of the Warrior, she begins reclaim her own self-worth.

This process can be both liberating and incredibly difficult. Sustaining the necessary awareness can, in itself, take a tremendous amount of energy. A woman cannot do this all the time, or in every facet of her life. She needs to carefully prioritize and choose her battles. But the liberation here is in being conscious of when she is putting on a mask, when she is veiling herself—and knowing she retains the ability to choose otherwise.

In time, the voices of self-betrayal lose their force. She discovers that she no longer needs to compromise or prove herself. She is able to reach out, to let her vulnerability be seen by trusted others—because she *knows* that she is deserving, loving, and loveable. She discovers she can develop trustworthy relationships that liberate and empower her.

But firstly, she must recognize and confront the voice of the Inner Critic, or Judge.

## The Inner Critic

The Inner Critic is the voice in a woman's head that shames her, blames her, berates her for anything and everything—her body, her car, her job, her marriage, her children. Almost certainly for the hell she finds herself in, in the aftermath of infidelity.

For many women, this voice is a familiar one. It may have been with a woman for as long as she can remember. It runs incessantly, assailing her with messages that she is "not enough"—she is not pretty enough, smart enough, thin enough, curvy enough, sexy enough, nice enough. Or, she is "too much"—too loud, too smart, too career-driven, too s/mothering. These voices reach an all-time high during the experience of infidelity. They can paralyze a woman into non-action, or drive her into depression.

Recognizing, once and for all, the debilitating and disempowering nature of these voices, a woman's sense of the injustice that accompanies her partner's unfaithfulness can awaken the fierceness of the Warrior Woman to proclaim *Enough. No more.* We will see this, again and again, in the pages that follow.

## Self-Compassion

Self-compassion is an essential element of the ground on which a woman must stand to challenge the voices of self-betrayal. When a woman feels compassion for others, her heart opens to them. She feels kindness toward them, empathy, and a desire to help alleviate their suffering. With self-compassion, she relates to herself with that same nonjudgmental, open-hearted empathy and loving kindness.

Many of those same women who can feel compassion for others, withhold it from themselves. Some women confuse self-compassion and self-indulgence, but the two are very different. Self-indulgence can mean numbing and denying the pain, or ruminating in it in a way that actually feels pleasurable—an unrelenting succumbing to the *"poor, poor me"* scenario. Self-compassion acknowledges and is present to our suffering. It is a deep acceptance of what is, in the moment. Self-compassion doesn't make the pain go away—rather it allows us to soften into it, to be fully present to it with the same loving kindness and empathy that we would offer a child or a friend who is suffering.

## Self-Worth

Self-worth is a deep knowing of one's intrinsic value. In the absence of self-worth, a woman will give herself away again and again. Living in the shadow of her authentic presence, not only does she lay the ground for betrayal, but she also forfeits her ability to fully express and share her gifts with the world.

Women often confuse self-worth with self-esteem. Believing *"I am right"* or *"I am good"* may correlate with self-esteem, but not necessarily with self-worth or self-love. They are different aspects of the way a woman views and relates to herself. Self-esteem is more common than self-worth, and many women have little sense of either. The experience of infidelity will leave virtually every woman—at least initially—bereft of both.

Good self-esteem comes from a woman being proud of who she is and what she does. A woman can have good self-esteem in some areas of her life and not in others. She might feel confident about her work, or know that she attracts people with her good looks, but not feel confident at public speaking or in forming intimate relationships. Self-esteem can change in a flash because it is dependent on externals—even on what other people say or think about her.

When a woman *knows* herself to be of value, then regardless of what anyone says about her, regardless of whether she appears to succeed or fail at any particular endeavor, that core knowing does not change. Even though she may deeply feel the pain and disappointment of being betrayed, this does not diminish her self-worth. It does not call into question her intrinsic value. Self-worth is a deep knowing that *"I am of value. I am loveable."* Self-worth is the foundation of an unshakeable self-esteem.

One of the most precious gifts that a woman who chooses to make good of this experience of infidelity may emerge with, is this deeper sense of her own self-worth, and of the strength and fulfillment to be found therein.

## Re-Sourcing Herself

Ultimately, each woman determines the meaning, the power, and the significance of any betrayal. The healing of her heart and the building of self-esteem and self-love requires she turn her attention inward, rather than outward. It demands she question and deeply reflect on the values and thinking through which she has disempowered herself. *Is this what this experience says about me? How may I, in some way, have done something to contribute to this infidelity? Where was I naïve?* Such questions will emerge again and again as a woman engages with the stories in these pages. She will begin to recognize the ways in which she has unwittingly allowed herself to be programmed.

A woman embodies the strength, courage, wisdom, and open heart of the Warrior Woman with her:

- willingness to accept what has happened;
- willingness to recognize her role in the infidelity;
- willingness to proclaim herself as the source of her worth, happiness, and fulfillment; and

- adamant refusal to give the power to determine her worth, happiness, and fulfillment to anyone or anything else.

Each step toward the reclaiming of that power engenders confidence. A woman begins to experience herself in a fuller, more embracing way, rather than from a place of inadequacy or lacking. She realizes she has a choice in how she interprets what is happening. She realizes she has the power to re-source herself and to re-contextualize her experience—and with this new realization, to access the liberation of standing in the beauty and potency of her own authentic presence.

# CHAPTER 4

## *In the Aftermath of Infidelity—The First Year*

Here, we open a window into aspects of the experience of one woman, Gail, as she lived through the first year or so after the discovery of her partner's infidelity. While every woman's experience will differ according to a range of factors—from her own personal history to her personality, her age to her financial status—there is always the shock, the grief, the shame, the anger ... the disbelief and outrage. While a woman will carefully prepare for her graduation, marriage, the birth of her children, even for a trip overseas, she is never prepared for the discovery of her partner's infidelity—and the devastation and fall out in the months, even years that follow.

It is important that she realize the emotional swings, friends avoiding her, fantasies of wishing her partner dead and the other woman "in hell," and suicidal thoughts are all normal responses and reactions to a woman's being betrayed. Knowing this does not diminish the raw intensity of the emotions, but it can alleviate at least a little of the fear that she will not be able to survive ... that she will never heal this broken heart. It can ease some of the bewilderment she feels as she finds herself thrown into an alien world.

Again, while the details are different for every woman, the threads remain the same. In the coming chapters we will follow other threads, in other stories, of women moving through and well beyond the first year.

### GAIL:

*Mark called me from the conference center to tell me he had met a woman who "took his breath away." He said he had never experienced anything like this before. He told me that he wanted to be up front about it ... that she wasn't a replacement for me— she wasn't his "type"—but they wanted to explore this "magnetism" that was between them. They wanted to know how I would feel about it. Why would he even ask! I told him he was playing with fire; we had no idea what the repercussions would be. I was shaken, really shaken, but I didn't believe he would go ahead with this. He was a sane, rational man. We had been married for over two decades. It was only months later, talking with a friend, that I realized how naïve I was not to have said, "Do Not Do This!"*

*A couple of days later he phoned to tell me that he was with her. I was shocked. Stunned. It was as if a bomb had been dropped on my home, crashed through my heart, landed smack in my solar plexus. I didn't believe it. This couldn't be happening. I couldn't think. It was horrible, horrible.*

*Shocked, devastated, I shut myself in, curled up on the bed, sobbing, my mind whirling out of control. I couldn't believe it. Shock moved to disbelief, to grief. And back again. For days and days I was like a zombie, lost in a nightmare. I would stagger up to shower, to get dressed, but more often than not I would collapse back on the bed. I couldn't function. I didn't want to eat. I didn't want to see anyone. I had never, never experienced anything like this.*

The pain center of the brain responds to shock and becomes physically distressed when one is betrayed and abandoned. It's a very frightening and disorienting time for a woman, feeling she has lost control of not only the physical aspects of her life, but also of her mind and body.

It is very important for her to know that she can "be real" at this point, to experience and express the full range and depth of the emotions cursing through her. Kay Rutherford, author of *Infidelity: Not A Pretty Picture* writes, *"She may feel as though her soul has been stolen, stopped dead, and frozen in its tracks."*

*Three weeks have passed. Every night when, exhausted, I try to sleep, there's nothing but the aching heart, the pit in my gut, the grief, the disbelief. Whenever I wake in the night, it's there. Every morning, it's what I wake to. The days are an endless fog of meaningless actions, doing only what I must to get through the day, all the time this incredible weight in my heart, sickness in my belly, ache in my head, nausea in my throat. I keep trying to remember to breathe, to ground, not to allow this to destroy me ... the never ending effort of trying to let go, to find the right*

*balance of feeling the feelings … feeling the anger but not letting
it consume me, feeling the grief but not drowning in it …*

*When he first called me to say he was being intimate with this
other woman, I thought this couldn't be happening. He would get
over it; we would talk about it and work it out. Now I was lost in
shame and humiliation—the likes of which I had never known
before. Captivated, in the heat of the affair, Mark was openly
sharing with others his passion for this woman, and my inability
to "meet his passion." I asked him, pleaded with him to stop, but
he insisted on his commitment to "transparency," to "being
real." He told me that he didn't believe in monogamy anymore
and wouldn't be constrained by such "patriarchal" values.*

While honesty and transparency certainly have their place, the pain and
humiliation of having intimate details of one's life (sex life no less!)
revealed to others can be devastating, most especially when a woman is
already feeling helpless and out of control. When she believes those
details to be misleading or manipulative, it can be crushing—and
misleading details are inevitable, given human nature's inclination to
carefully select information to confirm one's own biases and self-interest.
Hurt feelings are inevitable, and cause tremendous distress that can take
an age—if ever—to resolve.

As Brené Brown writes in *Daring Greatly*, this transparency can also be a
means of getting attention, or engaging in the *"shock-and-awe behaviors"*
that are so widespread in today's world. Not only is it demeaning to be in
such a light that Mark put Gail and their years together, but his "story"
also affected people's relationship with her.

*He told me he was following his heart. He said he "could not
control the timing of his heart," and he "couldn't stop." He told
me that he took responsibility for what he had done, but I was
responsible for my experience of what was happening. He said
that we had co-created a situation that was presently causing me
more pain than him. He said, "I know you are hurt by my
actions, but that's different from I hurt you." Only months later,
he decided he didn't want to continue in counseling together. He
said that he didn't know why I was so angry. If I had found
someone I loved so much, he would be happy for me.*

His belief that he was *"following his heart"* gave Gail's partner
permission to break his marriage vows. *"You can't go wrong if you follow
your aliveness,"* from the popular Abraham teachings, and Joseph

Campbell's *"Follow your bliss,"* are but two of the many popularized expressions that have been taken out of context and indiscriminately used as justification for all manner of what might also be perceived as self-indulgent behaviors.

Truth is relative. While from one perspective it can be said that no one is responsible for how another feels, it is equally true that what we do can harm another. When centered in the wisdom of our heart, we avoid doing something that would bring another pain. When in true heart, we do not need to be told to be kind, to be thoughtful—we simply are.

Shirley P. Glass, Ph.D., observes that one of the difficulties in following the trail of caring and honesty to the point of clean resolution is that it is unrealistic for the unfaithful partner to expect his partner's emotions to go away anytime soon. To keep holding that *"he made me feel like this"* perpetuates a woman's inability to recognize what she can do to alter her relationship to the situation, and so perpetuates the suffering. However, to even consider that no one else is to blame for her feelings is a rational thing, and it is unreasonable to expect a woman to be rational while in a state of shock and distress. Until her pain is heard and validated, and until her partner empathizes with the pain his infidelity caused and takes responsibility for his actions, it can be exceedingly difficult to move on.

> *He said, "It was a tradeoff. I certainly didn't want to hurt you, but I was presented with a rare opportunity, unlike any I've ever had in my life, and had no evidence it might be presented again if passed up this time." I listened, stunned. How can he be saying this! He said that he felt sad for how I felt, but remorse would imply that he had made a mistake and would do it differently if he had the chance, which wasn't the case. He said, "I couldn't help it, I had to do it. It's been that powerful. I continue to feel blessed for this happening." How can I hear "sorry" in that?*

It can be particularly difficult to move past the hurt if he persists in claiming *"I never meant to hurt you."* Such a statement conveys a failure to take responsibility for avoiding or consciously resisting an affair.

> *The cavalier way he would say, "Everything is the same for me. I still feel the same way about you except for no longer wanting you as my sexual partner, my wife." That "except" was so enormous! Myself as his wife, as his partner, was such a big part of who I was. How could he so nonchalantly dismiss our marriage and the intimacies we had shared over our many years together, with the likes of "I want to continue as good friends,*

*business partners, parents—let's keep all that as it was. I still value it and want it." How could he expect us to remain friends, how could I possibly remain friends with someone who had betrayed, abandoned, and humiliated me? I told him that for me, a friend is someone I know and trust who cares for me, loves me, will be there for me. He had disqualified himself on every single point of friendship. Yet he persists in saying he wants to be friends. It was incomprehensible to me that he could not get why I said no. How could he even ask?*

Frank Pittman, author of *Beyond Betrayal: Life After Infidelity*, sees the craziest and most destructive form of infidelity as being the temporary insanity of falling in love. In the throes of an affair, the infidel will erect impenetrable walls of denial in order not to hear anything that may threaten the relationship, and their right to continue the affair.

Pittman notes that men tend to attach too little significance to affairs, ignoring their horrifying power to disrupt and destroy lives. Often surprised at the intensity and duration of their betrayed partner's anger, they rarely appreciate the devastating long-range impact of their infidelities on their partner and children. Romantic affairs lead to a great many divorces, suicides, homicides, heart attacks, and strokes, but not to very many successful relationships.

*I knew from the very beginning that the only way I would get through this would be to adopt it as my spiritual practice. One of the mantras I chose to work with was, "It's all about me." But my intention to get my attention off of him—what he did and is doing—and onto me, often felt impossible to sustain in the face of the trauma I was experiencing. I took an hour morning and evening to sit with my trusted form of guidance, asking what am I not seeing, what is the right action, right attitude, what am I learning ... ? Each morning I wrote down a few of the most meaningful phrases that came to me and reflected on them throughout the day.*

*The challenge was not in resisting the guidance, but in integrating it into my emotional, mental and physical worlds. It was fine when I was immersed in the wisdom of that guidance, but when I emerged to step into the real world, all that I had embodied could fall away, sometimes with the speed of lightening, sometimes as gradually as butter melting in the sun. I could observe it happening but felt powerless to stop it. It was startling to see how suddenly I would find myself right back in*

52

*the drama of the infidelity. Exhausted, despairing, I struggled to feel compassion for myself.*

*Every two hours, or whenever an intense wave of emotion gripped me, I would lie down, clock by me, for a minimum of twelve minutes and allow myself to be fully present to the emotions coursing through me, breathing with it. Sometimes it extended well beyond those twelve minutes to a half hour, until the emotions had run their course, and I would emerge, calm and grounded. That was such a helpful practice. Still, so often, I found myself struggling to decide what to do with the intensity of the energy I felt—the rage, despair, shock ... when to breathe through it, when to release it with tears or outbursts of rage ...*

Beneath her anger is the sadness, the fear, and the grief. The experience of infidelity is like a death, but it's the death of more than a relationship and of a woman's expectations of a relationship; it is the death of the whole reality about who he is. It's shocking, traumatizing, because her whole world rested in that, and the emotional and cognitive dissonance is very disorienting.

While not in any way minimizing the deep distress a woman experiences at the death of a partner, with death a woman receives the unconditional support and sincere condolence of others. With infidelity, she can find herself the subject of condemnation—for anything from not being "good enough" to keep him, to her inability to "control" her anger and rage. She may find herself the subject of derogatory and humiliating gossip that she can only choose to ignore, or to confront—at cost of further escalation of the drama. She finds that women who she had thought to be her friends avoid or shun her.

As we will see, there are many reasons for this—ranging from their feeling awkward and not knowing what to say, to their being uncomfortable with the depths of emotions she is experiencing, their fears infidelity may be "contagious," and their own unfinished business with infidelity. However, for the woman who has been betrayed it is so very hurtful to feel she has been abandoned not only by her partner, but also by those she thought were her friends.

*Mark Adams was his name. The litany would emerge spontaneously and keep playing over and over in my mind. Sometimes I would chant it quietly. "Get fucked Mark Adams. Rot in hell Mark Adams. Get fucked Mark Adams. Die in hell Mark Adams. Get fucked Mark Adams. Die. Die. Die." Other times, with no one to hear me, I could scream the words into the wind. I got a certain satisfaction from it, a sense of empowerment. Many a time it was what brought me out of collapse. I was shocked and fascinated how it could spew out of me. Sometimes I would froth at the mouth. I could spit. I could pound. I could kill. It felt great.*

The rage, outrage, thoughts of hatred and retaliation must be allowed their responsible expression. The fierce energies of a chant of rage such as this passing through a woman's voice and body, can begin to awaken the Warrior energy in the physical and emotional body. This energy is immensely supportive and can function as both a form of purging, and also the first kindling of self-reclamation—a step toward taking her life back. With time and support, she can begin to recognize her part in what led to the infidelity. Self-inquiry as to how she wants to work with her own suffering, and her reactivity, is essential to understanding and insight—as is her questioning what happened, and why, and allowing time for insight and wisdom to arise and inform her how to proceed.

*When I first heard of his affair, it felt like a bomb had exploded in my heart. Six months later, my life torn apart, I still could not see how to put the pieces back together. I didn't have a picture of what the "me" after all this was over would look like, to guide me. It had all happened so suddenly. Overnight, the life I had known was gone, ripped out from under my feet. There were so many unknowns facing me, so suddenly. I was so, so scared.*

*Now, our home was to be sold. Stunned, I obsessed about where and how I would live. I couldn't afford to buy a place alone. I was no longer sure who my friends were, and who they were not. Perhaps most heart wrenching, I didn't know how to guide my children through the shock and disorientation of this.*

*I struggled with how to get my head and heart around the fact that this man, my confidante and intimate of twenty-six years, father of my children, had wittingly hurt me, abandoned me, virtually overnight, into the arms of a woman he had just met. I thought we would ride this out together.*

*Now I slept alone, I woke alone. For him it was one seamless move—from one woman, one bed, one home, one family, one community—to another. Just like that. He took his job with him, and his computer. I could not stop the relentless circling of my mind. I felt powerless to stop the questions that had no answers—why had he ended it this way? And I was left with the dreams, the nightmares with them together. I felt so afraid, afraid that I was not able to cope with this.*

As distressful as a woman's preoccupations, dreams, nightmares and flashbacks are, they serve a valuable purpose—reliving the experience in order to gain a sense of mastery and control over an overwhelming event. *"I can't cope"* is a very normal response to the loss and disorientation.

Hopelessness and severe withdrawal, flashbacks, extreme sensitivity and reactivity, irritability, and anger are hallmarks of trauma. In time, in the process of shifting focus from her partner's behavior, over which she has no control, to her own, over which she has some control, she will begin to gain a sense of inner strength and empowerment. Having had her known world torn apart, the process cannot be hurried. To attempt otherwise is counterproductive.

Psychologist Molly Layton, writing of her own efforts to comprehend the loss of her marriage and the obsessive litany that would replay over and over in her mind, writes, *"I began to appreciate my obsession's grinding mission: the effort to hold an absent and often unrepentant person accountable... In the absence of the perpetrator's accountability, injured people work with the only material they have: their minds. Indeed, it is the essence of obsession to try to handle something in your mind when you believe it cannot be resolved in the outer world."*

*It was dusk. He had come to collect some things. I saw him walk by the window. I screamed. So loud my throat was throbbing in pain. I screamed like I have never screamed before. He looked at me. And walked away. This gave him cause to tell me again, later, that he was angry that I was so angry.*

A woman who has been betrayed has a deep sense of having being violated. Her body may react to the sight of him—or even a phone call or email from him—as if she is still in danger, even when she is safe in her home. It is natural for her nervous system to vibrate with shock. Her brain is on alert, watching out for signs of danger and flipping into high gear at the slightest certainty.

*Ours was a marriage of almost three decades and now it's been nine months since he told me of his infidelity and no, I'm not ready to forgive. What does "not ready" mean? I can't find a place in my mind or in my body where I want it, where it feels possible—perhaps for a fleeting moment here or there, but nothing sustainable.*

*I know what it means to carry anger, rage, in my body. I know so much about it, the damage it does, it scares me—and yet it doesn't make me any more able to just "forgive, get over it." Here I am again, feeling like a victim, not feeling like a victim, trying not to feel like a victim.*

While so many women are judged and judge themselves for their inability to "get over" their partner's unfaithfulness and move on with their lives, it can be extremely difficult to get emotional closure until or unless they believe their partner truly gets the *gravity* of what they have done.

*He chose to move in with this other woman, without making real effort to come to any level of completion with me. I felt abandoned as well as betrayed. It takes time to heal. I knew this intellectually but oh, the pressure I felt to "forgive," to "get over it." The shame of knowing, or imagining, that people were judging me for not being over it. I wanted to hide, to disappear. Other times, the shame moved in the blink of an eye to anger. Fury. Disgust. Questioning, why is it me that feels this shame? How was it that he got to be out there lauding his virility ... while I felt humiliated, shamed. Forgive him? Most days I didn't even want to entertain the possibility. Other times, I worried about this. I knew it was poison to harbor this hatred, but how to "just forgive ..."*

The discovery that one's partner has been unfaithful strikes at the core of a woman's innermost being. It is understandable that she should find herself preoccupied with the injustice of it. When someone implies that she should "get over it," or cautions her to stop acting like a "victim" in the face of her grief, her anger, and her outrage, they are either totally ignorant of or dismissing any recognition of the impact of the violation.

*I hated what he did. No sincere apology ... he was full of defenses, rationalizations, his pride in the stud he had proven himself to be. How could I just "get over it"? I wanted to yell, "Fuck it! I just need to be mad, to grieve! I am not ready to be reasonable or forgiving!" It was he who had betrayed me and here I was the one feeling shamed, feeling like the worm, the lowly critter ... where is the justice in that? Oh, I hated him ... and her.*

Mind and body in shock, not only has a woman lost any sense of control over her life—she has lost her self-respect. She will swing from one

56

extreme to another: confident and determined one moment, humiliated and collapsed the next. She finds herself behaving in ways that engender confusion, grandiosity, inferiority, self-hatred and regret. All of these are normal responses to an acutely traumatizing experience.

When the unfaithful partner leaves prematurely, in the absence of any form of mutual resolution, it is very difficult for the woman who has been left to come to closure. Abandoned as well as betrayed, she will never know the full story of what happened. Certain stages of recovery from trauma, such as getting the facts, and searching for meaning, may never be completed.

> *I will eternally give thanks for those women who essentially said, "Yes, I see you. And I love you. I see your pain. You have every right to be right where you are, right now. And you will come through this. You will."*

The support and comfort from a woman's trusted friends bringing recognition, validation, and respect to the rawness of her emotions cannot be overstated. While it is important to refrain from supporting those feelings of victimization or helplessness that so readily arise, another woman's empathy is crucial at this time.

> *He kept saying how much he valued the many expressions of intimacy and connection we shared, but that I didn't offer the sensual/sexual passion he had discovered with this other woman.*

> *It wasn't until he had left that I read, "You can have trust without intimacy, but you can't have intimacy without trust." In that moment, I understood why, over the years, I had withdrawn from that area of intimacy ... Perhaps most significantly, he had slept on and off with three other women over the past eighteen years. He said it "wasn't sexual," and after all, I thought, he has a right to get his needs met. The third woman was six years ago.*

> *It was only now that it fully dawned on me, how his transgressions with these other women was impacting both me and our relationship. My first intuition of this had been when I realized I did not want to kiss him. He agreed to a counseling session. It went nowhere, in that he maintained his right to share a bed with another woman, as his "affectional needs" were not fully met with me.*

> *I didn't understand then that even "sleeping with, without sex" is a breach of trust and respect; an act of betrayal. Yes, my body*

*had been telling me this for many years ... I no longer reached orgasm, but I hadn't comprehended the enormity of what was happening here. I loved him. I valued so much of what we shared, and to maintain peace and harmony in our home, I kept compromising on what I felt to be acceptable.*

*He had suggested we see a sex counselor to talk about our different needs with respect to "passion." I had said no. It is only now I realized why. I was afraid it would mean that I was to have more sex with him. But my neglect to attend to these issues, contributed to the demise of our marriage.*

The counseling session went nowhere not only because he maintained his right to share his bed with another, but also because Gail was naïve—numbed to naming what was being dishonored and dismissed in their marital relationship. In all those years of losing respect for him, and not knowing how central that was to her growing inability to be intimate with him, Gail only now recognized what needed to be attended to—in this case his disrespect of her when he pursued intimate relationships with other women. It's so easy to constantly put aside what needs to be recognized because there appears to be safety in what is familiar. And because to recognize what's needed—which may be to take a stronger stand with him, to request they both go to counseling, or that she leave him—may demand she move out of that familiar zone.

*Some fifteen months had passed. I received a brief email. He said he was now ready to talk about what had happened and get some closure between us. That was it, a sentence or two. Heartless. No I am so, so sorry for the anguish, the pain that I brought to you and our daughters. Please, I want to talk with you, and to ask how I can in some way make amends. Please, can we do this?*

*Nothing like that. No semblance of caring. No invitation. Just like "I'm ready now. This needs to be done. Let's just do it."*

To offer a genuine apology would require that the unfaithful partner really feel, really empathize with the pain and anguish his actions incurred. He would need to acknowledge that he had done something wrong. And so often, he can't do that.

*This morning, again, the grief in my body. I question myself continually. Is it now indulgence, to go into that emotion? Should I get busy, turn my mind elsewhere, or should I work with this to allow more of it to come forth? This morning I simply sat to be present to what is there ... no judgments, no need to deepen or deny, just to be present to what is there. It was quite beautiful ... the grief moved to compassion, and the compassion brought a softening, a gentling, within me.*

*I came to realize that to be with the despair, the anguish, the grief, the disappointment ... demands a strength and willingness so much more than that required not to go there; to repress it or to stand above it.*

Buddhist teacher and author Pema Chödrön, *The Places That Scare You*, writes that staying with the volatile energy gradually becomes more comfortable than acting it out or repressing it. She says this so beautifully: *"Staying with it is what heals. It allows us to let go of our self-importance. It's how the warrior learns to love."*

*It seems that life roars on for everyone else, as usual. Life, for me, has become such a lonely, lonely experience. There came a time when I felt I couldn't keep sharing my pain with but one or two of my closest women friends. Increasingly, I felt that I just had to be with the pain of the experience, alone. Whenever a wave of grief, of anger, of fear came over me, I simply had to be present to myself, alone. Breathing, grounding, being present in my heart, present in my body, became my sanctuary.*

*I reflect back on the year that has passed. Initially it was the shock, the disbelief, the disorientation. I vacillated between rage, despair, shame, and grief. And this deep, deep disappointment, a sadness, an acceptance in my body that this man is now, indeed, a stranger to me. Yet, it still hurts. I have lost all respect for him. He disgusts me. Ironically, there is a gift in this—it is easier to let go ... So yes, ironically, I am thankful for this ... but I still feel so sad, that it ended this way.*

*The ground continues to shift beneath me. In my better moments, I can catch glimpses of a new life, but I soar only to crash again. Suddenly it returns with a vengeance ... the grief, the bewilderment, and the shame. Shame. Shame. Shame. Why did he have to end it this way? That's what hurts, hurts so much.*

Growing in strength and recognition of the need to take responsibility for her emotions and the situation, in time a woman may find herself drawing closer to her true self; her essential being. Or, she may numb herself— whether through substance abuse or getting busy and pretending nothing happened. Sometimes it feels impossible to do otherwise—and then, rather than engage in the ruthless self-judgment that a woman is so prone to, she will be best to give herself a break and to simply be with what is—with whatever loving kindness and compassion she can muster for herself in this painful predicament.

> *Now it's some eighteen months later. I am here in our home, now sold, to pack and move. Every direction I turn holds a story … memories of hopes and dreams we had shared, of the decades we had lived together. On the walls, the photos of so many precious times shared. Will I keep them? It pains me to think of keeping them, and it pains me even more to think of throwing them away. There is the wooden carved wall hanging of Ganesh that we had seen in Bali and I loved, that he and our daughter bought as a surprise for me. And there are the pillows covered with the fabric that we bought in Peru, to brighten the day bed on our deck. The photo albums filled with photos of the time from the birth of our first child to this time, the end time. The lamp that we bought to have burning through the period of the labor; the chopsticks he hand carved for me so many years ago. At last, something I will discard … but not without tears.*

> *I realize there is nothing, nothing left. "We" are done. He speaks as though there never was a "we." I am a discarded object he has no need to even recall or dispose of with gratitude or care. All those years together, dismissed. There is nothing. Nothing. Nothing. I cannot believe that we could end this way. Strangers.*

Jungian psychoanalyst Clarissa Pinkola Estés, *Women Who Run With the Wolves,* writes that while for years it was believed that grief was a process you did once, preferably over a year's period of time, and then it was done with, what we know now is that certain things can never be done being grieved … People may recover from the worst of their soul grief in the first year or two, but afterwards they continue to experience periods of active grieving. Although the episodes become farther and farther apart in time and shorter in duration, they have close to the same intensity of gut-staggering grief as in that first year. This validates the normalcy of long-term grief … *"When we can grieve and grieve hard, and come out of it tear-stained rather than shame-stained, we can come out deepened, fully acknowledged, and filled with new life."*

Here we end Gail's experience of the first year after learning of her partner's infidelity. While the details of every woman's experience will of course differ, the threads will be similar. Having some recognition, some awareness of the emotions and the devastation a woman will experience is important in normalizing the experience—for many a woman may feel she is going crazy.

While Gail thought the second year would be easier—and it may be for some—others will find themselves getting more depressed and ashamed of who they have become ... of the self-pity the self-hatred. Some women will at some point find themselves preoccupied with thoughts of suicide.

For those offering support, Kate Rutherford, in her article *Infidelity: Not a Pretty Picture* offers these suggestions:

> *Listen to her story—for the 1,000 times she will need to tell it.*
>
> *Believe her story. Patriarchy and society rarely support her; her self-esteem will be all but gone and shame takes its place.*
>
> *Respect her grief—she cannot make it smaller than what it is to her.*
>
> *Tell her not to sleep with him—very directive but necessary—for safety. She will want to sleep with him to keep him; he will have convinced her it was lack of sex that made him do it.*
>
> *Suggest a Clarissa Pinkola Estés's wolf pack of solid supporters who know and understand the "cunning, wary, feral, observant women."*
>
> *Encourage unforgiveness to keep her safe at first. Wade and Washington (2003) say forgiveness is not always the answer— dignity and self-respect come first.*
>
> *Let her anger be her strength, for it says, "Stay away from me."*
>
> *Remind her that infidelity is not simple; it is dangerous and it is abusive.*

In the following chapters we will see how the story of a partner's infidelity goes much deeper than the betrayal. We will see how a woman can choose not to fall passively into the role of victim. She does not have to accept others' judgments or opinions. She can end the disempowering cycle by refusing to play her expected part.

We will see elements of all of these patterns in the stories that follow. We will see how the patterns repeat—and repeat—and how through awareness, and with compassion and courage, a woman can sow the seeds for a new ground and the journey home to herself.

Before moving on to the stories of the many other women you will meet in the pages of this book, let's look briefly at where the seeds of self-betrayal were first planted—in the very earliest years of life.

# CHAPTER 5

## *The Early Years and the Adults We Become*

### Shame: Unworthy of Love

Many of us, even those who present as intelligent and accomplished women, carry from childhood the belief that we are in some way lacking, unworthy of love. We pretend that we are okay, but there is something in us that feels that we are not.

Most of us learned as very young children that our worth is not a given; it must be earned. We were left feeling who we were was disappointing, "not enough," and that we were not worthy of love. Shame may have been silently communicated to us as children, either verbally or physically through the disapproval, ridicule, or absence of care and attention from caregivers.

> *"Shame ... tells us that we are fundamentally flawed, no matter what we do and despite all evidence to the contrary. Shame discounts our good deeds and interprets any mistake as proof of our basic, unalterable unworthiness."*
>
> —Jalaja Bonheim, Ph.D., *The Hunger for Ecstasy*

While shame is most often the result of old messages from childhood, shame messages are continually absorbed—unconsciously—from the culture. As Brené Brown writes in *Daring Greatly*, *"While our first shame messages came from our childhood, as we grow we learn to do it all by ourselves."*

Shame locks a child, and the woman she becomes, in a state of disempowerment. We learned as children that, as one woman said, *"betrayal is the name of the game."* Fearing she is "not enough," fearful of being wrong or of being belittled—or worse—a woman may withdraw, hide, or silence herself. She may become aggressive, seeking to use shame to fight shame. She may seek to please and appease.

Succumbing to the demands or expectations of others as to who she "should" be and what she "should" do, she betrays her own instincts, intuitions, thoughts, and feelings. The ways a woman adapts and the roles she plays confirm her lack of worth and perpetuate the betrayal. At times, any one of these roles may be the best or even the only choice—but we need to recognize how they diminish us.

While self-compassion is an essential element of the ground on which the Warrior Woman must stand to challenge the voices of self-betrayal, alone, it is rarely enough. This is because these voices are rooted in shame, and as Brené Brown writes, shame is a social concept—it heals best between people. Healing is difficult because, as Brown writes, shame thrives in secrecy. What keeps shame alive is that a woman doesn't want to know about it or feel it—and she certainly doesn't want to talk about it.

As we will see, shame reaches an all-time high during the experience of infidelity. Self-compassion enables us to be gentle and kind with ourselves when in the grip of shame, and this makes it more possible for us to reach out to one another. We all have shame, and this shame is compounded by the fact that pretty much no one wants to talk about it. And the less we talk about it the stronger it becomes, so we don't even realize we are carrying this shame and we live our lives feeling as if we are flawed. When we can share our stories with someone who responds with empathy and understanding, shame can't survive.

We will see this in Chapter 16: *Reaching Out for Help—The Gift of Empathy*. But first, a window into how a woman may recognize, understand, and confront the source of these disempowering beliefs and patterns.

## The Early Years and the Adults We Become

Early neglect and abuse—and the shame that flourishes in such an environment—translate into the belief that we are somehow intrinsically bad, not worthy of love, and that people cannot be trusted. These negative experiences form our childhood wounds and factor significantly into the adults we become. The unconscious defenses that we developed as children to avoid feeling the pain associated with unmet needs or abuse— such as the repression of our feelings, needs, and wants—become part of our personality, part of our "act."

While many women have experienced blatant physical, emotional or sexual abuse and shaming, for others the abuse was subtle: for example being left to cry alone and uncomforted, or being repeatedly dismissed or ignored. While an adult woman may have no conscious memory of neglect or abuse, she may find herself unable to trust others, or to develop and sustain intimate relationships. She may live trying to please or impress others, to prove her worth. Or she may simply withdraw, feeling she will never be understood.

As adults we have an Inner Child and Inner Parents. How a woman's Inner Parents relate to her Inner Child is shaped by how her parents and caregivers treated her. There is no blame here. Our caregivers were the products of their time as were their parents before them, and like us, doing the best they could with the information and resources available to them. Today the schools and the media play an ever-increasing role in shaping a woman's self-image and self-esteem, her perceptions of what is natural and normal and what is not, and the voices she carries in her head.

If, as a child, a woman's caregivers were loving and affirming, her Inner Parents will likely care lovingly for her Inner Child. If they were judgmental, critical, or neglectful, her Inner Parents will likely relate in a similar way to her Inner Child. The Inner Parents may be identified as the Critical Parent, the Nurturing Parent, and the Protective Parent.

## The Nurturing Parent, the Critical Parent, and the Protective Parent

The Nurturing Parent listens to the Inner Child's feelings and needs, and responds with care and compassion. She encourages a woman, as needed, to give herself a break, to gather or buy herself a bunch of flowers, to take a walk on the beach, or do something creative for no particular reason at all. The Nurturing Parent is the voice in a woman's head that says, *I love you. You are beautiful. You are a gift to the world.* Or, when a woman is upset she may say, *I'm so sorry you are hurting. No wonder you are upset. You didn't do as well as you had hoped. It's okay. You did your best and I am proud of you.*

The Critical Parent is the voice of the Inner Critic or Judge. This is the voice in a woman's head that tells her she will never, ever, be good enough. In many women, the voice of the Critical Parent runs relentlessly, day in and day out.

A woman may believe that she needs the voice of the Inner Critic to keep her motivated and pressure her to do the right thing. Rather than genuinely motivating a woman, or strengthening her ability to accomplish what she wants, the Critical Parent causes her to fear failure and lose faith in herself. It prevents a woman from accessing self-compassion. It compromises her creativity and can paralyze her into nonaction. Even if she accomplishes great things, she will never be happy—nor fulfill her true potential—while driven by the Critical Parent.

The Protective Parent is an advocate for the Inner Child's wellbeing. Not concerned with seeking the approval of others, she doesn't hesitate to stand up to any form of dismissal, disrespect, or abuse. She stands strong in the face of over-demanding people or situations.

Many women have virtually no experience of the Nurturing Parent or Protective Parent. We hear the stories of some of these women in the pages of this book—as adults they lived for years in an inner world of ruthless self-judgment that they accepted without question, as readily as the fish today accepts the polluted water it lives in.

Shame and anger reach an all-time high in the experience of infidelity, carrying some women over the threshold of what can be denied, to the point of *Enough. No more.* No more of this ruthless self-judgment and self-denial. This is the voice, the wake up call pounding so loudly that it can activate the momentum for a woman to step out and onto the path to doing what is needed to reclaim not only her self-esteem and self-worth, but also her inner authority and personal power.

## A Voice of Loving Kindness

It takes courage for a woman to say *Enough, no more,* to the mean and abusive voices of the Critical Parent rather than silence or numb them with substance abuse and process addictions. It requires responding to any uncomfortable or distressing feelings with the loving kindness of the Nurturing or Protective Parent. It requires a woman talk to herself the way she would talk to someone she loves and wants to support in the midst of a breakdown. Changing the habitual voices playing in her head requires she do this again and again, day in and day out. When she forgets or has no time, or simply can't find the energy to do it, she acknowledges this— no shame, no blame. And she begins again. She does this again and again until the voices of love are louder than those of fear and condemnation.

### Exercise: *Cultivating the Voice of Loving Kindness and Compassion*

Today—this week—pay attention to the voices in your head. Whenever you hear the voice of the Critical Parent, meet it with, *Enough. No more.*

Ask yourself, *What would a Nurturing or Protective Parent say?* It may be as simple as, *I love you*, or, *It's okay.* It may say, *Please stop being so mean to yourself,* or, *Don't say yes, when you want to say no.*

As well as noticing the voices in your head, notice the energy and sensations that arise in your body as you listen to the different voices. With your breath, intention, or imagination, create space around any tensions you may notice. Whenever you are aware of the energy moving towards love, relax into it. Notice that as you put your attention on that loving feeling, it expands.

This is what our Inner Child wants—for us to feel, accept, and love her. It's exactly the same as what we want for ourselves. We don't have to wait for anyone else to give us the love that is our birthright.

It takes courage for a woman to say to herself the three-word statement that should be the most natural thing in the world for a human being to say to herself: *"I love you."* As she does this, in time she will discover it comes more naturally and, often, unbidden.

Then, she might ask, *If it's the most natural thing in the world, why is it so damn difficult?*

## Why *Is* it So Damn Difficult?

Human infants are born with approximately 25% of the brain's patterns already formed. The remaining 75% are formed through accumulated experiences during the early years. The most important of those experiences have to do with an infant's relationships.

Our earliest experiences form neural pathways in the brain that profoundly influence the ways in which we view ourselves and our world. During this early formative period, our nervous system learns whether to trust or fear, and whether to love or protect. Without the loving and consistent care of primary caregivers, the brain literally doesn't develop in a complete and healthy way.

The good news is that thanks to revolutionary discoveries in the field of neuroscience, scientists now have a greater understanding of neuroplasticity—how the brain can change throughout a person's life. Simply put, this change is directed by our mind's focus and attention.

With persistence and repetition, we can gradually and over time create new neural pathways in the brain—pathways that replace the familiar fearful and disempowering patterns with new and empowering patterns. We are not the victims of the past. We are not irreparably damaged.

This reprogramming is set in motion whenever a woman replaces the voices of the Critical Parent with those of loving kindness and self-acceptance. We will see it too, when a woman calls up the Warrior in her and replaces the disempowering voices running through her mind with voices of encouragement, strength, and affirmation.

The impact is strengthened when a woman engages her feelings and her body in the process. This may mean, for example, imagining how it might feel to experience that loving kindness in her body, and adjusting her body as needed into a position that accompanies these feelings of loving kindness. She may feel a softening in the body, more energy around her heart, and an easing of some of the tension she is holding. Or, perhaps she may need to imagine how it might feel in her body to align with the thoughts and energy of the Warrior Woman, and move her body into a position to reflect that energy. She may find herself standing straighter, taller, and breathing more deeply. The more deeply the feelings and the body and thoughts are engaged, the stronger the imprint.

We will see that when a woman is feeling so disempowered that she is unable to access any experience of hope or of strength, even the awareness that she is in the disempowered mind rather than in the heart and mind of the Warrior, can be something to be grateful for. This recognition and acceptance of where she is creates an opening into another possibility.

# CHAPTER 6

## *Women Betrayed—The Beliefs and Illusions that Blind Us*

We begin here with Helen's story to introduce the myriad ways in which the absence of self-love and the accompanying beliefs, illusions, and self-betraying patterns expressed in a woman's life place her in a position to be betrayed. The mindsets that appear repeatedly through the earlier part of Helen's story—looking to a man for security and fulfillment, not knowing what she wanted or needed, not knowing anything about boundaries or how to set them—are epidemic among women.

All of this leaves us disempowered, with no voice—not knowing what we want, and unable to take a stand for ourselves. Thus we live—most often unaware—a life of self-abandonment and self-betrayal. Here we see how infidelity may be the wake up call, and the beginning of a woman's journey home to herself.

### HELEN: *"I didn't know how to express what I wanted and needed"*

*When I married him, I didn't know myself ... didn't think to ask, did I really love this person? I didn't like myself, so how could I know if I liked him, or if I wanted to marry him? I had not yet learned not to say yes unless I really meant it. I had developed the belief that no matter what, I would not get the support I needed. I had learned to give myself away, to get just a little something. I just did what was expected of me, as I always had.*

*I had not been taught how to be in relationship. I wasn't taught at school, I didn't have good role models at home. So when things started getting bad, neither of us knew how to handle it. We didn't know how to have a conversation about what was happening, or how to repair the damage that had been done. I didn't know what I wanted and needed from the relationship, and if I did, I didn't know how to ask for it. It wasn't until some eight years after we separated that I could really say I love myself, and I know what I need.*

*I was with him for eight years, and most of it was awful. He wouldn't talk to me about what was wrong. Why did I stay so long? I was ashamed. I believed that I was ugly, undesirable, not worthy of love. He treated me so poorly. When I was pregnant, he wouldn't touch me. He wouldn't see a counselor with me.*

*I knew Peter was a chronic liar. Still, I refused to believe he was cheating, even though the signs were there. It became clearer and clearer that he had no attraction, no care for me. It was all about him. Why the denial? I thought this was what I was supposed to do, that he was just going through a phase and that we would stay together through thick and thin. This was the way it was with my parents. They were my role models and no one taught me any different. I always believed when there are problems you work it out, you don't separate. I couldn't grasp that he didn't love me.*

*It makes me sick now, that I would put myself in such a relationship. It mirrored the relationship between my parents. What my dad said, we did. My mother was unhappy, lonely and unconfident … she taught me that a woman was supposed to stay in a marriage, no matter how bad it was, and to give herself up in the process. I feared that if I left my husband, I would have nobody and that was scary—so scary that I was not willing to leave the relationship. His emotions, everything, were with the other woman, but we had still been having sex together. That was the sick part. I was giving myself up sexually to try to keep him, and he was with another woman.*

*I had so much shame at this point because it was so clear he didn't love me anymore. I remember one evening in the living room, I asked him to come to me. I told him I wanted to hold him. I said, I don't know what has happened, but I can work on this—I can make it work for us. I was blaming myself. I felt so bad about myself, I was willing to take crumbs. I didn't know anything about setting boundaries. After we hugged, he walked away … he wouldn't have anything to do with me. I felt like I was a screw up. The reality was he was not treating me well.*

*My parents were both functional alcoholics and not available to give me what I wanted and needed. When I was four years old, my mother was told by the pediatrician to ignore me when I had my temper tantrums, so as not to reinforce them. I would wonder, What did I do that was so bad, that no one is here when I am crying? No one was there to hear me when I was sad, so I quit feeling. I learned my needs were not important.*

There was nothing in Helen's family that opened any window into her even entertaining the notion that she was worthy and deserving of love, of knowing what would nourish her, or who was worthy of her trust. In fact, to the contrary—Helen learned her needs were not important. She learned that she didn't matter, and that no one was there for her. These beliefs, taken in so very deeply as an infant and young child, will infiltrate her every thought and action and continue to play out throughout her life— until she learns otherwise.

While the human brain is neurologically wired for connection, shame is rooted in our fear that we are unworthy of love and connection. Nothing strikes more deeply at our existential fears, than the fear of being involuntarily alone. Helen's shame was deeply established long before she married Peter. She lived her whole life believing there was something wrong with her—that she was flawed, not good enough. She had always done what was expected of her, without ever really knowing or asking what she herself wanted. She had not even thought to question this.

Setting boundaries requires a woman be clear about her needs and expectations of a relationship. Helen, like so many women, learned as a child to disconnect from her body as a means of not feeling the helplessness, fear, and pain she felt. In the absence of self-love, disconnected from the instincts and intuition of her own body, she does not know what she needs and wants. She is enmeshed in the values she has absorbed through the patriarchal, male dominated society she lives in—just as her mother and her mother's mother before her, through millennium. No wonder she was unable to set the boundaries that are necessities in relationships. She didn't even know what a boundary was.

All of this played out in a mostly loveless eight-year marriage. Helen knew Peter was a liar and that he didn't care for her, but her habitual ways of thinking kept her imprisoned. She believed that this was what marriage was—you stay no matter what. Why wouldn't she think this? It was what she saw with her parents. There was no love, no communication, and the same was true in her marriage.

We numb to avoid feeling fearful, disconnected, inadequate, and "less than." For years Helen did what so many women do: she blamed and shamed herself rather than entertain the notion of leaving her partner. This actually makes a lot of sense if you consider our neurobiology. We are social animals. We need others to survive. With rare exception, this is at the heart of many of our behaviors. We create patterns of behavior that help us to stay connected with others, even when it's just a bare thread of a connection, or even if those others are harming us. It's not rational. It's survival. And when it works, even partially, it becomes automatic. Rarely do we question it—and even more rarely do we recognize it. For Helen, this went on for eight years until, one day, something rose up in her to say *Enough. No more.*

### HELEN:

*One day I put my boundary up. I was forty-eight years of age, teaching full-time at university, and still I didn't know about personal boundaries. For months now, he wouldn't do anything with me or with the kids. I would ask him what was going on. What did he need? What did he want? Usually he wouldn't say a word. If he responded, it would just be, "I don't know." This time, I looked at him. I wanted to shake him and yell, "What are you doing?" I got so mad, which was new for me. I smashed something, and then I marched out and slammed the door.*

*I had finally seen that there was nothing left. That night, I told him I was moving to another city. I see now how narcissistic he was, how much I took, and how I will never do that to myself again. And yet at the same time I was praying he would say, "Don't go, I'll work on it with you."*

*He didn't. I packed up and left with the kids. I felt so, so awful.*

When a woman doesn't feel heard or validated—when she feels shamed and unseen—she will often resort to pushing and provoking her partner. Helen's husband responded as most men will. Men who feel shame when they are criticized for being inadequate either shut down, as Peter did—which brings a woman to poke and provoke even more—or come back with anger.

Lamenting the behaviour of her partner but still taking it; expressions of anger, rage, complaining, whining, feeling threatened or victimized are all clues that boundaries are needing to be set and enforced. At first, setting and enforcing boundaries can feel scary. A woman may feel guilty. She may initially need support in stating and holding her boundaries.

After years of being not only unable to express her wants and needs, but of being *unaware* of her wants and needs, finally, in the face of her husband's unresponsiveness, Helen's frustration and anger could no longer be repressed. It suddenly hit her that things were never going to

72

change in this relationship—and that this was no longer tolerable to her. Frequently, the driving force behind this kind of intense emotional reaction is the unmet needs of our Inner Child being triggered. However, just what brought her to this point Helen herself doesn't know. Like with a pot of boiling water, it can be contained for so long and then—no more.

Her praying that Peter would stay, even while telling him she was leaving, reflects the struggle between the newly awakened self that longs for freedom, and the habitual voice of self-betrayal that lives in the familiar safety of the known. This is the struggle between the newly awakened self that recognizes it is over, the part of her that still wants the relationship to work, and the tremendous fear that can arise in the face of stepping up and out into the unknown.

In Helen's leaving, we see the immense courage and resolve of the Warrior energy that, so long suppressed, now propels her into action—even in the face of her fear. The more consciousness, the more embodied presence she can bring to that experience—and to her recollection of that experience—the more deeply it will imprint on her body and psyche. It will be reinforced and strengthened whenever she calls that experience up in herself, and, using her breath, grounds it in her body.

### HELEN:

*When we separated I went right into another relationship. I knew that it wasn't good to do this, but I did. I truly believed this other man was interested in me, cared for me, adored me and for that, I chose to be with him. I didn't ask myself what I really wanted.*

*I stayed with him because he was a man who told me I was beautiful. I later found out he was a liar. He told me what he knew I wanted to hear. He was, however, also a man who was willing to work on issues. We went to counseling together, which was a good step. I liked him, but I couldn't handle his inauthenticity and lack of positive values. I would tell him I was done, but found I still was not capable of setting firm boundaries.*

*We continued to break up and get together again. We even got married—I somehow thought marriage would make it better. Six months later, I finally realized I had to end this. I was dying inside. Not because of him, but because we weren't good together. We weren't good for each other.*

*He told me that if I ended the marriage, he would never talk to me again. That was the best thing he had ever said because I wasn't able to stay away, but I didn't want to be with him. We never spoke again.*

Helen's heading straight into another relationship, even while knowing it wasn't good to do so, reflects the tenacity of self-betraying ways of thinking and behaving. And so Helen repeats her earlier patterns, succumbing to the belief that she could find her worth in the eyes of a man who told her she was beautiful, told her what he knew she wanted to hear. While Helen now had a taste of the Warrior within herself, it was not yet enough to sustain her in the face of her habitual patterns. Even though Helen recognized she needed to leave, she felt herself incapable of setting boundaries. Again, we see the strength of the voices of self-betrayal relentlessly pounding in her head saying, *You can't, you can't leave.* This is even after she knows, for she has proven to herself, that she *can* leave.

A woman will need, time and time again, to call herself back to the path of the Warrior . On those occasions when she simply cannot find it within herself to do this, she calls up an acceptance of *what is* in this moment, and compassion for herself in the plight she faces. Even calling herself to a place of acceptance and compassion requires an element of fierceness and will to resist the old and familiar; not to give in. *I will NOT go there. Breathing in self-acceptance, I choose compassion … I choose love.*

She will need, time and time again, to bring her attention back to what has been newly awakened, to call up and embody those qualities that she is sensing from deep within her, long to be reclaimed. She will need to do this until these qualities are thoroughly integrated into her being. Helen had the sense and the strength to seek counseling. Until the new is established, it is simply in many cases wise to seek support.

**HELEN:**

*Now I haven't been with a man for a whole year. That's a first for me. I began a program that put me on a path of deep healing. I found this part of me that carried the belief that I was ugly, a belief I carried over from my childhood and from my marriage. I noticed every time I looked at myself in the mirror, I would feel nauseous. I wasn't buying clothes for myself. Whenever I saw him with his lover—his now wife—I got nervous and felt old and ugly.*

*In the past, I would have ignored these feelings and moved on. But I realized I didn't want to feel that way anymore. I wanted to heal the part of me that believed I was ugly. I began to notice that part of me whenever the feeling came up, to accept it, and to give my attention to the feelings and to where I felt them in my body. I found the deep shame that I carried there. A memory came to me of when I was a little girl, and a boy called me a boy.*

*I went home and told my mom, but she didn't validate my feelings of upset about this—she just said not to worry about it. I don't think she ever told me I was pretty. I didn't know validation as a child.*

*As part of my healing program I learned to witness, to accept, to validate, and to empower the many aspects of my "inner child" that I had earlier rejected. I gave my inner child a voice. The process is about taking every feeling like this that comes up, and accepting it as a gift. I was empowered.*

*I realized I had lost my connection to my femininity. Allowing Peter's lack of attention to victimize me, I had begun dressing in a more masculine way, to wear the pants in the family. Now, I began to shift these feelings. Today I don't need other people's approval. I don't need to "prove" my femininity because I am actually feeling more feminine.*

Helen had tasted enough of her newly awakened self to determine that she would never return to the old. At this point she not only recognized the importance of not heading into another relationship, not falling back into the old patterns and influences—but also of setting forth on a path of deep healing.

It could be said that this program truly turned things around for Helen. But this is only partially true. It was Helen's strong intention and determination not to return to her old patterns but to forge a new ground for herself, that set her firmly on the path of the Warrior Woman. This rarely happens overnight.

Helen speaks of taking every feeling that comes up and accepting it as a gift. This is a very powerful practice. By accepting every feeling that arises with gratitude, the energy shifts not only from blaming others, but also from blaming oneself. Negative tendencies are experienced calmly— simply observed. The energy moves from the fear and contraction that underlies blame and anger, into gratitude and expansion.

Helen came to not only recognize and name the inner voices of shame and the other parts of herself she had earlier rejected, but to feel where that shame was in her body. Even as an adult, when shamed a woman will revert to feeling "very little." As a child, it was too painful to feel those feelings … survival required numbing or suppressing them. Now, Helen learned to feel and witness and give voice to those feelings. Awareness is always the first step, and by accepting and feeling rather than denying those inner voices, Helen is no longer unconsciously at the effect of them.

She can question them—question the values they reflect, and the reality they affirm. *Is this what I choose?*

Witnessing, accepting and validating the hurting parts of herself requires a strong commitment to be mindful of the debilitating, reactive patterns that emerge spontaneously and with tremendous force at a moment's notice, and to call up the courage of the Warrior Woman to be in her body and present—to it all. Feeling the feelings in the body is essential, or the awareness and acceptance is only conceptual.

Joining this program was an important step in Helen's reaching out and sharing her story with trusted others. She can now receive the empathy that is so crucial to dispelling shame. Today, she doesn't need other people's approval. She has learned to talk about how she feels and to ask for what she needs.

### HELEN:

*Even today, eight years after Peter and I separated and after this year of personal growth work, there is still anger in there, and shame. Shame of how I stayed with him and gave my body to him to try to keep him, even when there was no love there. I still feel so bad about how he left, how he did it ... It really hurts if a man or woman doesn't know how to leave; it really leaves scars. The way Peter left, it totally scarred me. He would never talk about what was wrong.*

*I was never able to really feel the anger, to let the anger out, until about eight months ago. I had been too afraid of that part of me. And it had been pushed so far down in me, when I was a child, that I had no access to it. Now I let it out. If I see a picture of him, or something that triggers a memory, I let it out. I scream. "Fuck you, you fucking bastard ..." whatever comes out.*

*I can feel the shame under the anger ... the deep, deep shame at the piece of crap I was in that moment when he treated me like that—all the while he was with this other woman and I continued to have sex with him. I feel nauseous when I think about it. It's that deep, deep shame that rises in me. I know now that it was my shame, and how I felt about myself that kept me in the relationship. I didn't think I deserved any better. That's the part that's really hard, the part that really scars.*

And so, eight years after leaving Peter, Helen still finds herself to some degree at the effect of the shame that she has carried through her entire

76

life. What is radically different is that she is now very aware of the shame and how it works in her. How a woman responds to any debilitating feeling or reaction that arises in her depends in part on her awareness of the dynamic itself and of how it catches her. With awareness, there can be a level of objectivity—an ability to witness, rather than totally be at the effect of it—and so, to choose appropriate action. The fact that the shame persists testifies to the strength of these patterns that are so deeply entrenched in the body, mind and psyche, and the determination and courage of those women who, like Helen, persist.

The fact is that Helen has come a great distance. The anger and shame that she still feels is understandable. There was never any closure to her and Peter's relationship. Unacknowledged, the anger a woman will feel at the abuse she has experienced and all that she carries with that—her shame in her own role in the situation—has never been given space for its expression. Helen now recognizes the value of expressing her anger, and the sense of empowerment that comes with allowing this energy to move through her.

It is essential that a woman does not succumb to the false sense of power she may experience when projecting her hatred onto another (see Chapter 10: *Projections—What We Resist, Persists*). This is not to say that what her partner did was right, but to recognize the need to come to that place in herself where she no longer blames another; where it's no longer about "what he did," but rather about her standing in her own place of empowerment in relation to this.

The first step in using anger wisely is to recognize that she has a choice in how she expresses and experiences it. She will learn that she has a choice to be angry, to be sad, to be happy—her feelings do not depend on the external world appearing as she wants it to be. But for now, expressing this anger is also a form of purging. The body needs to eliminate it. By allowing it to come up—to be expressed—it can be released, making space for new possibilities to enter.

What could ease the way for Helen is for her to bring awareness and compassion to those parts of herself that still carry shame, and to that voice of the victim that continues to project her anger at herself, onto Peter. Again, this is not—not *ever*—to say that what he did was acceptable, but to recognize that in harboring these thoughts it is herself that she is hurting and disempowering.

Since the initial uprising of the Warrior Woman, and her taste of freedom and empowerment, Helen has persisted in reclaiming this aspect of herself. Rarely is this process of transforming the familiar voices of self-betrayal to voices of deep self-acceptance and self-empowerment a linear, straightforward one. It is more often a matter of a woman's patiently and persistently acknowledging the conflict between the two tendencies, accepting rather than resisting or struggling with this conflict, and choosing to align with the voices of empowerment rather than those of self-betrayal.

### JESSICA: *"Whatever I thought they needed, I would provide it … to get the love I wanted"*

*Initially we had a monogamous relationship. I was supporting the family, working full-time. He was the house husband and trying to keep the family together emotionally. Throughout the relationship he'd always been restless, but because he wasn't earning money, he wasn't secure enough to leave. It was a very stressful time for both of us. I was on the verge of an emotional breakdown. He started saying he didn't want to stay with me.*

*We had been married for fourteen years and shared a very beautiful musical relationship, we traveled a lot, and in many ways we had a good life. Now, with all these stresses, we began questioning whether we wanted to be together, and over the next five years went back and forth between a monogamous marriage and an open marriage. He was into drugs and partying. I wasn't, but I accepted he did that. I loved him. I told myself, We can do this. We are adult people and we can be intimate with others as well as each other.*

*Finally, at a weekend workshop, I got a very clear understanding of myself and how and why I got hooked in with men. In me, there's always been this feeling of being incomplete. My mother died when I was very young. My father was very emotionally unavailable. I saw at this workshop how I would look to my father to try to fill the hole in me. I would ask myself, How can I be the right person for my dad? Who do I need to be so my dad will pay attention to me?*

*I learned how to psychically draw someone to me so they would pay attention to me. With my first boyfriend, I became exactly the kind of woman he wanted me to be. It was totally unconscious—I didn't even know I was doing it. I soon found I did this with all men. I would find things I had in common with them, and then provide them with what they needed. I would fulfill all they wanted in a woman—the smart one, the artistic one—whatever I thought they needed, I would provide it. I now recognized that this was what I thought I needed to do, to get the love I wanted.*

*At some point, it came out that in the two years we had recommitted to each other my husband had been going to prostitutes and to sex clubs with group sex, having every kind of sordid experience he could have. He had been with over thirty women. I just had to trust I'd be okay. I was in shock, so weak that I was really afraid for myself. For three years he had been deceiving me, using my money, putting my health at risk. It's been eighteen months since we separated but even now, talking about it, I feel the shock in my body. Even now, there are tears falling down my face.*

*My husband openly shared the experiences he was having with these other women. Everyone knew our business, our story. I felt incredibly violated by this. He totally dismissed my request he not talk about it with others … it seemed he couldn't go anywhere without sharing. All of this contributed to the further deterioration of my health. Knowing people were talking about me, and us, I felt really embarrassed … I was full of shame. I felt people looking at me in a different way. I was very vulnerable, very unsure, very insecure about myself as a woman. Even now, eighteen months after we've separated, I tend to isolate myself. I'm not sure I can stay in this town.*

*That one insight I had gotten at that weekend workshop didn't change anything, because I still didn't know what it meant to know myself as complete. I understood how I was looking to fill the hole, but the hole was still there. Intellectually, I understood that I was complete, and that's how a woman "should" be in a relationship. I could now see what I did, but I hadn't actually recognized who I was. I could see I had been with men because I hadn't felt complete, but I didn't yet know how to feel complete.*

*My husband came home from a work-related trip to Israel to tell me he had met the love of his life. He told me she was coming to join him in six weeks. I agreed to keep living with him, to support him financially. It was crazy, but I was weak and on the verge of an emotional breakdown. I kept thinking, I have to be as calm and loving to my husband as possible. I just want to see our son get through his final year of school. I don't want him to get caught in all this craziness.*

*Meanwhile they were communicating all the time by phone and Skype. I emailed this other woman. I told her that this was the biggest thing that had ever happened to me. This man who has been my rock, who is the father of my child, is leaving me to be with you. Please give me this little time before you arrive here, to get used to this. I am not well and this will make me even more sick.*

*I was afraid for myself. She didn't reply, and they continued to communicate. I emailed her again. I said, I am asking you woman to woman, I understand you want to be with this man, but please give me this little time to close down my family.*

*I didn't know what I was going to do when she arrived. I didn't think I had the strength in my nervous system to stay, to having her running around town, to see her. She didn't write back to me. I said to my husband, I will love you, you are the father of my child. And I can forgive you. But I don't understand how you can be with such a woman, a woman who will not hear my request that she give us this little bit of time.*

*We kept it together through the six weeks. I footed the bill. I didn't want to blame him. I don't think I could face that I had invested so much in him, and he had let me down. What I came to realize at the end of it was that I had let myself down. In time, I realized that I was really no longer interested in supporting my husband. It was time for me to support myself.*

*I was like a wounded animal when I left town. I was down to ninety-seven pounds and looked so, yes, wounded. A lot of women who have been through betrayal look like that—they don't look well. It takes a long while to recover. Oh, it's really, really awful. I feel so, so much compassion when I hear of a woman in this situation. Oh my God, I've been through it. It's terrible, horrible. My heart goes out to her.*

*My mother died when I was very young, but this betrayal by my husband was the deepest grieving I had ever experienced. I was grieving the loss of not only my husband, but myself. I had thrown myself so deeply, so innocently into marriage with this man when I was only twenty-five, and I lost who I was. At twenty-five I was adventurous, strong, courageous, independent—and I became this unwell, thin, insecure mess. It was hard to accept that I had let myself go that much, that I had lost myself and come to this.*

*Some time after separating from my husband, I went to India. I was still grieving one minute and angry the next, and I wanted to get to the bottom of this. I was introduced to a course which systematically took me through a very deep exploration of who I was and who I was not. I began to inquire: What am I grieving, why am I so sad, what has this role of wife and mother and homemaker meant to me? What is the loss that I am grieving?*

*I came to a very deep realization of who I was. I came to recognize I did not need to be in a relationship with another person to complete something in me. I still fall into my old patterns, but now I can recognize when I am there. I know I can be myself and be fine.*

Generation after generation, girls and women have been seduced by all manner of subtle and not so subtle means into making sure they know everything about "their" men: their fathers, their husbands, their boyfriends. This is in direct opposition to asking the question Sri Ramana Maharshi, widely recognized as one of the greatest Hindu gurus of modern times, said to be the most important question of all: *"Who Am I?"* What would it mean if a woman chose to live into that question, rather than seeking to know everything possible about "her" men?

Again, Jessica was one of so many women looking outside of herself to find the love she wanted, the love that she never received as a child, the self-love and self-worth that is further denied her in a patriarchal and media-driven culture where a woman's worth is seen to be sourced outside of herself—and most often, through the eyes of a man.

The depth of the longing for that love she has been denied, the desperation that drives that longing, the belief that she can indeed find the love she yearns for both outside of herself and in the arms of another is so evident in Jessica's statement, *"I would fulfill all they wanted in a woman—the smart one, the artistic one—whatever I thought they needed, I would provide it."* Even after discovering that her husband had been deceiving her—using her money, putting her health at risk, denying her request he not speak openly about his affairs with others—she stood by him, unable to take a stand for her own physical and emotional wellbeing.

Many a woman will find it easier to deny the reality of her partner's behaviour, and to continue living in her illusions and hopes of what may be. She will continue allowing her partner to cross boundaries because *"I love him," "in time he will change,"* or, *"forgiveness is spiritual."* Does his great body or the value of sharing the same interests compensate for all the times he doesn't act like a responsible and respectful adult, or in other ways repeatedly disrespects you and your relationship together? A woman wants to be optimistic, to "think positive"! Is it possible that at times, "positive thinking" can be another form of self-betrayal? Is it possible that before a woman can connect authentically with a "positive thought," she first needs to meet herself authentically, where she is? In searching out there for what can only be sourced from within, a woman will inevitably, as Jessica found, lose herself.

During those periods of open marriage, Jessica's statement, *"I told myself, We can do this. We are adult people and we can be intimate with others as well as each other,"* would suggest that this was something she did not feel sure about and did to please her husband—to keep his love. Her reticence is warranted. It takes a tremendous amount of maturity to be in an open marriage. As became evident between Jessica and her husband, unless a couple knows themselves to be whole and complete within themselves—and they would be one rare couple—it will inevitably and insidiously breed the jealousy, suspicion, and mistrust that destroys intimacy.

Even couples in open marriages have assumptions about their outside relationships. The spoken or unspoken assumptions and agreements of an open marriage may be that each may have multiple partners but not become emotionally attached or have secret liaisons with others. More often than not, emotional attachments and liaisons develop. The sense of betrayal and devastation is felt as acutely as when there has been an assumption of monogamy.

Jessica's husband openly sharing his experiences with other women, even in the face of Jessica's request he not do this, and even though it further contributed to the deterioration of her health, is typical of that narcissistic sense of entitlement of the unfaithful. The dilemma here is that at the same time Jessica needed to stand up for herself, to set effective boundaries and say *Enough*, not only was she feeling full of shame and very insecure, but she was also on the verge of an emotional breakdown. She was grieving—deeply. Grief alone is exhausting. When grieving, a woman simply doesn't have the energy to do things she usually does. It's not that she *won't*, it's that she *can't*.

Boundaries are limits that a woman defines to identify what are reasonable, safe and permissible ways for other people to behave around her, and how she will respond when someone violates those limits. Setting boundaries means taking responsibility and being adult in a relationship. Effective boundaries emerge as a woman learns to inhabit her body and to trust, value, and listen to herself. Boundaries emerge from her knowing what she deserves and what she doesn't deserve, and from her knowing that what she wants, needs, likes, and dislikes are important.

Mind and body depleted, it is impossible to think clearly. The first thing a woman needs do is to recognize this, and to take what steps she can to return to a place of calm. Calm first and then, in time, clarity. It can be invaluable to reach out to a trusted other, get support, get counsel.

While Jessica was not able to set effective boundaries in her relationship, she did step out to assert and protect herself and her family. She confronted, in no uncertain terms, those women she knew were partnering with her husband. Given her health, this was no small thing to do. It is a compelling indication of the power of hitting that wall of *Enough*, to activate that Warrior energy—even when a woman is exhausted. This part of Jessica's story is told in Chapter 9: *The Other Woman—Sluts, Bitches, Whores!*

We don't know why Jessica did not turn to others for support. Many women will not do so because they are ashamed that their partner's infidelity is somehow their fault, or because they believe their distress is a sign of weakness. However, while conventional beliefs hold that a "strong" and "mature" woman should be independent and self-sufficient, research points to the fact that being able to turn to others for emotional support is a sign and source of strength. It takes courage to acknowledge our weaknesses, our so-called "imperfections."

Jessica's dilemma as to whether or not to stay in her town, and her experience of people looking at her differently, is shared by most women. It requires a huge amount of strength for a woman to stand in a place in herself from which she is able to meet the gaze of these people with the silent declaration, *I have been betrayed and here I am.*

While this may be something to aspire to, in many cases it is simply not kind or reasonable that a woman demand this of herself—at least in the early aftermath of infidelity. Many women will choose to leave their known community, to begin a new life away from the stories that are circulating; away from the eyes perhaps judging, perhaps ridiculing, perhaps pitying them.

Jessica said that her insight that she was "complete" and that's how a woman "should be" in a relationship, didn't change anything in that she didn't yet know how to feel complete. However, she had now named and could recognize that the source of the unhealthy patterns she fell into in her relationships with men, was within herself. This recognition, this awareness, is huge. When Jessica is able to recognize the hold of this pattern over her and how it gets activated, she can begin to change the pattern—to choose differently—and in doing so lay the circuitry for new patterns to emerge.

Jessica's wanting to be keep things together through their son's final year of school is very understandable—yet no teenage boy will be oblivious to what is happening. Born of their love, his parents' conflict is inevitably reverberating through every cell of his body. While he may bury his head in his books, or party with his friends, every moment he will be absorbing what is being reflected to him of his mother's self-respect and ability to stand up for her own physical and emotional wellbeing.

What is being reflected to her son with respect to a woman's ability or right to demand her husband's responsibility to her, and to the family? What will he carry from this into his relationships with women, and with his own children?

When a woman finds herself betrayed, she may have no idea what to say to the children. Most every mother is caught completely off guard. As we see in Chapter 17: *Children of Infidelity—How They Hurt, and How They Heal*, the bottom line is that when parents are role models of infidelity, their children can't help but react. They may have a particularly hard time with issues of trust and intimacy, and finding their way through the challenges of dating and marriage. Others may extend themselves in their determination to *not* be like their father.

While Jessica didn't want to blame her husband, she had every right to expect that he would act with respect towards her and towards their son. She came to recognize that in standing by him, in not taking a more forceful stand, and not facing the truth of what was happening and of who he was, she had let herself down—she had betrayed herself. Yes, her health made it exceptionally difficult at this stage for her to do this. This dynamic between her and her husband—her inability to recognize what boundaries needed to be set, her inability to set those boundaries, and her husband's self-absorption—had been at play for so very long, that it is no wonder she had little of herself left. Her realization that she was no longer interested in supporting her husband—that it was time for her to instead support herself—was her declaration that she had had enough.

Recognizing that she was still grieving one minute and angry the next, Jessica engaged in a process of self-inquiry. While grief may be accepted, as children we learn that anger and rage are "not nice." A child can even be punished by an angry parent or teacher for being angry. Yet a woman can use this energy to see into places she cannot usually see, aspects of herself that have long been buried or simply never seen the light of day. Rather than trying to suppress her rage—or using it to burn down everything around her—these energies can open a door into new ways of being and new possibilities.

Self-inquiry may also be explored in the form of journaling, meditation, counseling, therapy, prayers, or women's circles. It requires the willingness, courage, persistence, and compassionate heart of the Warrior to invite into consciousness areas so long denied, so deeply buried. It is one of the keys to a woman's returning to life with a new knowing.

The empathy Jessica speaks of feeling for other women in the aftermath of infidelity is one of the many deepenings that comes with a woman's not repressing or projecting her anger, not dismissing her grief in order to "get on with her life." It is this empathy that gives a woman the capacity to be fully with another woman through the shock, the anger, and the grief of infidelity.

The relationship ended, but looking at herself and the unwell, insecure mess she felt she had become, Jessica found it hard to accept that she *"had lost (herself) and come to this."* What can be helpful is for her to hold herself in compassion, for simply not knowing how to have done it differently at the time.

As is true of many women sharing their experience of infidelity, Jessica realized that even now, years later, she still feels the trauma of it in her body—to the point of tears. Infidelity can cut so deep that even after addressing it to the degree Jessica has, a woman can carry a residue of this trauma that surfaces, to be met again—and again. Each time, another layer of the onion. Each time a woman accesses ever deeper levels of empowerment and presence.

Several years after Jessica had shared her story with me, manuscript finally near completion, I sent it to her for any corrections or comments. Below, she shares with me an update of her life since we had last spoken.

### JESSICA:

*My life has changed immeasurably. Having a very kind and considerate partner has really helped, but ultimately I have done the work ...*

*I have a very new relationship with intimacy now—intimacy with myself. My tendency had been to look to a man for happiness. I didn't know any better. I didn't know how to be alone. I was an independent person in many ways, but whenever I was by myself I would be afraid, insecure. I would fill the space with whatever I could ... friends, activities, etc.*

*After my time in India, a deep unraveling occurred. I saw that no matter whom I was with or what I was doing, someone was always there and that someone was me. I was present in every single moment. Not only that, but the very fact that I was there gave meaning to the moment I was experiencing. It was just so obvious and simple. It's such a relief to no longer feel I need someone else to make me feel complete or whole.*

*I also have the strength to ask for support from friends. I see how important friendships are and I'll never go it alone again when things get tough. The main thing I am working on now is restoring my son's trust in me and rebuilding our relationship.*

Self-love naturally expresses outwardly in an innate desire to take good care of yourself, and to focus on what brings you happiness and fulfillment.

### MAGGIE: *"To try to make that marriage work ... I did not always take a stand for what I knew was right for me"*

*My ex-husband was a spiritual teacher, and with that, there was so much hypocrisy. He was in a lineage—a spiritual lineage—of teachings that was also my lineage so it really confronted the way I was seeing my world spiritually, and fractured my understanding of what a spiritual life was supposed to bring us. There was, in fact, so much physical and emotional abuse in that relationship.*

*To try to make that marriage work, to bend around his infidelity, I did not always take a stand for what I knew was right for me. I watch that pattern in myself still, all the time. It may at times be subtle, but it's there.*

*My first son had just been born; he was maybe eight hours old. My husband insisted on a blowjob. I'd just been in labor, I had just had a baby ... I was on a different planet. I resisted. He got very angry. I resisted more. He got angrier. He stood up, zipped his pants, and said, "Well then, I'll go to a prostitute."*

*While he was standing there, fastening his belt, this incredible peace came over me. It was undeniable ... it was such a presence, and I think that if I'd hung out in that presence I would've let him go find the prostitute, and let him sink his own ship because he would have felt so guilty. I didn't have to acquiesce. In this moment there was this peace, this choice point, where I could have let him fall on his own sword—but I got too scared. I begged him to come back and I gave him what he wanted. That scene will forever be burned into my memory—I didn't have to do it, I didn't have to give him what he wanted, I didn't have to have him in my life. If I had hung out in that other space, things would've turned out so differently. I would have left ... rather than staying for ten more years.*

*That was a really big moment for me. I was aware I was not making a stand for what was right, but I was frightened. There were thousands of those choice points, those moments, every week. Little ones where I bent from what I knew was right for me. Each time it disempowered me, it disconnected me from my own life-force that would've carried me, and it kept me in a victim role. I did a lot of work with Byron Katie's very simple and profound process of self-inquiry, and came to see that while on one hand my husband did all those things to me, on another hand I was really good at treating myself that way and he was just an extension of the way I treated myself.*

*It's tricky. It all comes down to being able to discriminate between Lucifer and God. Lucifer is the angel who looks just like God, and because he stands closest to God, many choose him over God because he looks so godly. This is what makes him so dangerous. There were so many moments where I thought I was choosing God, I was choosing Lucifer. I was misled—I hadn't been taught to tell the difference between the Light of God and the seductive light of Lucifer. And that's what made it tricky. The blowjob moment was very clear, but there were also a thousand other moments where I was choosing Lucifer.*

*He had numerous extra-marital affairs. There were many breaches of trust, and yet he had no interest in healing our relationship. Finally, I left. I hated him so much—I was absolutely wrathful, full of rage and hatred. I even had fantasies of eviscerating the children and throwing the excrete on the walls so he would come home and see what he had done to us. With time I came to some place of peace with his infidelity, but it remains like a cigarette burn on the skin.*

*The divorce is where I got to wear the consequences of his actions. Today I live with the results of the decisions I made during that time of trauma—decisions about child support, finances, etcetera. I didn't want to appear to be one of those women who are seen to "take their husband to the cleaners." I gave too much. Already shamed by the experience of his infidelity, I didn't want to look like the wrathful wife. I made my decisions from this place of trauma in me rather than from a place of dignity. Our years together are still a part of me, threads in the tapestry of my life … at any point it can be plucked by any number of triggers that might set me off again.*

*I am only now becoming aware that so much of something I thought had been resolved, has not. The experience really was traumatic—and that has never been acknowledged. The wounding of betrayal is so deep. Now I am aware again of my anger at how this is perpetuated ... and of the number of women betrayed through infidelity, and how deep the betrayal goes. I am seeing how, as women, we can enable that violence to continue ... There is so much brewing in the collective wounding.*

Many women learned, as children, to disregard their inner knowing of what felt healthy, or safe, or right. We learned to be nice, to please others, to maintain peace and harmony in the home—often at huge cost to ourselves and to our loved ones. We learned to endure; to silence our instincts and intuitions.

A woman's awareness of those situations in which she feels disempowered is a crucial element in setting boundaries. Maggie was very aware of those many moments of disempowerment, but she did not sufficiently value herself and her right to be treated with respect, to set the necessary boundaries. There was perhaps also a naïveté in her not knowing what she had a right to expect, even demand, in regard to what was and was not respectful or honorable action from her husband. While this naïveté is endemic in the feminine collective, it is particularly difficult for a woman to recognize it as such when the behaviors are clouded in "spiritual" or cultural attitudes that justify and normalize what are surely no less than acts of disrespect and disregard—in a word, betrayals.

Even when she *had* tried, her requests had been ignored. It is impossible to be in a healthy relationship with someone who dismisses her requests, who has no boundaries, or who cannot communicate honestly and directly. Often a woman is more worried about her partner rejecting her than her right to be treated with respect, and her need to be in a healthy relationship. What is often overlooked here is that in the end, if she refuses to accept her partner's boundary violations, it's *her* doing the rejecting, *not* him.

Already shamed by the experience of her husband's infidelity, Maggie made her decisions from this place of trauma, rather than from a place of strength. When shame is triggered, the conscious use of the breath can bring a woman strength and clarity of mind. The first step is to recognize that she is at the effect of her shame. Then, using her breath to center herself in her body and connect to the earth, she can attend to what needs to be done from a grounded and centered state of being. As with all things, practice enhances the effectiveness of this skill.

Self-empowerment comes through setting personal boundaries. No woman deserves to be treated abusively. No woman deserves to be abandoned, lied to and betrayed. A strong emotional reaction will often be an expression of the Kali force; the declaration of a woman's outrage at the transgression that has not been recognized.

Who is Kali? Kali, in Hinduism, is a manifestation of the Divine Mother. Those not appreciating her complexity call Kali the goddess of destruction. She is represented with perhaps the fiercest features amongst all the world's deities—however she destroys only to recreate. She demands the truth be told, and what she destroys is ignorance of the ego, and the transgressions that bring needless pain and suffering to self or others. She then metamorphasizes into another aspect, that of a loving and comforting Mother.

When there has been a betrayal of trust, feeling the violation in the depths of one's being, asserting the truth of this and demanding amends, is an expression of this Kali energy. It is not playing victim or "the wrathful wife." Any such assertion is a very linear, rational, masculine view, with no recognition of the nature of the feminine descent and the depth and potency of such an experience. We blame those who refuse to close their eyes for "making a scene," while the victimizer is ignored, sympathized with, or forgotten.

When the strong emotional reaction is still present some years on, what look like bursts of indulgence or playing victim is Kali screaming out for the truth to be seen, to be heard, to be recognized. When there has been no genuine apology, when there is no, *"Oh my God, I see how I have hurt you, how do I make this right?"* but only justifications and rationalizations, *this* is the core of a woman's outrage.

In sharing her story, Maggie recognized the degree of collective wounding amongst women that is a result of the unresolved trauma of infidelity, and the ways in which women perpetuate the violence of infidelity.

For some women there will also be an awareness of the fact that her rage is not for her alone. It is also her outrage at the fact that each act of betrayal further normalizes and legitimizes these behaviors. This Kali energy is a wake up call; it must not be dismissed. Regardless, a woman's point of power—at least initially—is to recognize her role in what led to her own predicament. This will require her recognizing her own self-betraying patterns. It will require she forgive herself for not knowing how to do it any differently at the time, and that she surrender to the compassionate heart of the Warrior Woman within. It will require that she move beyond that storyline to creating a new reality, a reality that affirms the value of self. Now—a woman who has come to terms with her rage— she returns to life with a new knowing, a new depth of wisdom and compassion to bring to herself and to her world.

## ELIZABETH: *"I hadn't wanted to see the signs because he was saying how much he loved me ... I wanted to believe that"*

*I always entered a relationship feeling very open hearted, and also feeling—I guess with my Irish Catholic upbringing—that whatever this sense of happiness, it's an ever after kind of thing that will ultimately sustain both of us. That's that whole romantic version of mating. I wish I could raise a generation of girls and boys who could be satisfied with less, not have to have that romance let them down. A generation that would be satisfied with self-love and intimate sharing that is practical and based around mutual satisfaction of need without that "ever after" portrait. Is it possible?*

*When I look at my own life, I've been to the altar four times. The first was with a college roommate. That lasted three years, and then we decided it was time to move on. We shook hands on the courtroom steps and I never saw him again.*

*The next was with my meditating, guru worshipping husband, who I had my two kids with. He was always off to his Indian guru to advance his consciousness. He wore beads from his guru to decrease his sex drive so he wouldn't taint himself with the body of women, who his guru claimed at that time were less evolved than men. I lost so much self-esteem in that marriage, and so of much of my sense of my feminine self.*

*I was a journalist. I went to this conference where I met a guy who swept me off my feet. He asked me what I was doing with this guy who doesn't want sex. I was thrown into "Oh, look at how he looks at me, I must be worth something. This is solace, bliss!" I divorced my husband, and married this guy.*

*That ended up being a seven-year marriage with a sexaholic. He had multiple affairs over the time we were married. He had been through five marriages before ours, and insisted we renew our marriage vows five times. We had so many ceremonies in so many different places—Hawaii, Oregon, even in the Elvis Presley Chapel. He said that this way "I won't cheat on you. I've cheated on everyone else I've ever married." It wasn't long before it became very clear that he was a sex addict, but I refused to face the truth of it. The clues were there; they were so very obvious. I refused to see them until friends took me and shook me and I finally saw the reality of how horrible it was. Even today, some ten years later, when I recall being told my husband was fucking around, I can go into such humiliation and embarrassment with that memory.*

*I finally got that this marriage was over. The betrayal, the agony, it was so awful. But until then I was always making good of his lies, thinking there is a devotion under this, thinking he loves me, that I was really traumatized by getting a divorce, and losing half custody of my children. I couldn't allow myself to consider the possibility that I had made a mistake with this addicted character.*

*To be cheated on was always my biggest nightmare. I remember saying when I was in college, "No one's going to cheat on me. I have a good bullshit detector in me. I can tell if some boy is the kind that has a cheating heart. That's not for me." Then when it happened to me, I was kicked in the gut. I hadn't wanted to see the signs because he was saying how much he loved me, how committed he was to me. I wanted to believe that.*

*I wanted the marriage to work even though I had no respect for him because I had two children, and he had two children from our previous marriages, and the four of them had really bonded. I felt sad I had to break up the family. It was really a hard decision, but staying with him had become too detrimental for me*

*My next partner had taken a vow of celibacy when he was twenty-one years old, some twenty years earlier. I knew this when I married him, but I was so turned off by sex I didn't care. And so, by marrying this celibate, I fell on the double-edged sword of betrayal. I didn't just turn on the betrayer, I turned on myself. I didn't do very good self-care, put it that way.*

*The continual longing to find a life partner had never left me. I though, Maybe my ultimate mate is this celibate. Maybe we will have a purely spiritual mating of the heart and this will be divine, and lasting. When he moved his domineering mother in without asking me, I realized I had had enough. I had never intended to marry his mother. That relationship lasted four years.*

*Then there was a terrible marriage with a right wing republican, anti-feminist, anti-environmentalist, former navy pilot. I was in some kind of amnesia state for that one. It lasted three years. Each man I left, I left him with a house and everything in it. I would leave the marriage frustrated and not penniless, but without all my material possessions.*

*I later learned why, in therapy. I was the youngest of three children; a menopausal baby. My mother was really sick with me, and stayed in hospital for a month after I was born. I was a crying baby. I was propped up with a bottle by neighbors who would check in on me. I had an older brother and sister who would sometimes put a pillow over my face to stop me crying. My father was working during the day and at school at night.*

*I learned that I am so quick to run, to leave everything behind me when I feel unloved ... when I feel that there is nothing left. You can have the home, the yacht, the bank account ... I just need to get out of here. I run so fast when I think the love is gone, or if there is betrayal. It was always a precipitous ending and my feeling I'd be smothered to death if I stayed in the person's presence another moment.*

*After my leaving this guy who was anti everything that I was pro, who was the exact opposite of all my values, my family sat me down and asked me why ever did I marry him? What I saw was that I was so afraid of being alone. He had shown me kindness and attention, after my breakup with the celibate. What was this driving force in my life that I would choose to marry the devil incarnate rather than be alone? I realized I was in some kind of trance and needed to awaken. My whole orientation to intimacy and mating and relationship was on invalid ground.*

*I saw that I was falling in love faster, more furiously, and with men who were less and less compatible with me. So it wasn't love, it was addiction on some level. Addiction to, "Oh my God, I don't want to be alone. Oh, look at you, you look good, you make me feel good ..." And there I was, off again.*

*Each time I self-abandoned even more fully. And that self-abandonment, I couldn't run from it anymore. That was the ultimate challenge, the ultimate part of my healing journey. "Oh for crying out loud, come home to yourself now. This is getting horribly embarrassing." In my professional world, I have a certain level of success and it was hard to have this personal biography accompany me on my professional ventures.*

*I went into therapy. It was wonderful to finally be doing this self-work. Now, I had five years alone. I had to work hard to find who I was and why I mistreated myself that much. I bought a town house on the water, joined a sailing club, began taking long walks on the beach, singing, joining meditation circles, making new friends, practicing yoga. A lot of healthy stuff.*

*My healing came through therapy and honest reflections with women in my life who accepted me for being vulnerable and naïve, but who also held my feet to the fire. I was committed to not dating through that period. It wasn't a perfect five years. I would stick my toe in the waters, I would take a date ... but they would challenge me: "Hey, what are you doing even thinking of dating that guy? I thought you weren't going to do that again!" They had confronted me before, in gentle ways, like, "Really, getting married again? Are you sure?" I was now able to better hear them.*

*I learned how to be alone on a Friday and Saturday night. I used to think that was a death mark. Oh my God! Me and the TV again, how can I do this? I learned to enjoy myself and have a sense of safety with myself, and to have an emotional connection with myself and what I was feeling and doing. I learned to like myself, to appreciate my alone time, and prefer my own company to the company of just some guy. That was beautiful.*

*Strangely, this desire for intimacy is right side up with despair and depression and death. Those neurons are really close together in my brain—maybe they're coming out of some real desperate urges or imperatives. It's taken me sixty-two years to have an understanding of intimacy that is relaxed. I always had this urgency about it: "Oh my God, fill me, fill my soul, take care of this anguish, take care of this loneliness." It was this existential fear of being alone that was momentarily satisfied by intimacy, instant marriage, rapturous love affairs, ungroundedness. I think I probably suffered more in love than most people should ever have to suffer. I don't think I was ever truly in love—it was just another high anxiety disorder. I am thankful that I now understand my accountability and co-creation for the many failed relationships.*

*At the end of those five years, I met the wonderful man I am with now. We share values, enjoy each other, we sometimes work and travel together. And even if he was to say goodbye today, I would say bless you, I love you. This has been wonderful. I've finally come home to myself. I feel the anima and animus has had the marriage within, and whatever that desperate reaching was, whatever that karma was, it's finally over.*

There are many women who, as was true for Elizabeth, have done a great deal of self-inquiry and personal growth work over the years but still get triggered by recurring variations on a situation. There is an enormous difference between conceptually knowing what your triggers are, and *really* knowing. The triggers will activate a woman as long as the knowing remains primarily, if not exclusively, in the realm of the conceptual. Resolution takes hold when the knowledge has been sufficiently embodied.

Discernment is a woman's ability to recognize what is not healthy in a relationship, and whether to stay and work on the relationship or to get out. It can be very difficult, when she is in the situation, to be able to see the costs incurred and to seriously consider what is the most supportive of her wellbeing. When a woman is not able to do this, she will find herself in unhealthy situations, unable to make a stand for herself—even in the face of broken agreements. She will usually need support to recognize what she needs to do to change the situation, or to change her relationship to the situation.

As we have seen, the tendency to stay is high—even when it is clear that the costs are debilitating and the potential for a healthy relationship is virtually nil. It will take tremendous courage to step out of the familiar and into the unknown. This may mean tearing the family apart, it may mean facing the disapproval of others, and often confronting frightening financial difficulties. Many women stay because they don't know love any other way. This is as true of women who have been betrayed as women who betray, as we will see in Chapter 12: *Bad Girls—Looking for Love In All the Wrong Places*. At what cost does she stay?

It was only after four failed marital relationships sourced in the *"whole romantic version of mating"* and feeling that *"this sense of happiness, it's an ever after kind of thing,"* that Elizabeth questioned its ability to sustain us. This very questioning will in itself put cracks in and eventually break through the assumptions and feelings that lead a woman to overlook the fact that when happiness is there, relationships will take care of themselves.

While not an explicit part of this telling, the fact that Elizabeth is a very attractive, intelligent, accomplished woman in her own right, is testimony to the tenacity of the beliefs that drive this compulsion to look outside of herself—to complete herself in the eyes of another—that is embedded in the very circuitry of the female brain and fiber of her body. The belief in that "ever after" kind of love, the belief that *"how he looks at me, I must be worth something"* is so seductive, so deeply imprinted it overrides not only her intuition and instincts but also the rational circuits of the brain.

Elizabeth's "anxiety disorder" took her to the altar four times, and all the while losing her self-esteem, she persisted in her search for worth in the eyes of another. Even when it was clear her partner was betraying her, she continued making good of his lies, unable to allow herself the possibility she had made yet another mistake. This is true even for a woman who was awake to the reality of cheating and had determined no one would cheat on her. Elizabeth's preparedness and determination not to be cheated on, and her having been cheated on twice before, fades into insignificance in the face of that wiring that is hell bent on wanting to believe how much he loved her. Because there was no insight into her role in perpetuating these patterns of betrayal—and self-betrayal, they continued. It was only after leaving the celibate did Elizabeth realize that she had not just turned on the betrayer, she had turned on herself: *"I fell on the double-edged sword of betrayal."*

In Elizabeth's case, it took family and friends sitting her down and questioning her, shaking her, before she could face the reality of how horrible it was. In none of the other stories of women betrayed, did their awakenings come through their being called to accountability through family or friends. However, here we see the role that women, as sisters, can serve as each others keepers, looking out for each other when we are deceiving—betraying—ourselves.

Would Elizabeth have headed for the altar, yet again, if not for her family questioning her? Her family's questioning led to the self-inquiry through which a woman can awaken to the fact that she is in *"some kind of trance"* from which she perpetually turns against herself. With the recognition that she would *"marry the devil incarnate rather than be alone,"* Elizabeth went into therapy—and five years alone. She engaged in honest reflections with women who held her accountable to being her best self.

Mistreating herself had so much become the automatic drive for Elizabeth that she had to work hard to find who she was. Choosing to fill her life with enjoyable and "healthy stuff" was a wonderful way to both balance the hard work and affirm and rebuild her body, mind, and spirit.

*"Even today, some ten years later, when I recall being told my husband was fucking around, I can go into such humiliation and embarrassment with that memory."* Even when a woman thinks she is prepared for bad news, even when she has suspected her partner is cheating, hearing the worst sends a blast of adrenaline into the body. All the body's systems are aroused and they stay aroused for a very long time. Again, the degree to which the *"double-edged sword of betrayal"* slashes through a woman's body, mind and spirit, is evident in the fact that even after years of therapy and a new and fulfilling relationship, that pain can still be reactivated.

Even ten years later, while able to say that she has finally come home to herself, as we will see in Chapter 14: *Once Friends—Colluding in Our*

*Silence*, Elizabeth still gets triggered by the memory of her partner's infidelity. Likewise, Jessica, even while having found a new form of intimacy—intimacy with herself, found herself tearing up while telling her story. This highlights the fact that not only does betrayal hurt, but the consequences are profound, deep, and long lasting.

What may be helpful for Elizabeth, at this point, is when those memories and the associated feelings emerge, to simply feel them, without the labels. To simply feel the emotions as energies in motion, letting them move in and through her. The labeling keeps a woman in the old story, keeps her victim to the feelings. The feelings emerge until they have fully run their course. Engaging with the humiliation and embarrassment feeds the feelings, and the old story. By simply experiencing and witnessing these feelings as energies, in time they will begin to dissipate in intensity. This is a practice that requires a certain level of skill and mastery, and one that—for the most part—a woman can or even should do in the earlier period of infidelity, when the feelings are screaming to be felt and validated.

## Awareness Opens the Door to Freedom

Each of these stories echoes the absence of an embodied sense of self-worth and self-love that underlies the heartbreak and the self-betraying acts of so many women. It is infidelity that will drive many to point of proclaiming *Enough, no more* and to the readiness to engage in some form of self-inquiry to decode and rewire those disempowering patterns. What we have seen repeatedly is that insights alone are not enough. What we have seen in each of these women's stories is that despite her numerous insights, a woman will find herself—once again—seduced by the unrelenting pull to return to the familiar disempowering way she sees herself, holds herself, and reacts to many of life's challenges.

Awareness opens the door to freedom, the meeting with the Warrior Woman, and a woman's journey home to herself—but as we have seen, again and again, this demands confronting the inner voice of the self-betrayer, its messages passed on to us in childhood, reinforced through the media, unconsciously carried into and through adulthood … and often, never silenced in a woman's life time. This will be so until a woman engages wholeheartedly with the energies of the Warrior—to do whatever is needed to stand on her own sacred ground, heart open in hell and certainly in heaven.

Here we have shared the stories of women who, after experiencing infidelity, left their marriages. In Chapter 8: *Choosing to Stay*, you will read the stories of those women who chose to stay. First, let's look at how a woman may begin to unravel those patterns of self-betrayal.

# CHAPTER 7

## Unraveling the Patterns of Self-Betrayal

### Practices and Processes

The patterns of self-betrayal that a woman succumbs to are usually unconscious. To begin to understand how she betrays herself, she will need to engage in a process of self-inquiry. In doing this, she is seeking to understand what is true for her, and what it is that she wants—and needs—for herself. As women, we carry so many illusions about life: *It is through a man I will find my worth and fulfillment; I need a man in order to feel secure and loved; If I make him happy, I will be loved and taken care of; If I look beautiful, he will love me.* Seeking to claim what is true for her will require a willingness to recognize and look through these illusions, and to discover what lies beneath her shame, her rage, her "taking crumbs."

This may not be easy. It may be like coming through that birth canal—again. However, just as the fetus is primed to make that journey down that birth canal, so is a woman primed to do what is needed to come home to herself. The fact that modern birthing practices have destroyed women's confidence in their ability to give birth naturally does not for a moment alter the fact that women are designed to do so. *And woman is born—to love and be loved.*

Again, she may ask, *Then why is it so damn difficult?* We have seen in Chapter 3: *Coming Home to Ourselves,* that reprogramming happens in the mind—however it also happens in the body. While the mind has a huge role in both sustaining and changing habitual patterns, stimulating the growth of new neural pathways requires feeling the feelings and sensations in the body—not simply thinking or talking about them.

This chapter is replete with exercises and practices that are designed to engage a woman in the process of identifying and changing self-betraying patterns, healing her broken heart, and reclaiming her inner authority and personal power.

The exercises and practices you will find in this chapter include:

*Feeling the Feelings:* a gentle but effective process to support you in feeling, rather fearing or repressing, your feelings

*Reclaiming Your Instincts and Intuitions:* those that are innately yours to guide, inform and protect you

*Grounding:* an essential component of wellbeing, especially in times of trauma and stress

*The Inner Dialogue:* developing an awareness and means of shifting the inner dialogue

*Anger:* your right to be mad

*Boundaries:* setting and enforcing the boundaries that are essential in any healthy relationship

*How a Woman Betrays Herself:* an initial inquiry towards recognizing the ways in which you may have betrayed yourself

*Reclaiming the Authentic Self:* the journey towards reclaiming your inner authority and personal power begins with a single step.

Engage with these exercises at your own pace. It is not intended that you do them sequentially—although you may. It is certainly not intended that you do them all in one day. The practices that will be of the most help to you will differ on different days and stages of your journey. You may choose to read through this chapter in its entirety, and to identify the exercises that will be helpful to you, right now. Or, you may skim this chapter for now, choose one or two exercises that call to you, and return to read the rest later. I hope that this is a chapter you will return to many times. This healing process will take time—it cannot be hurried. This is perhaps one of the hardest lessons a woman will learn. Be sure to acknowledge yourself for every small step along the way. In time, you will learn to live, laugh, and love again.

# Feeling the Feelings

As infants and young children dependent on our parents and caregivers for love and sustenance, we learned to suppress or repress any feelings that were met with words or looks of disgust, contempt, or dismissal. Whether because it hurt too much to feel the feelings or because expressing them was not allowed, those unacknowledged and rejected feelings were relegated to the shadows, where they remain hidden—until triggered, or activated, by a present-time experience. The experience of infidelity excels at activating these feelings. As horribly painful as this is, it offers a woman the opportunity to unravel layer after layer of these repressed feelings—and so liberate more and more of her authentic presence.

Because repressed feelings are held in the body, one of the most direct paths to releasing them is simply to connect with and welcome the feelings that arise, unbidden—rather than ignore or judge them. As a woman does this, the feelings will respond positively. She can often feel the softening, the dissolution, the release of these energies in her body— her Inner Child is finally being given the love and acceptance she has been yearning for, all these years.

### Exercise: *Feeling the Feelings*

Find a comfortable place where you can sit or lie and take some slow, deep belly breaths. Simply be aware of the gentle rising and falling of the belly, until you come to a natural rhythm that feels good to you. Now, gently direct your attention towards feeling the sensations in the body. Breathe into them, meeting them as best you can with loving kindness and acceptance. If you can't identify where the feelings or sensations appear in the body, simply imagine where they might be.

If you notice any resistance—perhaps your body is tensing, or you are breathing more rapidly and shallowly—return your attention to the breath. Breathe slowly and deeply. When you are ready, imagine or visualize some space opening in and around that sensation in the body. This in itself can relieve some of the tension that is bound up in that feeling. If any tension or resistance remains, simply allow it to be.

If you find your attention drifting back into your mind, engage your mind in the process. Ask yourself, *Where am I feeling this in my body?* There are no right or wrong answers. Simply be present to the feelings. Is this energy big or small, hard or soft? Is it light or heavy? If your attention drifts back into the mind, call yourself back to naming the quality of the feelings, not what they may mean.

There is no victim or perpetrator in this inquiry; there are no judgments and no stories. There is only the energy that's been triggered and the sensations in the body. Simply bringing attention to the feelings and sensations is, in itself, healing.

A woman cannot do this all the time, with every feeling that arises. She does it when she can, and to the extent she can, knowing that every moment love is offered—and received—healing happens.

A woman's ability to be present to these energies requires her being in her body, and past traumas can impede her ability to do this. However, every time she is able to remain gently present to the sensations in her body, her body will begin to release these locked energies. When she finds it overly stressful or frightening to consider doing this, it can be important to seek professional support.

When a woman becomes skilled in remaining present to these feelings and sensations, she can tend to them at a moment's notice, wherever she may be. She can do it while walking, or talking with others—a part of her attention is in the body, and she gives any distressing or debilitating feelings the acknowledgment and love they need. Of course, ultimately, as with all things, it is love that is the healer.

## Reclaiming Your Instincts and Intuitions

Women are innately informed and enlightened by a very different intelligence than men. This may be what Jung was implying when he said, *"Women, with their very dissimilar psychology, are and always have been a source of information about things for which a man has no eyes."*

Within a patriarchal culture, the search for knowledge—and for the sacred as taught by traditional religious and spiritual lineages—is centered almost exclusively in teachings and practices that foster both control *and* transcendence of the body, of the emotions, and of the earth. We are taught that wisdom and fulfillment are to be found in the linear, external, masculine dimension of *doing,* and that the body is the place we leave in order to soar with the spirit.

This is the antithesis of a woman's way of knowing. The way of the feminine is that of the receptive realm of *being*—honoring and attuning to the imminent, that which pervades the physical world, the human body, and the universe. For a woman, the path resides within her body and psyche.

Most women live primarily in the head, rarely present to the feelings and sensations in the body. We live the way we learned to live and survive as a child—until we decide to choose otherwise.

### SONIA:

*I was a psychologist. I had clients coming to me with issues of sexual abuse, and in learning how to support them I discovered that—like them—I was a co-dependent. Just as physically or emotionally abused children learn to be co-dependent to survive, just as a young child growing up in a family with a handicapped sister, I learned to get attention by being the perfect child. The idea of me saying "no" was not in my worldview of how to survive.*

*At thirty-four years of age, I learned I had a right to my feelings, thoughts, and my own choices. It took me seven years of emotional work—feeling my feelings and telling the truth about what was real for me—before I felt comfortable doing this. Now I recognize that not being able to say what is true rules out a woman's whole intuitive, instinctual, and emotional guidance system—and, of course, her ability to know what she wants and needs.*

In the absence of self-worth, disconnected from her own instincts and intuitions, a woman cannot know what she wants and needs. She is driven by the values she has absorbed through the patriarchal male dominated society she lives in—as did her mother and her mother's mother, though millennia.

A woman rarely stops to ask, *Is this what I want? Is this true? Is this really true, for me? What more is possible?*

We have seen the importance of connecting with our feelings as a means of releasing the energies otherwise imprisoned in the body. Inhabiting the body is also essential to a woman's reclaiming access to the instincts and intuitions that are innately hers to guide, inform, and protect her.

*The body never lies.*

So, let's begin there.

## Grounding

Inhabiting the body requires being grounded. A very immediate way of doing this is, while breathing into the belly, to image, sense, or feel roots extending from the base of the spine and souls of the feet, though the floor, into the ground, and deep, deep down into the center of the earth. Another way to do this is to allow her attention to fall from the head to the base of the spine, and anchor deep, deep in the earth. Walking can be another way of grounding as long as she doesn't "stay in her head," but instead breathes into her belly and, with each step, feels the ground beneath her feet. While one woman may ground by walking in nature, another will do so by beating a drum, or swimming in the ocean.

How a woman chooses to ground doesn't matter. What does matter is that she learns what works for her and practices it so that she can send down those roots at a moment's notice. In time, and with practice, she will always retain a portion of her awareness in her body. Grounding, sending those roots down, feeling connected to the earth beneath her feet, anchors her in the body and renders her receptive to its impulses and intuitions, rather than the automated machinations of her head.

It is from this point of stillness in herself that a woman can access the clarity and compassion to be able to inquire more deeply what it is in her that triggers a particular intense emotional reaction, and what in her needs to be acknowledged in order to release this. Ideally she grounds when she gets out of bed in the morning and as needed, throughout her day. As with developing any new skill, this takes persistence, patience, and practice.

### Exercise: *Grounding*

Consider taking a few minutes now to do this simple grounding practice. Sit or stand, spine relaxed and straight. Take three deep belly breaths—in through the nose to a count of three, out through the mouth to a count of three. Allow your attention to fall into your body—perhaps like a leaf falling from above, gently drifting down through the crown of your head, and all the way down to rest at the base of your spine. Imagine roots extending from the base of your

103

spine and soles of your feet, through the floor, all the way down into the earth. Feel the welcome of the Earth Mother. Say, *Thank you.* You will likely notice that, as you said these words, you took another deep breath, and your energy shifted yet again.

Take a minute or two—or as long as you wish—to breathe, simply being present to the energy in your body and the earth below supporting you. Be aware of how your energy feels now. Is it different to how it felt a few minutes ago? You might want to stand and walk around, paying attention to how this, too, feels different when you are grounded.

Grounded in the body, knowing what she needs and wants, a woman is best able to speak with strength and clarity—without being defensive or aggressive. This enhances the likelihood of another person being able to receive her communication as an invitation to meet and engage in a place of mutual respect. Grounded, a woman can remain firm in the face of confrontation or the conflicting opinions of others. Along with self-awareness, this is key to her being able to set and enforce boundaries.

## Self-Awareness: Your Inner Dialogue

We began this process in Chapter 3: *Coming Home to Ourselves*, with an exercise to identify the voices of the Inner Child and Inner Parents. Here we look at some more exercises a woman can use to become aware of and begin to shift her inner dialogue.

The exercises may seem awkward at first, but will come naturally with practice. I suggest choosing one or two of these, and practicing them over the course of a week. Try to do, at the very least, one each day. It can be helpful to set an alarm to ding every two hours, or whatever feels comfortable, and take even a minute right then to check in on that inner dialogue.

It is best to ground yourself before doing any of these processes.

### Exercise: *Simply Noticing*

Set an alarm or place a note somewhere that will remind you on occasion throughout your day to pause and notice what you are thinking are saying to yourself, and what you are feeling. You are not judging or focusing on the thoughts and feelings, you are simply noticing them.

If your thoughts and words are kind and self-affirming, wonderful! Notice how good it feels in your body when you think and speak to yourself in these ways. Notice how this influences your perception of what's needed and what's possible.

If your thoughts are critical, shaming, or debilitating, notice how they have a life of their own. They go on and on, of their own accord. They are mean, nasty, abusive, and disempowering. Notice how they influence your perception of what's possible.

### Exercise: *Witnessing*

Breathe into your belly as you notice the thoughts running through your mind. Continue breathing, aware of your thoughts but willing to let them be ... not judging, thinking about or focusing on them. You will notice, as you begin to witness your thoughts, that you will be able to gain some distance from them. Their intensity dissipates and you are no longer so strongly at the effect of them. In fact, you may not be at the effect of them at all.

### Exercise: *Welcoming*

Breathing into your belly, acknowledge the thoughts and the feelings that accompany them. Perhaps something along the lines of, *I see you. I'm so sorry this is so hard right now. I know it's scary, but it's going to be okay. I love you.*

If it's sadness or disappointment, meet it with love. If it's grief, meet it with love.

If it's anger, acknowledge the anger and meet that, too, with love: *No wonder you feel angry. Of course you feel angry.* Take some deep, forceful breaths. You are not simply releasing the anger; you are using it to ignite a Warrior-type energy in your body. You are igniting the strength of the Warrior Woman—*"I can and I will."*

There is no need to do any more with this for now, other than feel that strength in your body. If you are unable to access any strength right now, that's fine too. Simply acknowledge and validate the feeling: *No wonder you feel exhausted.* The heart of the Warrior Woman will meet you there.

### Exercise: *Refuting the Thoughts*

When you find your thoughts are critical, shaming, or debilitating, you can choose to refute them. Here, you are not fighting the thoughts; you are not arguing with them—you are *refuting* them. *Enough. No more.* You are refusing to give power to these debilitating, disempowering voices in your head—they are not true, not helpful, and certainly not kind.

### Exercise: *Writing and Journaling*

Writing is a valuable way to connect with your thoughts and feelings, and to discover new insights and understandings. It can be as simple as writing, *"Right now I am feeling ..."* or *"Right now I am thinking ..."*

List all of the things that may be triggering a specific emotion. For instance, if you're sad, or afraid, write down all the things that are making you feel this way. If you're angry, write *"I feel angry because ..."* and list everything that comes to mind. Simply write—do not judge, censor, or edit. Keep going until you feel emptied; until there is nothing further to add. It may take two minutes, and it may take ten—or twenty.

You may feel complete, or you may want to take this a step further. Place your hand over your heart, and read what you wrote. Don't judge the words, simply read them as if you were reading the words someone else wrote. Notice how you feel as you read these words. Ask yourself, *What would a voice of loving kindness say, right now?*

You may want to write a list of what you want to think or how you want to feel. Don't question whether or not it's possible. You are simply allowing yourself to name what you want— and sensing and imagining how it would feel to have that. You can, in this moment, experience this in your thoughts and in your feelings. In doing so, you are developing the new neural pathways that will facilitate the embodiment of your more authentic self.

Or, if you don't want to write, then scribble, draw, or paint. Just connect with those feelings and thoughts and let your fingers lead you in putting what wants to be expressed onto paper or canvas.

When you have done this, you may want to burn the paper or flush it down the toilet—you will be surprised how good this can feel.

You can also do this exercise with movement. Ask the questions above and let your body respond.

The following two exercises can be done alone, or to follow on from one of the exercises above.

### Exercise: *Igniting Self-Love*

Bring your attention to the area around your heart, or heart chakra. Imagine your breath moving into and out of your heart as you breath in, and out. You may find it helpful to place a hand over your heart. Continue breathing until you find a natural inner rhythm that feels good to you.

Bring to mind someone or something you really love. Notice, as you allow your heart to open, that it begins to soften ... to fill with love. It may fill a lot, or only a little—either is fine. Notice, as you gently focus your attention on this feeling, that the love expands. It may feel as if there is a soft, warm glow around your heart. Receive it with gratitude. Stay with that feeling for as long as feels good to you.

This is a wonderful exercise to do several times throughout your day. You can do it at any time, wherever you are—while you are walking, watching a movie, or lying awake in bed.

Heartfelt emotions activate a cascade of neurochemicals and restorative processes in the body. Intentionally accessed heartfelt emotions diminish the harmful effects of stress and the sensation of pain, and play a key role in rewiring dysfunctional neurological pathways.

### Exercise: *"What Do I Want, Now?"*

Ground, breathe, center in your heart, and when you are ready, ask yourself, *What do I want to be thinking?* or, *How do I want to be feeling?* The answer may come in words, or as a feeling. Don't question whether or not it's possible. You are simply allowing yourself to name what you want—and sensing and imagining how it would be to have that. Simply allow it to be what it is, and receive it with gratitude. You will find gratitude invites more of the energy in.

You can further embody this energy with your breath, your imagination, and your will.

With time it will come naturally to do these exercises as the need arises. Taking responsibility for our energy in this way is true self-care—of body, mind, and spirit. Furthermore, it inevitably ripples out to touch everyone and everything around us.

108

# Anger: Your Right to Be Mad

You have an absolute right to your anger. It's important to give yourself permission to feel and release your anger in a way that doesn't hurt yourself or others. In doing this, you are shaking up your body's vibrational state, and breaking disempowering patterns that keep you from seeing clearly. You will find you have much more life-force and energy available for accessing your inner authority and personal power.

Many women don't know that they can express anger, and stand in their truth, without losing love. Many are afraid that if they let that anger out, there will be no end to it. When something pushes a woman to express her anger, she may feel a huge sense of liberation and even surprise to find she is not destroyed by it. One can only wonder what new possibilities might open for her when she releases that energy, and is no longer consumed by its suppression. Anger, when suppressed, can turn to rage, then to addictions in an attempt to mask the rage, or even to suicide if enough of it has been turned inward. This is how incredibly harmful suppression can be.

Physical expression is a healthy, natural, and powerful way to release anger and stress and to activate the vitality and momentum of the Warrior energy. However, a woman must release her anger in ways that do not to harm herself or another.

## Exercise: *Physical Expression*

Find somewhere you can go and safely throw rocks. Pound a pillow with your fists. Stamp on the ground. Get out and walk—walk purposefully, striding rather than strolling. A woman may be surprised to find that anger can also be released through a good cry—here a woman is accessing the fear that underlies that anger.

If there is nowhere you can go and safely express your anger at the moment, or if you just cannot allow yourself to do that right now, use your imagination. The body and mind can't tell the difference between reality and imagination, so while this might not feel as satisfying, it does help. Using the imagination can often be a first step in giving yourself the permission to express your anger.

Know that as well as physically expressing this anger, it is also important to explore the underlying feelings.

### Exercise: *The Underlying Feelings*

What are you angry about that is causing you to react so strongly? Can you identify a fear that lies beneath this anger? What do you need that you are not receiving, that may be causing you to feel this way? What can you do to fulfill that need? Journaling can be a valuable way of exploring and coming to understand these feelings.

When the above processes don't help—when a woman consistently feels stuck with her anger or other feelings, or when her feelings are messy, unclear, all-consuming—it can be important to get the support of a counselor or therapist. This is a powerful statement of a woman's intention to make good of this experience of infidelity.

## Self-Awareness: Boundaries

Here the focus is on a woman's developing an awareness of the presence, or absence, of boundaries in her relationships with others. Initially, she may want to ask the following questions in relation to someone other than her partner. It can be helpful to write down any responses. These will almost certainly change—becoming clearer and stronger—with further reading and reflection on the stories of other women in this book.

There are no right or wrong responses, and no thoughts or feelings that are not acceptable. It is vitally important a woman gets to feel what she feels and think what she thinks. There is no need to answer every question—this is not a test and she is not to be judged by anyone. The questions are best explored from a place of curiosity, without self-judgment, shame, or blame. When a woman finds herself in any of these mindsets, she can appreciate herself for noticing, breathe, and continue—or, if needed, take a break. It can be helpful to do this exercise with the support of a trusted friend.

Now, where to begin?

### Exercise: *An Awareness of Boundaries*

Firstly, of course, breathe and ground. Take three deep belly breaths—in to the count of three, out to the count of three.

Allow your attention to center in your body. It may help to place a hand somewhere on your body—perhaps on your belly, or on your heart or heart chakra. Now, bring to mind someone who drains or upsets you. When you feel ready, begin this process of inquiry:

*How does the presence of this person affect me? How do I feel when I'm around this person? How does this feel in my body?*

*What are the thoughts running through my head? Does my heart feel open, or closed—or does it fall somewhere in between?*

*Do I like how I feel?*

*What am I afraid of? What more, am I afraid of?*

*Do I feel loved, and respected, by this person? Do I feel able to love and respect myself when I am with this person?*

*What do I need to do in order to feel empowered in this situation?*

Note that this isn't initially about what you want from the other, it is about what you yourself need in this situation—perhaps more space, or to give yourself more respect, love, or compassion.

*What can I do to get that?* This in turn requires your knowing what attitudes or behaviors are unacceptable to you, and what you have a right to ask for.

*What more do I need? What else is possible?* If you don't know right now, that's okay. Simply allow the question to be.

For now, allow some time to simply be with all that has arisen in you. Take a deep breath, and appreciate yourself for completing this process. You may want to take a break before moving into the next section.

A woman can develop and refine her awareness of her instincts and intuitions, perhaps at some later time, by bringing to mind a person with whom she feels strong, clear, and empowered, and working through these questions again. This inquiry can also be explored in relation to a place or situation.

Paying attention to the impact of different people, places, and situations on her energy is an important element in self-care. As a woman becomes clearer about her own worth, and the value of self-care, she becomes more sensitive to the people, places and situations that are healthy for her—and those that are not.

## Setting and Enforcing Boundaries

In an ideal world, surely a woman could assume and expect that people will be respectful, but this isn't the way it is. Still, many a woman persists in assuming that because *she* thinks, feels, and acts a certain way her partner will do what she expects. Many a time her expectations—and assumptions—are sourced in her ideals, hopes and wishes. She assumes boundaries are not necessary; her partner will do the right thing because he cares about her, loves her, shares a bed with her, or says all of the things she wants to hear.

In the absence of boundaries that are articulated, clear, and realistic, believing her partner will be trustworthy is not reasonable. What trustworthy means to her partner may not be what it means to her. Assuming and expecting she and her partner have a shared understanding of what constitutes a breach of trust, or of what being faithful means, has led to many an infidelity.

Initially, setting boundaries may be difficult. A woman may feel guilty for putting herself first; taking care of herself. She may feel uncomfortable and uncaring. The unrelenting voices of guilt and of shame surge to the forefront of the mind: *You can't do that; that's not nice; you'll disappoint him; he will think you don't love him; he won't love you. Be good, make him happy.*

### Exercise: *"What is True, for Me?"*

Spend some time each day exploring what is true for you— what you are feeling, and what you need. Become aware of what supports your wellbeing, and what does not. Often knowing what you don't want will precede knowing what you do want. Practice saying what you really feel, and stating your needs in situations that are safe.

Putting herself first, choosing to set boundaries that affirm her self-love and self-respect, is *never* about disrespecting the other person.

Can you identify one, or more, absolute yes's with respect to behaviors that are essential to you; and absolute no's with respect to behaviors that are deal breakers?

It is not enough to just set boundaries—they must be enforced. This requires a woman setting consequences that she is willing to enforce. If she is not ready to leave the relationship if a particular boundary is violated, that is not to be given as the consequence. Repeatedly claiming she is mad and done with him is not an effective consequence. An effective consequence means owning that she is angry, and why, and taking action to show that she indeed means it.

A boundary violation can be an opportunity to clarify needs and expectations, and come to a shared understanding of what the boundary is in this situation. There may be conditions for continuing in the relationship—perhaps not coming home unless he's sober, or entering counseling together, or no longer being involved in a group that the woman he is attracted to is part of.

Some violations may be totally unacceptable; others a wake up call. The absence of a genuine apology indicates a person is not willing to take responsibility. With a genuine apology, a woman may choose to address it and accept no more breaches. A core boundary violation means no matter what, we are done. *Enough. No more.*

Regardless of the degree of the violation, it's crucial it be addressed. Yes, she may love him, he may have some great qualities or be simply gorgeous on his good days—but to ignore actions that violate agreed to boundaries is a set up for disaster. A disaster like infidelity.

What does it mean when a woman's partner won't commit, doesn't act like a responsible and respectful adult, and talks or acts in ways that disrespect her and their relationship? When a woman repeatedly takes another person's disrespect, she is teaching them that this is acceptable to her. How often can a man dismiss a woman's concerns—*"It meant nothing," "It's you I love"*—and persist in this behavior, before she recognizes that *Enough is enough?*

What does it mean when a woman is with someone who is repeatedly crossing the boundary lines, or when a woman keeps letting him come back when he persistently disrespects her? A woman may let a violation pass on the grounds that *"We all make mistakes," "Let's forgive and forget,"* or, *"I love you, let's just start over."* Perhaps because she fears leaving the relationship and standing alone, or losing the only love she knows. In the absence of consequences, why would he stop? Why would he do any differently? At some point a woman needs to recognize the insanity in not enforcing consequences. It is true that it is human to make mistakes—we all do—but repeated actions of disrespect, especially when boundaries have been made clear, are not mistakes. They are the very substance of this man's character.

Remember, a woman's putting herself first, choosing to set boundaries that affirm her self-love and self-respect, is *never* about disrespecting the other. In fact, to the contrary—it is a woman's affirmation that *I love and respect myself; I love and respect my partner; I love and respect and will care for and protect this relationship that we share.*

A trusting and respectful relationship liberates a ceaseless flow of creative energy that is otherwise consumed in endless cycles of blaming and shaming, conflict, and power struggles.

Note: While here the focus is on the woman, of course it is equally important that her partner, too, is able to do what is needed to set and enforce boundaries. Boundaries are best put in place very early on in any relationship—and reviewed at regular intervals. Boundaries are best clarified, articulated and shared in a space of collaboration and mutual respect for each other, and for the intimacy and potential of the relationship.

## How a Woman Betrays Herself

When a woman has a healthy amount of self-worth and self-love, she naturally sets and enforces boundaries. She does not question whether or not she has a right to be respected. Sadly, this is the exception rather than the norm. It is important a woman recognize that the absence of this knowledge is widespread—is not hers alone, rather it is endemic in the feminine collective. It is the ground on which self-betrayal flourishes—and endures. There is no shame or blame here, only an invitation to choose otherwise.

Before exploring some additional questions that will further unravel the patterns of self-betrayal that were almost surely a factor contributing to any infidelity, it will be helpful to consider the ways in which a woman typically betrays herself.

- A woman betrays herself whenever she judges herself, sees herself as "less than" or not enough, or as being unworthy of love and respect.

- A woman betrays herself when she lives in her head rather than her body. Most women learned at a very early age to abandon awareness of the body as a means of avoiding feelings of helplessness, fear, and pain. Many women live, almost habitually, with their attention out of the body.

- A woman betrays herself whenever she turns to addictions to relieve her pain, rather than accepting responsibility for her feelings and what needs to be done.

- A woman betrays herself when she laments or criticizes another's attitudes or behaviors, and blames others rather than accepting responsibility for what is asked of her, to right the situation.

- A woman betrays herself when, aware she is betraying herself, she persists in doing so.

Read back over this list, noting on a scale of 1 to 5, where 1 is never and 5 is always, where you fall on that continuum. Again, no judging—simply noticing.

The many ways a woman will betray herself, and the many ways she will discover to call herself back and reclaim her inner authority and personal power, will become more and more evident with further reading and reflection.

Remember, for many women, infidelity is the wake up call. It takes courage to wake up—and even more courage to call herself back from the roles she plays each time she drifts away from the truth of who she is. Yet when a woman has been betrayed, courage may be difficult to access. She will find herself at an all-time low with respect to self-worth and self-love.

Cultivating self-love and self-worth begins with her accepting herself just as she is. It requires that she make the decision to forgive herself for simply not knowing how to do what she did any differently. It requires a willingness to inhabit the body, and to accept responsibility for her feelings, thoughts, and actions. It is crucial that she does not succumb to the relentless voices of the Inner Critic and the habitual patterns of self-judgment, shame, and blame that are so endemic in the feminine collective.

The following exercise can serve as an initial inquiry into how you may have betrayed yourself. This can be done alone, or with the support of a trusted friend. As we see in Chapter 16: *Reaching Out for Help—The Gift of Empathy*, the support and empathy of others is essential.

### Exercise: *"How May I Have Betrayed Myself?"*

Take a few minutes to check in with the feelings and sensations in your body. Are you ready to move on?

When you are ready, and remembering there are no right or wrong answers, consider the following questions. It can be helpful to sit down with pen and paper, or fingers to keyboard, and write whatever comes—no editing, just writing. Write a few words, a few sentences, or a few pages. This is only an initial inquiry and your responses will shift and deepen in the weeks, months, and even years to come.

If you feel stuck, you might want to work through these questions with the help of someone else. It may be helpful to reflect back on some of the patterns and beliefs we have seen in the stories to date. Simply respond with what emerges as true for you, in this moment. It may be that you simply don't know. Asking the question, in itself, opens the doors to insight and discovery.

*How may I have, consciously or unconsciously, done something in the past to lead to this infidelity?*

*How may I have given my partner permission to treat me the way he did, and to do what he has done? How may I have perpetuated his disrespect, deceit, even abuse?*

*When have I felt something was wrong between us, with the action he took or wanted to take, and not taken any effective action to remedy that?*

*When was it that I did not, or could not, stand up for myself and set and sustain firm boundaries?*

*What were the consequences of my not doing this?*

*Where was I naïve? Where did I remain silent? What was I afraid of?*

*What was the belief or experience, beneath this fear?*

*What was it that I needed, and wanted? How did I feel, when I didn't get that?*

*How could I have taken a stand for my getting those needs met? What did I need to ask of myself, and of my partner?*

*What do I know now, that I did not know then, that may have empowered me to do this differently?*

*How have I compromised myself, day in and day out, to be loved and accepted?*

*What lessons, what new awareness, and what gifts might I be taking from this experience?* It is likely that of all the questions, your responses to this question are the most likely to evolve more deeply, over time.

*What matters more than anything to me, in this moment? What do I value, above all, in this moment? How do I want to live my life?*

*What beliefs, behaviors, and actions would support me in moving into this possibility?*

Take a few minutes to appreciate yourself for doing this process, and check in with the feelings and sensations in your body. You might want to return to one of the exercises above, such as *Witnessing* or *Igniting Self-Love*. You might want to take a walk, or talk with a friend—or your own Inner Child.

---

A woman may need to come back to this process again and again to get to the core of the betrayal. The stories that follow will shed additional light on this initial inquiry. It can be helpful to talk with insightful others who have earned her trust, to meditate, pray, or engage in some form of counseling.

The journey home to herself requires a woman move beyond the conceptual insights discovered in the process of self-inquiry, to embody those insights. When a woman awakens to the fact that she has, again and again, betrayed herself, she is ready to inquire into what is needed in order to affirm and embody the newly awakening self.

We will see more of this in the stories that follow. For now, let's look at some practical ways a woman can begin this process—at her own pace, and in her own time.

## Reclaiming the Authentic Self

Recognizing the ways in which she has betrayed herself opens the door to a woman's reclaiming her authentic self. Sustaining the necessary awareness demands a woman inhabit her body and stay present to her experience. Aware of the potential of her mind and body to source her experience of reality, a woman is able, with persistence and patience, to master the art of changing consciousness at will. However, the first step towards sourcing her experience of reality is recognizing what she, herself, wants and needs. Oftentimes, recognizing how she has betrayed herself, and knowing what she doesn't want, will come before knowing what she does want and need. These knowings can emerge in a flash, or over a long period of time.

### Exercise: *Identifying and Changing Disempowering Patterns*

Note any glimpses, dreams, insights, or intuitions you receive of your newly emerging, more authentic self. Whenever you receive even an inkling of this, move your attention there and notice how, as you do so, that inkling of insight will often expand. Your imagination is a powerful way to create and nurture the new neural pathways that bridge the gap between where you are today, and where you want to be.

Keep identifying the behaviors, beliefs, and patterns you want to change, as well as the new ones you want to develop. Each day or each week, choose to focus on one or two of the behaviors, beliefs, or patterns you want to change. Choose the behaviors or beliefs you want to replace these with. Do something to remind yourself to monitor these throughout the day—perhaps write a note to remind yourself, or set an alarm to ding every few hours.

Consider what else you can do to support yourself in making these changes.

Support may include anything from practicing any of the other exercises, to spending time in nature, talking with a friend, praying, meditating, making an altar, taking an assertive training course or yoga class, getting a massage, or putting photos or images or objects that inspire and encourage you in places where your eyes will fall on them throughout the day.

It is almost always small and simple steps that are the most sustainable and effective. Do not take on too much at once. Accept setbacks as part of the process. Reframe them as evidence of the commitment made, rather than as failures.

What is crucial is that the Inner Critic does not take over any review or evaluation of progress. When a woman finds it impossible to silence or shift that voice of ruthless self-judgment, or any other aspect of the Inner Critic, it will be important to seek support. In fact, every woman needs the support of others to get through this.

### Exercise: *Embodying the Authentic Self*

Each day, each week, or whenever you are drawn to, ask:

*What would it feel like to embody that newly emerging way of being—however slightly I may be sensing it—today?*

Imagine how you would stand or sit, how you would hold your head. Imagine walking, confidently, sure of yourself in this new way of being.

What would be different in your life if you carried that new way of being, and the self-esteem and self-worth that accompanies it, into your day? Would you feel differently in your body? Would your voice change? Bring your attention into your body and allow yourself to feel that way, now. Has your breathing shifted?

Notice your posture throughout day and adjust it as needed to reflect this newly awakening, more empowered and authentic self. Can you allow yourself to feel love for yourself? How good does *that* feel?

The more a woman feels and engages with the imagination, the stronger the imprint. Feelings can be strengthened by aligning the posture and breathing to be in accord with these feelings. The clothing she wears, the objects in her environment, the people she connect with, all reinforce and strengthen—or diminish—this process.

It will likely take several years before a woman will feel established and confident in her new identity. Again and again, the habitual thoughts and emotions will return. She may need to call herself back one thousand times a day. In time she will realize, with gratitude and wonder, that the balance has shifted. Those habitual disempowering patterns that were once so prevalent, appear as naught but a shadow to be dispelled on sight. Now she is able to stand centered in her own wisdom, strength, and equanimity. This reclamation does not happen overnight; it is a process that continues to morph and evolve and deepen throughout a woman's life.

In the following chapter, you will read the stories of women who chose to stay and renew their marriages. We will see how the self-betraying patterns evident in the preceding chapters repeat again and again, albeit in ever varying shades in a woman's life, and how with awareness, compassion, and courage she can do what is needed to shift these patterns.

These stories are of special value not only to those women who have chosen to stay, but also to those who are uncertain or have separated from their partner. It may be that, for a woman whose marriage ended after infidelity, to read the stories of women who rebuilt their marriages may simply be too difficult. If this is the case, skip over this chapter for now and perhaps return to it another time—for these stories, too, are every woman's story.

# CHAPTER 8

## *Choosing to Stay*

This chapter contains the stories of women who chose to stay and work through the issues that came to the forefront with their partner's unfaithfulness. Regardless of whether a woman stayed, left, or had no say in the matter, these stories, and the wisdom gleaned from them, offer insights that are of relevance to us all.

### MELISSA: *"If I walk away from this marriage, will I regret it one day?"*

*The discovery of my husband's betrayal knocked me for a sixer. I wasn't expecting it. Our baby was just eleven weeks old when I found out. I had a gut feeling something was wrong. Then I saw emails alluding to something going on romantically between him and a friend. He said it was nothing, it was all in my head. I returned to her one of the emails she had sent to him, asking her to explain this. She said, "Every dog has his day, and I guess I've had mine. I'm in love with him, but he wants to be with you, not me."*

*He told me he had been spending time with her, but they hadn't had sex. I told him he had to end the friendship. Then it all started to get very nasty. She phoned my husband in hysterics, crying, "I'm in love with you. I can't live without you." He was really afraid of what she would do. She was very unstable. It was horrible. Even prior to this, I was suffering from postnatal depression.*

*We had planned to take the baby to my parents' house and go away together for the weekend to celebrate my birthday. I cried the whole time ... I couldn't stop crying. Still, I had thought we would work through it, but then driving back to my parents' home to pick up the baby he revealed to me that it had also been sexual. I was totally devastated. Up until then he had told me they hadn't had sex. This had meant it was "just" an emotional connection, although as I learned later an emotional affair is every bit as painful as any other. Now I totally lost it. I yelled at him, why had he lied to me? He told me that he didn't want to spoil my birthday.*

*I demanded he leave me at my parents' house for a few days. I said, "You tell me that you don't want to be with this other woman, but here you are telling me lies. I don't know what to believe." I needed reassurance that the relationship with her was over, and the space to think about what it was that I wanted. I told him to take a few days off work to think about what it was that he wanted. He went to his parents' house and explained what had happened. He later told me it was terrible to see the disappointment on his own mother's face.*

*The other woman started sending me horrible text messages. I gave my phone to my mother and asked her to only tell me if there was anything I needed to know. I just couldn't stop crying. I would look at my child and decide this is the most important thing to me. I only got through those few days with my parents' support. He and I exchanged emails about how we felt. We decided we needed to go home, and that we would work through this together.*

*I had always said if anyone ever cheats on me, I am out the door. But when you love someone, you need to ask, If I walk away from this marriage, will I regret it one day? You might discover no matter how you are feeling right now, you still have a lot of love for this person. I had to ask myself, What do I want? Do I have the strength to look at this person, to try and work this out?*

*We had been together a long time—seven years—when Seth was born, but we knew we needed help from other people. His parents brought him over to my parents' house. We all spoke around the table. He revealed that he had been seeing the other woman since the early part of my pregnancy, and that when he spoke about leaving her, she would start to go crazy. He agreed he had to stop seeing her and to cut off all contact with all of her friends. That was hard because many of her friends were also our friends.*

*He began looking frantically to find a counselor to help us. He found one and she was really good, but it was still such a very,*

*very difficult time. I felt I was living in a bubble. I was trying to push out all the negative things happening in the outside world and focus on myself. Taking every day, a day at a time, was all I could do.*

*While he was searching for a counselor, I looked up resources online. I found an article from Dr. Frank Gunzburg explaining the phases a couple needed to go through after the discovery of infidelity. First there was individual healing—each of us had to look deeply within, sort through our emotions and feelings and reflect on what we wanted. It was good to have these guidelines because I felt so powerless, so out of control. It was good to have something to focus on. The article helped me see that my pain was different to my partner's pain. It helped me to better understand what he was going through, and what he needed. The second stage focused on healing as a couple, working together to identify issues within the relationship and to effectively communicate with each other. This required learning to listen to what it was that we needed from each other, and the kind of agreements we needed to make. The final stage was healing as a couple—putting the problems of the relationship in the past and renegotiating a new relationship. Our therapist helped us a lot with that. She helped us get really clear about our expectations of each other, and the kind of agreements we needed to make. This was crucial in building new foundations and learning how to trust again.*

*My mother had often reminded me that I'd always known what I wanted, and I had been ready to go out there and get it, and to strive for good results. And I remembered this now. But I don't know ... if not for the baby, maybe I would have fallen into a heap with this experience—it was so horrible. I decided the responsibility of being a mother to this beautiful innocent baby was of first and foremost importance, and the pain had to come second.*

*We began counseling right away. It was really crucial for us to have another person who we trusted and connected with. She helped us to understand, week by week, where we were in that cycle of grief. She helped us understand what to do at home when we felt uncomfortable talking about what had happened, or when I felt I couldn't restrain my need to ask questions that were too graphic—like what kind of sexual positions they had used. The first couple of weeks I obsessed with wanting to know how, when, where—all those questions.*

*I learned to remove myself from his presence when I couldn't control myself. It was frightening, my heart could be pounding ... sometimes it felt like I couldn't breathe. I learned to take time out when even being near him made me really angry. He was frantic, willing to do anything to save our family. Counseling helped us to come back down—we couldn't wait until the next session.*

*I also grappled with confronting the other woman. Counseling helped me to understand that her behavior was irrational and abusive, and there was no benefit to approaching her as she never accepted responsibility and maintained that she was the victim in all this. Then the time came when our counselor suggested we only needed to come every other week, and then once a month.*

*It was how my husband responded that really helped me get through this. He was willing to do whatever it took to save our marriage. I saw he was really sincere in his apology, and I saw his remorse. He took responsibility for his choices and never made excuses. These were crucial pieces.*

*He was intoxicated each time he had been physical with her and yes, he was scared that she might flip out if he left her, but he still made that choice to do what he did. He had to work really hard to look at himself, and make the decisions he needed to, to make things better between us. This included doing what he could to make me feel secure. He would tell me where he was going, and why, and what time he would be back. I would still be thinking, Is he going to meet her? Knowing these details was important to me. It was, and still is at times, really hard trusting him—especially when alcohol is involved.*

*He stopped all contact with the woman and the friends that were still hanging out with her. This was like a double whammy for me. So many friendships were severed. It was such an emotional time—being betrayed by my partner and also losing so many other friendships, including his lover. She had been my friend, but refused to take any responsibility for betraying me. She turned it all on my partner, saying he wouldn't leave her alone.*

*I really valued those friends who did choose to cut contact with her. A few friends were so negative about what he had done and about our staying together that we had to sever contact with them. The friends who were really helpful to us were those who didn't take sides with either of us but were there for both of us.*

*Some were disappointed at first in what my partner had done, but they were here to support us no matter what—while others had very strong opinions of what we should do.*

*It's usually very hard for a man to talk about his emotions, but my partner learned to do that. Now when friends are going through problems in their relationship, he will help them put things in perspective. He told them he made a terrible choice. He said, "Now I know that my family and my relationship is what is most important to me, and I am going to do everything I can to make everything work."*

*It took a good couple of years to get through the very worst of it. There were times when I was scared that if I looked at his face I might see her. Even now, six years later, the affair is still always there in the background. I can still get very angry when something happens to remind me of what he did.*

*I learned not to let anger overtake me. Sometimes when I looked at him, I just wanted to punch him. I found the strength to instead say, "Right now I just want to punch you," and to breathe through it all. I found the strength to be able to look at him and connect with him even while I was really angry. I am learning to focus on the here and now, and the improvements we've made along the way. We have better quality friendships with others now. We weeded out the ones that weren't so healthy for us.*

*I am now studying counseling and psychology, wanting to make a positive out of this. I hope I will be able to help others. It's so very horrible, and there is not a lot of information for people going through infidelity. It happens so suddenly and it's like, oh my god, what am I to do? I felt like running out onto the road and under a car. I was so fortunate to have my mum. When I called her she told me to breathe. She asked me where the baby was. She covered those basics. I also rang a close friend who told me to breathe, not to overreact, get the information about what's really going on.*

*I changed as a person. Before this had happened, I hadn't invested a whole lot in the relationship. I didn't realize that that was necessary. We had many heated arguments and there were certain things we just didn't deal with. He was a very immature man. None of his friends were married and here he had a marriage, a child, and a mortgage. The other woman had started telling him he deserved better, and he fell for it. But that was his choice. I can take responsibility for what went wrong in the marriage but not for the decisions he made to have an affair. There was so much pressure through these years. Looking back at the path we were on I can see that this had to happen to wake me up to who I am. Unfortunately we tend not to learn until catastrophic things happen.*

*We still see our therapist every six months. It's a place where we know we can go and talk, though it's no longer primarily about the affair. It's more about how to talk about resolving conflicts within the family, how to balance work and time together, and how to take care of ourselves as individuals, independent of the other.*

*I had thought you get married then the man would look after you, take care of your worries. You look at the movies, and think this is how a relationship is supposed to be. You look at other people around you, and their relationships look better than yours—but when you get down to learning about the nuts and bolts, that's not the way it is.*

*A big question for me after the affair was, Who am I? What is it about me, that's valuable? How has this horribly painful experience helped me? I learned to watch my negative self-talk. And I worry a lot less now about what others think of me. I learned a lot about looking after myself. I learned it's not all about the relationship—a marriage also needs to be about me, and who I am, as an individual. Before, I had viewed the relationship as me. I did not know who I was, apart from that. Now I can say, "This is who I am."*

Upon learning of her partner's betrayal, Melissa had the good sense and fortitude to demand they take a few days apart. As she found, unanticipated details given after the original disclosure add fuel to the betrayed partner's feelings of mistrust and distress. Honest answers about who the affair partner is and the extent of the betrayal relieve some of the pressure a woman feels to know everything, now. In the absence of these facts, the imagination runs wild.

Intense emotions and post-traumatic reactions make it difficult for the betrayed partner to act rationally or with self-control. Delving into the intimate details of the affair right away will inevitably lead to escalating arguments and accusations. While any semblance of care for the other may seem impossible to access, respectful communications as one might speak to a stranger, minimize further damage. An honest discussion

126

about what happened is best left until a constructive conversation is possible.

Rebuilding trust lies at the heart of recovery, and the first step is establishing safety and cultivating goodwill. This is a monumental undertaking requiring tremendous courage, resolve and patience. Post-traumatic reactions need to be recognized and validated, with neither partner denying or minimizing the painful feelings.

It's hard to know how to live through another day without adding salt to the wounds. It's hard to know how much to say and when to say it. It's hard and at times impossible to control the emotional outbursts and accusations, and to know how to remain supportive when a partner is hysterical or depressed. And as Melissa said, even months later, it can be hard to look the other in the face—whether this is because it activates a desire to attack the other, or because it is such a painful reminder of the heartbreak that lives in and between them.

Melissa's husband met the need of all betrayed partners for the relationship to move forward—her questions were answered, the intensity of her emotions validated, he empathized with the pain his choices caused, and offered a sincere and heartfelt apology. He also took those steps essential to rebuilding a sense of trust: ending all contact with his lover, and being open and accountable for where he was and what he was doing when away from home.

Post-traumatic reactions can last days, months, even years. As Melissa found, symptoms often include an obsessive need to hear the intimate details of the affair. Her hyper-vigilance in monitoring her partner's actions comes from the fear of further hurt and trauma. It can be difficult to find the balance between validating these reactions and trying to contain or manage them.

Melissa and her partner took another really valuable step: reaching out for the support of a wider network—parents, a counselor whom they trusted, and others who proved to be friends of the marriage. Friends of the marriage are those who accept and support a couple's decision to stay together, whether they are in the stage of ambivalence or in the process of reconciliation. They don't speak badly of either partner, even if they are angry with or disappointed in them.

Melissa asked the question that will serve every woman who has betrayed or been betrayed: *"If I walk away from this marriage, will I regret it one day?"* This was one of the first steps towards her having—as she does today—a richer, deeper and more committed relationship with both herself and her husband.

## EVA: *"The hardest part … was seeing my part in what had happened"*

*This was my second marriage. I had to leave my first marriage to my childhood sweetheart and that religious, small town and small-minded community we lived in. One day I just blew up and left. I felt tremendous guilt in tearing my own nuclear family apart. My son was eight at the time. We moved 3,000 miles away, to California. My whole life changed.*

*I fell deeply in love with another man. We had planned to marry and invested in property together, when he suddenly broke off our wedding plans. That was a huge loss, emotionally and financially. I decided I would no longer be held back or controlled by convention and the thoughts of others. I accepted responsibility for the decisions I had made in the past, and decided to move forward from this point with my eyes open.*

*I was single for the next two years. I made a commitment to praying and meditating regularly, and met my husband after a very forceful series of meditations and prayers. I had read a book—and it wasn't that popular book, "The Secret"—that basically said when you ask the universe for what you want and assume you deserve it, you will get it. So I prayed. Something like, "Dear god, universe, when the time is right, let me meet the right partner. I want to be free but when the time is right, I want to meet this person. It can be soon or in ten years from now." I had made a list. I wanted him to be six-foot-two, about 200 pounds, really well traveled, a citizen of the world, as smart as hell—in fact an ivy leaguer, really smart. I wanted him to have a sailboat.*

*About a week later I get this email. Mutual friends had decided to connect us. He wrote, "I am six-foot-two, about 200 pounds, lazily intellectual, athletic, I like to travel, I like to sail and have a sailboat …" Literally there he was.*

*It was amazing. I know this sounds hokey but I felt that my prayers had been answered. I had met my soul mate. I'd planned a trip to Europe as part of my metamorphosis, and on a whim I invited him. We had ten wonderful, wonderful days traveling together. On the tenth day he asked, "When should we plan the wedding?" Within six months we were married. It was all really fast. It was this amazing meeting of heart and mind.*

*Six months after we married he had an opportunity to do some contract work in India for two years. I was in a job I didn't like, so I quit and with my son, we headed off together. I was so passionate about him and our new life together. I started teaching music and English to street children. I ran into all these beautiful children and felt I wanted to have children with him. I was forty-three, so we decided to adopt.*

*He was born in Kenya. I was from the Deep South. We had both moved far away from our family home. He was from a more traditional Indian family, but quite global in his travels. We were both risk takers, warriors—we believed anything was possible. We believed through sheer will, when we wanted something to happen, we could make it happen.*

*We returned to the U.S. with a beautiful foster son and daughter, natural siblings, three and five years of age. The adoption was official a year later. When we arrived back in the U.S. in 2005, it was a tight economy and we had lots of concerns about money. My husband was offered some consulting in Prague. He would be in Prague a week or two, and then here for three weeks, and then back to Prague. So that seemed reasonable. We were still newly married, and I thought we would be able figure this out. I wasn't working at the time. I was the anchor for our new family and still unpacking boxes from India.*

*He phoned me from London on his way to Prague. He couldn't find his hotel booking, so he asked me to sign into his account to find it. He seemed antsy. Here I was—innocently looking, looking—and then it was this big giant shock. I could hear his voice saying, "What's the matter, what's the matter?" but I couldn't speak. I was looking at several email exchanges between him and three different women he was looking to have dinner with in London. He must have been desperately worried I'd see these but also desperate to get to his meeting at his hotel …*

*What was incredibly hurtful to me was that he was literally reaching out to total strangers—women like on Craigslist, people passing through—for these quick affairs. I don't think he ever formed a serious connection with any of these other women, and there were many of them. I think these affairs were distractions. He had massive insecurities, he had lost money on investments, and he wasn't supplying the anticipated lifestyle for his family. These relationships were like any addiction—a means of escape.*

*Despite my decision to take responsibility for myself, a part of me died. I did what I needed to do to survive and take care of kids. I was totally dependent on him for income and didn't want to break up this vision of this awesome new family we had created which included two children who were totally dependent on me. They had had an incredibly horrific childhood in India. I felt it would kill me to rupture their view of the security they had with us. We went to counseling. I honestly can't say I forgave him, but I figured I needed to move on from his betrayal, to keep this family together for now and—in time—to figure it out what was best.*

*After the first affair he told me he was really sorry, that he knew he had done wrong, and he didn't know what came over him. He was really loving and helpful and I thought he was done, but I later discovered he was having other affairs—mostly internet-based meet ups. I stayed through two or three years of this. I stayed for a lot of reasons. We went through hell with the economy falling apart, we almost lost our house, I was financially dependent on him, and I have such a fierce love for and desire to protect my children.*

*Then he was struck with a pretty massive heart condition. He couldn't keep his job and things really fell apart. I was working as best I could, but the family scene was deteriorating very horribly. There was lots of drinking, and we were arguing a lot. He moved out of the house and onto an old sailboat. The kids were falling apart. I was falling apart. I didn't have the energy to get divorced. He wasn't able to function; he looked horrible. He lived alone on the sailboat for about a year and half. It was grim. Then, slowly but surely, as he came to visit the kids I would notice him starting to look and to act better.*

*Things began improving. We were given a referral to a therapist who worked with us as a family at a very special rate. I credit her with saving my life—rebuilding my self-esteem and sense of self. I was very happy to blame my husband for everything, and the hardest part of my time in therapy was seeing my part in what had happened. Seeing my clinginess, my need for him to validate me, the amount of emotional energy I demanded from him to reassure me because of the fear of abandonment that I carried with me from my own very tumultuous childhood. I saw my need to be responsible for validating myself. She helped us to recognize the patterns that we had both brought to the marriage that had contributed to the blow-ups and loss of emotional connection.*

*Our current therapist is masterful in providing a safe setting in which we can both share. Therapy helped both of us to talk through a lot of things, though there is still a great deal we need to work on. It has helped me to be more empathetic and understanding of why he did what he did, but whole parts of my trust system are still shut down. I could go into all kinds of theories as to why he did what he did, but in the end, I'm in a healthier place now.*

*Therapy has really supported him in opening up more in communicating with me. Our therapist recognized that if things get very intense, he backs away—so she moves carefully. He is dropping his guard because he feels less threatened, less put upon by me. I saw how he had never had a chance to be a child—there were tremendous demands placed on him by his family. And there I was likewise putting demands on him, counting on him to shine for me in all those areas that I aspired to reach myself. He saw me as a career-driven woman, which would mean that he didn't have to be entirely responsible to provide for the family. We both traveled many, many miles to get away from our families, and I came to realize how we had both come into the relationship with our own baggage, our own unresolved issues.*

*My children are very protective of him and so happy when he is at home. They need the stability so much. And we both want to keep this family together.*

*I can see now that from having been reduced to nothing, these past two years have forced me into a period of deep personal growth. My therapist speaks about how, as women, we tend to suffer too much for those we love. My husband still gets depressed, he drinks—and he loves me. Today I know that I am strong, and my happiness is not to be determined by who he is. I am determined to make decisions that are affirming of me.*

*Today I am very cognizant—and have told him—that I don't want to go through the rest of my life without intimacy; without a decent sex life. Now, as I am gaining my own financial independence, I no longer feel financially tied to him. I don't know where were we will be in another two or three years, or when the children leave home. We've just gotten to first base. Our family has survived together. We are all healthier than we were and our home is much calmer. I do believe that we are here for each other on a very deep spiritual level, and that we are passing through a period of immense growth together.*

*Betrayal is such an incredibly painful experience. I feel that even now, eight years later. I think it is something a person never fully gets over. Trust is the central component in marriage, and putting your heart out there and counting on that person only to have that trust diminished is incredibly hurtful. I think it is irreparable. I don't think I will ever feel the way I once did for him. Today I have love for my husband and a deep camaraderie, but the rose colored glasses have been removed.*

*What would I add, in retrospect, to my wish list for my perfect partner? I would add strength of character, integrity, truthfulness, and gentleness.*

Each woman in this chapter speaks of the value of the support received from their counselor or therapist. This helped them to put the affair into perspective, work through what happened and the reasons why, and identify what was needed to move forward. The empathy for their partners that both Melissa and Eva developed in counseling, has been shown to be one of the best predictors of how successful a couple will be in reconciliation.

Eva found the value of recognizing the unresolved emotional baggage both she and her husband had brought to the marriage—all the unresolved emotional issues, all the disappointments, wrongs and traumas carried over from the past. Unresolved emotional baggage can take the form of negative expectations or beliefs created by previous relationships, perhaps from some form of abuse or betrayal experienced as a child, or a later relationship with a significant other. Problems that might otherwise be minor in a relationship become colored by and overloaded with negative associations from earlier times.

It is often said that a woman should not stay in a marriage because of financial uncertainties, because she feels too weak to end it, because she is afraid to be alone, or because of the children. Although each of these factored into Eva's decision to stay, she is certainly not going to settle for an empty shell of a marriage. Her choice was made after careful consideration of what was involved in leaving—or staying. She decided she needed time to figure out what was best.

The children's wellbeing was a major factor in her deciding to stay. Many parents end their marriage prematurely, believing that the children will "get over it." As reported in *The Unanticipated Legacy of Divorce*, by

Judith Wallerstein, et al., the whole trajectory of an individual's life can be profoundly altered by parental divorce. From the viewpoint of the children, divorce is a cumulative experience.

When the time comes to choose a life mate and build a family, the effects of divorce are exacerbated. Parental divorce affects the children's personality, ability to trust, expectations about relationships, and ability to cope with change. Ana Nogales, Ph.D., *Parents Who Cheat: How Children and Adults Are Affected When Their Parents Are Unfaithful*, reveals a parallel pattern in children of parents who betrayed. While martyrdom is not a healthy option for children to carry into future relationships, ending a marriage because the grass looks greener elsewhere—or because they are running from conflict, or it just looks easier—says little of a person's character. Ultimately children benefit from parents who show them how a conscious and loving couple can grow together, through good times and bad.

Eva recognizes that both she and her partner are continuing to learn and to grow. While progress may be slow, it is steady and she realizes allowances need to be made for the difference in their cultural backgrounds, and her husband's need to travel to support the family. She believes a woman should not throw the marriage away without work and deep introspection on both sides.

Whether for the sake of the children, or because she owes it to herself or to the relationship to see how good this marriage can be, staying requires the strength to ride an emotional roller coaster. It requires not walking away until all avenues for renewing the relationship have been explored over a period of months and there are no signs of any positive developments. Realizing relapses and new crises are part of the territory keeps them in perspective.

If, in the years to come, Eva and her husband decide to separate, they will be able to say to their children, with absolute integrity, that they are sorry. They will be able to say they explored every possible avenue for staying together, only to find they had grown apart, and that this was a necessary next step.

Eva speaks of "the rose colored glasses" having been removed. Following betrayal, there will never again be the blind trust that existed before. A woman is now seasoned, and wiser.

### SARAH: *"Even today I feel part of my life is in a shadow with my marriage"*

*I've been betrayed in several relationships prior to marriage so I know what it's like to be on that end. When I reflect on it, what strikes me as the most confusing was that when I met the other man, my relationship with my husband was in the best shape it had been. I was feeling very settled, calm and confident about myself—my marriage, my family—and then it was as though this relationship came out of nowhere and hit me like a meteor.*

*This hit me two weeks before my fortieth birthday. A whole culmination of things led to that implosion. There was a very strong and instant attraction between the other man and myself. We worked in the same field, had many shared interests, were both extroverts and able to talk easily and openly. And, it started with a kiss. It was alcohol induced, dreamlike, fantastical—but when I think about it I should have woken up the next morning asking myself, "Oh my god, what did I do? I kissed another man, how will I explain this?"*

*Instead, from that point on every moment was filled with, "When and how can I see this man again?" This was crazy given that I was in such a good place in my relationship, but on waking that morning, I was already beginning to think about how to cover up the event. I talked to the man that night about how we might see each other again. It is very scary even now to reflect on how I could've been so divided that I was able to play two very different roles and be a willing participant in this whole thing.*

*I think my earlier experiences of being betrayed played into it with a sense of entitlement, of minimization, telling myself it's not that bad. But once on that slippery slope, the level of self-deception grows and grows. We begin to look at our primary relationship in a very different light, and make up all kinds of justifications for doing what we are doing. We have to in order to continue to behave in this way. We must close the door on our primary relationship to open the window to allow the other relationship to flourish. There is incredible suffering for the betrayed spouse, who will likely know something is different, but not know what it is.*

*I felt like I was thrown under a bus by the other man, who told his wife about me. I was on family holiday with my husband and children when she contacted me. She was full of threats, saying I had to tell my husband immediately and that she would be relentless in pursuing me until she was sure I had told him.*

*This was a very painful, very traumatic period of my life. I did tell my husband the truth, and he was gutted. We went into couples counseling, and I had individual counseling as well. He*

134

*was very much fighting for our relationship and scared to death he could have lost me to this man.*

*My lover and I had only been together for six weeks. I felt we were just starting to communicate on a level of emotional intensity that I craved. I had such a deep longing to be in a relationship with someone who could really hold me emotionally, and had never had this in my marriage. I express myself in a very intense way when I want to and feel safe to, and I felt that this man offered me this one opportunity to really explore intimacy at a very deep level—sexually as well as emotionally.*

*I went through incredible levels of grief. The grief was, of course, about my having betrayed my husband—but there was also the grief my very wounded self felt at having lost this other man who I'd built up in my mind to be a savior in a sense; someone who was going to answer all those unanswered questions for me about what was possible in relationships and intimacy. I could talk with my counselor but otherwise there was no one I could confide in who could understand that kind of grief. I was overwhelmed by it. I couldn't understand whether I was grieving the loss of him per se or grieving the possibility that the whole thing was a fantasy. Meanwhile, I was still in this marriage. The inner turmoil felt unbearable. I can honestly say that I never ever stopped loving my husband, and I never ever wanted him to be in pain—but he was, as a consequence of what I had done.*

*There were four months of absolutely no contact between the other man and myself. Then we arranged to meet, to say goodbye. It was meant to be a closure. He had experienced a similar level of emotional intensity with me. We arranged to meet to honor what was, and to move on. Of course this is not what happened. Once we made contact, like with a drug addiction, we wanted more and more. We remained in contact, seeing each other once every five or six weeks in a park or somewhere. My husband didn't know. I felt unable to end the connection, as much as I knew it was the right thing to do. My investment in my marriage at that time was still compromised. I was longing for clarity about why this person came into my life, what was the meaning of this relationship? I was not prepared to let go of that curiosity, even though it was very painful to continue doing what I was doing.*

*I read books and really searched to understand the complexity of my feelings toward my husband and this other man. I believe that ultimately, though, this thing had to play out. I believe we have karmic life lessons and this was one of those—it couldn't be ended prematurely. It had to play out in its full sense to deliver the lesson.*

*So I remained in contact. We emailed a lot. There was some physical contact, but no sex. It was primarily an emotional connection now. He had become much more cautious as his wife knew of his betrayal, and also as he was planning to relocate to North America.*

*A little over a year after meeting my lover, I reached a breaking point where I couldn't play these two divided roles anymore. I couldn't continue to deceive my husband—and myself. I had done enough soul searching to know that I couldn't remain in my marriage while I had these feelings for another man. So we separated. I didn't tell my husband why I was leaving, but he probably suspected.*

*The separation in itself was a huge upheaval for all of us—my husband, children and myself. We worked out parenting arrangements for the children. I remained in contact with the other man. His wife and children had left the country to go on ahead and set up their new home, so he was here for three to four months alone. I was on my own, so this was a time for us to embark on a full-blown journey to discover what the relationship meant to us. Parts of this were glorious but there was always the knowing that he was leaving, and wresting with myself about accepting that and not accepting that and lots of pain and conversations about this.*

*He went to join his family for a six-week period and didn't me contact at all during that time. That wasn't what we agreed to. I became really, really irrational. I threatened to tell his wife. This felt like a betrayal of our relationship. I felt so very lost, hopeless. It's hard to talk about this even now, eight years later. I was suicidal and, when at my lowest, the only person who was there to pick me up was my husband. And thank god for that.*

*It's like you are wearing a thick hooded mask when engaging in this kind of deceit, and my husband coming in at that time was like pulling the mask off and remembering who I was again. I realized we had a very deep friendship, a very caring relationship—and how much I needed to honor that.*

*He carried me through four or five months while we remained in separate homes. He desperately wanted to reconcile, and we did* to some degree when I was at my lowest. I didn't want to promise anything but I desperately needed his support. Part of me felt it was not fair to take his support, but he was there and he offered it. He tried to persuade me to return home. I knew my relationship with the other man was ending as he was leaving the country, and I had to figure out what to do. It was a huge decision to make—whether to give our marriage another chance. Part of me felt I had betrayed my spouse to the point I couldn't repair it and I had to remain alone.

Our children were suffering horribly. We agreed it was in their interest to see what we could do and I returned to the family home. It felt so strange, I don't have words to explain it. I felt I was moving into someone else's house. It was really, really hard to do. We took it very slowly. My husband did not have unrealistic expectations about what we could achieve straight away. We were not sexually intimate at all in the beginning. Our relationship was platonic, but very caring. It was a very painful and very slow process of recovery for both of us. At times we both hit the wall, one or other of us got triggered by something and all the hurt and grief and pain would come up. I was overwhelmed with his pain. It was hard to hold his and mine at same time.

We went into counseling. We had a very supportive counselor— all the way through the last ten years of our relationship she has been very neutral, supportive; a saving grace for us.

There is no miraculous way to repair a relationship after infidelity, no one way of going about things—but there has to be transparency. Even today I feel part of my life is in a shadow with my marriage. Not in shadow meaning I deceive him, but we don't share a level of emotional connection that allows me to be completely open with him about my feelings in the way that I crave. We have a good relationship, but he is not able to receive me in that deep way. However, what he showed me was true love—real love, sacrifice, hanging in there through the entire turmoil. Even now, I find myself in tears as I think of how he stuck by me through all that, and taught me this huge lesson of what love really is.

I wish I had with my husband the level of emotional intimacy I did with my lover, but I don't know how much of that was a fantasy and how much was real. I accept what we have in our marriage and I am really glad we're still together and we found a way to get through it. He was the strong platform, unshakeable *through the whole thing, and that enabled me to find my way home.*

*I told my children the truth about what had happened. I wish my parents had had that conversation. My parents both cheated, but they never openly disclosed what they were doing, and we kids were always trying to figure it out.*

*Today I believe a successful marriage is built on a foundation of friendship—a foundation so strong that nothing is so bad you can't tell the other what is happening. It's important to know about the chemical changes that are activated in the body when you are physically attracted to someone and that this happens even when a couple are happily married. When someone is not aware of this and doesn't have clear boundaries, these things can get out of control very quickly. I believe each partner needs to be willing to be transparent and aware of their vulnerabilities and needs—and a couple needs to have open conversations about these things right from the beginning. There need to be very clear boundaries and conversations about what's acceptable between them.*

*Couples become very complacent, and learn to live with dysfunctional traits and an unhealthy level of dissatisfaction. This makes a person very vulnerable to outside influences. Some of those problems that need to be faced are not relationship problems but problems more directly to do with the individual. For example, my own parents' cheating and my being betrayed in two earlier relationships made me vulnerable to being unfaithful.*

*This experience changed the way I see myself, my relationships, and the world.*

*I am now a hell of a lot more cautious. I police myself. I watch what I do, how I interact with people. I am constantly checking myself all the time for anything that crosses a line I might not be comfortable with.*

*The one good thing that came out of it is that today I do a lot of really good work helping people—both the betrayed and the unfaithful partner—through infidelity. I see practitioners who are very uncomfortable working in the area of extramarital affairs. They come with their own personal judgments and values, and often take a shame-based approach that can be very harmful—a person who has betrayed his partner already has enough shame to carry.*

A period of ambivalence, of being torn between wanting to stay and wanting to leave, is one that many people—be they the betrayed or the unfaithful partner—endure. Walking out looks so much easier, but the painful emotions and fallout will need to be faced either way. Usually, leaving the marriage is not the best solution. The unresolved issues that led to the infidelity are carried into the next relationship. Leaving the marriage for a relationship that was sourced in broken trust and betrayal will likely develop its own problems with trust.

It may be months before ambivalence is resolved—even with therapy. However, in that ambivalence, there is hope. The first decision to be made by each partner is whether they will commit to working on the marriage; whether they have the resolve, care and respect for the other and their vows to each other, to commit to the process of rebuilding trust and intimacy. The decision of whether to stay or go is set aside for a time. Not living to regret an impulsive decision requires deciding to leave only when all options have been explored, and everything reasonable—which includes counseling—has been tried for many months and there is still no sign of progress.

A temporary separation, such as Melissa demanded, can sometimes be helpful to allow a couple to cool down and think through the issues involved. The problem, as Sarah found, is that unless the unfaithful partner ends the affair at least for the period of this separation, clear thinking is impossible. Even when there is a promise not to see the affair partner during this time, issues of trust arise, putting further stresses on the marriage. And when this separation is really a means of seeing the affair partner, this additional betrayal will need to be dealt with.

When a couple chooses to make a strong commitment to save the marriage, they have a high probability of staying together. Couples therapy is then usually the best option because individual therapy tends to focus on *me* rather than *us*, to the detriment of the couple relationship. In addition, the confidentiality established in the relationship between therapist and individual excludes the partner, and will likely exacerbate their fear and distrust. At other times, as Sarah found, individual counseling may need to run parallel with couples counseling.

A lack of progress may not be a reflection of what is possible in the marriage itself. It may be a reflection of the therapist or counselor's lack of skill or experience. Despite statistics clearly indicating that a couple is more likely to remain married when the factors surrounding the infidelity are thoroughly explored in counseling, Shirley P. Glass, Ph.D., *Not "Just Friends,"* points to studies revealing that 59% of couples in counseling said that their therapist mainly focused on general marital problems, not the affair; and 23% of the couples said their therapist encouraged them to quickly get over it.

As Sarah has seen, a counselor may be judgmental of the unfaithful partner or dismissive of the betrayed partner's distress. A counselor may be uncomfortable or impatient talking about the details of the affair and want the partners to forgive or forget what's happened, and move on. She may be shame-based in her counsel. She may be well meaning but simply not know the stages a couple goes through in moving towards reconciliation.

> *"We enter intimate relationships blindly, often effortlessly, swept up with passion and an idealized perception of our partner, often cocky about our ability to keep things hot. Most of us are totally unprepared for what lies ahead, and ignorant of what's required to last the course. The affair shocks us into reality. Fortunately, it also invites us to try again."*
>
> —Janis Abrahms Spring, Ph.D., *After the Affair: Healing the Pain and Rebuilding Trust When a Partner Has Been Unfaithful*

And so six plus years after the infidelity, although the affair remains in the background for each of these women, they have chosen to make good of this experience—both as individuals and as a couple. Each has emerged with a stronger sense of themselves, of their own personal worth and their personal boundaries. Each had the good fortune of having partners willing to walk the distance with them. Today, they are stronger both as individuals and as a couple. They have learned how to communicate their needs and resolve conflicts. There is an awareness of the vulnerabilities that created the environment that led to the affair, and what it takes to protect a relationship. And, I imagine that not one of them would disagree, they are still learning.

Each of the women spoke directly of believing that this had to happen, in order for them to in some way wake up. There is maturity and wisdom in this perspective. And yet, of course this in no way condones infidelity as a path to personal growth. Each woman regrets the pain and suffering this brought to others, including their children, and hopes that their children will not need to go through what they did. In part with thanks to their parent's choosing to stay, these children will grow up with a greater awareness of what it takes to shape and sustain a committed relationship and a love that lasts.

Now, to look more closely at the feelings a woman who has been betrayed may have for the "other woman." Regardless of whether a marriage ends or is renewed, the reality of the other woman is a force to be dealt with.

## CHAPTER 9

## *The Other Woman—Sluts, Bitches, Whores!*

A woman who has been betrayed feels deeply violated. The betrayal cuts to the core of her being. Most immediately the violation is that her partner, her intimate, would betray her; but also that another woman would partner with him in doing this. Even in the face of the competition, gossip, and betrayal that has become the norm amongst women, to be betrayed by another woman in this way compounds the violation a woman feels.

### JESSICA:

*What were my feelings about the women he was having affairs with? Basically, I hated them. I hated them. I wanted to kill them. They were sluts, bitches, whores. I made contact with all of them in some way, saying this is my man, stay away. He was pissed off I did this. I didn't ever hear from any of them. They were all young—none had ever been in a steady relationship.*

*I had so many angry, horrible feelings of hatred. I was so angry, I hated the woman who he finally left me for, hated her so much, that I wanted her dead. I was shocked that I could have that level of anger, hatred, disgust. I was really shocked to see I despised someone so much I could annihilate them off the face of the earth.*

A woman who has been betrayed may be shocked to see the depth of venom she feels towards the other woman—or in Jessica's case, women. This exacerbates her feelings of bewilderment, shame, and disorientation.

As we saw in Chapter 6: *Women Betrayed—The Beliefs and Illusions that Blind Us*, Jessica was on the verge of a breakdown. Here, again, we see that Kali energy (explained in Chapter 6) that compels a woman to demand the truth be told, and to confront transgressions that bring needless suffering to others. Jessica's stepping out to assert and protect herself and her family, rather than succumbing to despair or resignation, was an expression of the Kali force in her in that moment. Jessica garnered the rage she felt and directed it in a constructive way. The fact that the other women ignored her request they stay away from her husband, is secondary to this.

That the other women ignored her request is not surprising. This is a reflection of the degree to which infidelity has become legitimized and normalized, more so within certain communities than others—and while not shared directly in Jessica's story, this is certainly so of the area she lived in. It is also a reflection of the narcissism and sense of entitlement that accompanies this attitude—and probably of a level of naïveté, too, in that these women in all likelihood had not even a clue as to how their behavior impacted Jessica and her family. It was important that these women see her anger and hear her words—seeds were planted that, one day, may bear fruit.

As we saw in Chapter 6, Jessica went on to engage in a process of self-discovery that revealed what lay beneath her rage. When a good deal of time has passed and a woman still has trouble letting go of her anger or rage, it is often because she is using it to empower herself. While this may have been wise in the beginning, at some point she must be careful or it can hurt her—badly. It takes a Warrior's self-compassion and courage to recognize when *enough is enough;* and determination to relinquish those thoughts and feelings of rage and condemnation that, understandably, feel so very justified. Holding in her heart the intention to change her relationship to the situation will, in itself, set in motion the process that will in time release her from their grip.

### DEE: *"It was as if it was a contest"*

*I was so stupid, so naïve. She was my friend. She needed someone to drive with her on this long distance trip. I encouraged Jerry to go along and help her. They both later said they saw this as my giving them consent to have an affair. I couldn't understand. What were they talking about? She was in a jam and needed help. I encouraged him to help her. Nowhere in my mind was there any intimation of an affair; I never even thought of the possibility. I was her friend. She knew we were monogamous. That's how deluded the mind is when there is desire or temptation. Their minds just made stuff up because they wanted to. That's what hurt. I didn't matter to either of them.*

*I felt hugely betrayed by her. After the affair had ended I called her at a time when I was deeply upset and feeling that I'd lost everything. I told her that she had taken from me the thing that mattered most to me, and I asked her how she could do that when she was my friend. She said in a condescending way, "I didn't take anything from you." It was this cold, remorseless New Age message that "I can't make you feel anything. You are responsible for whatever you experience and choose how you feel about it."*

*It was as if it was a contest and this was a victory for her. She was unwilling to take any responsibility and showed absolutely no remorse. I hated her guts. She didn't care at all about how I felt. I had no further contact with her. I had reached out to communicate with her as a friend, to let her know I was in pain. She made it clear that she didn't give a shit. That was the ultimate betrayal—that she had no remorse for screwing my man! I was the one who had asked Jerry to help her when she really needed help and was out of options. It never crossed my mind that either of them would betray me. There has never been any indication she cared about me in the slightest or that she has had any remorse. I've not had any contact and mostly just tried to forget about her and let it go. Obviously I haven't succeeded very well.*

*That was decades ago but I still feel the sting of her betrayal. It's funny because I forgave Jerry a long time ago, but I'm still working on forgiving her. That's because he saw how hurt I was, and not only expressed remorse but did all he could to make amends. She showed no remorse or care for me. I think that makes a huge difference.*

New Age rhetoric or not, statements such as, *"You are responsible for what you experience,"* completely dismiss any recognition or responsibility for acting with integrity and respect towards another. Dee's friend's absence of care or remorse, and her refusal to accept any accountability for how her actions affected Dee, is the very substance of that which perpetuates the epidemic of mistrust amongst women.

As Dee found, time alone will not heal the many levels of trauma residing in a woman's body and psyche. Most women have suppressed the trauma so deeply that they are not even aware of it. It is often the news of another's infidelity that will activate the unresolved feelings. However, most women will not see any connection between her past unresolved experience, and the agitation she feels at hearing of another's.

It takes courage to *"take the lid off the chest that all of those feelings have been stored in for so long,"* as one woman expressed it. It may be that a woman deems it too painful to do so. This will be especially true when there has been no expression of accountability from her partner, and no genuine apology. Instead, a woman may push the feelings back down inside of her, believing that, having lived with them for so long, these occasional bursts into conscious awareness aren't worth attending to. However, her choice not to deal with them will mean that the trauma remains to some degree stored in her body, unresolved, depleting the fullness of the life-force otherwise available to her.

### MAGGIE:

*My ex-husband was a spiritual teacher, and with that, there was so much hypocrisy. Even though it was my husband who slept with other women, I always blamed the women. I think it's because even though he was a jerk and emotionally and physically violent, I never saw him as predator. He would never really chase women; that wasn't his thing. The women chased him, even though they knew he was married to a woman who was pregnant or breastfeeding babies. Had they not, he wouldn't have done it.*

*I tried talking to the women, but mostly they were very defensive. We were all within this same kind of conceptualized spirituality so there were a lot of justifications like, "This is all part of God's plan, of consciousness evolving." I found it pretty heartless really ... that was surprising to me.*

Maggie's blaming the other women and not seeing her husband as a predator released him, at least in her eyes, from any accountability for his actions. It can be easier, and less painful, for a woman to detest the other woman than to detest her husband, but accountability lies equally in the hands of both who chose to be unfaithful. As a spiritual teacher, her husband was in a position that draws women to him as surely as bees to a honey pot. He had no need to chase women; they were attracted to the *"Light of Lucifer,"* just as Maggie was (see Chapter 6: *Women Betrayed— The Beliefs and Illusions that Blind Us*). Additionally, the emotional and physical abuse she took from him was surely an indication of a predatory character. Had she recognized this, Maggie may have said *Enough* to the ongoing disrespect and abuse, and left long before she did.

Unlike Maggie, these other women had no license to partner sexually with this man. It is true that many spiritual authorities have succumbed to the temptation of the subtle, or not so subtle, invitations for intimacy from

145

women. However, this does not alter the fact that the teacher's availability, as much as the women's invitation, culminates in infidelity and—ultimately—hurt is inevitable.

One would wonder, given that surely a foundation of all sacred traditions is respect for the wellbeing of others and accountability for one's choices, how these women had no qualms about doing this. What does it say about their spiritual teacher in that he collaborated in this?

Spiritual bypassing, a term coined by psychologist John Welwood in 1984, is a dangerous and seductive shadow of spirituality. It can include exaggerated or harmful claims to detachment, overemphasis on the positive, emotional numbing and repression, and devaluation of the personal as relative to the spiritual. It allows us to avoid facing the bigger picture or truth of what is happening. It's endorsed with superficial, oversimplified, and out-of-context bites of wisdom such as, *"Don't take it personally," "Whatever bothers you about someone is really only about you,"* and, *"It's all just an illusion."*

The women wanted what they wanted, as did he, and the mind can justify anything it wants to when the desire is strong enough.

### JESSICA:

*There was one situation that was incredible to me. I couldn't believe it. At some point after my husband and I had recommitted, I had gone to Bali. A good friend of mine was going through a breakup with her own husband. She had written to my husband, asking him if he would sleep with her so she could get over her breakup. She had assumed because we had been in an open relationship, he was fodder for any woman. Obviously he had told her we were still in an open relationship and was still thinking about seeing other women. I wrote a long letter to her saying, "You are my friend. We've been friends a long time. You don't know the whole story, don't do this." She responded, "Oh my god, I'm so glad you told me this. He didn't tell me the whole truth—I thought it was all cool. I'm glad we didn't end up sleeping together."*

Jessica's contacting the other woman, and communicating with her in a careful and respectful manner, eventuated in this whole scenario turning out very differently than it may otherwise have. This is why directly contacting the other woman, rather than leaving the man to be the go-between, is so very important. What matters then, is *how* the communication is made. Jessica spoke from her heart in appealing to the friendship that existed between her and the other woman, and this doubtlessly facilitated the favorable outcome.

Setting the stage for the best possible outcome will require a woman being very clear about what it is she wants to request. It may require venting any strong emotions beforehand, perhaps with a friend. If a woman is at the effect of her own rage when communicating with the other woman, it is less likely that the other woman will be willing to hear or consider what she has to say. She may dismiss her as mad, crazy, or unstable. When the communication is person to person, it may be helpful to have a friend or support person with her, if that is acceptable to the other woman. Communicating in a firm and respectful matter, and asking questions rather than making assumptions, will more likely allow the other woman to be receptive to the communication. *"Are you aware that this man is married to me? Do you know we have children? What did he say, that gave you permission to partner sexually with him? Have you considered what your choice to do this means to our children and to me?"*

### MARILYN: *"I wondered what she had that I didn't"*

*When I was pregnant with my fourth child and my partner's first child, he had an affair with another woman. I was devastated. I didn't feel angry, just very sad. I didn't understand at that time that I had a right to feel betrayed or to be offended or traumatized. I don't think I felt worthy. I had been emotionally, physically, and sexually abused as a child, so I already was shame-based and felt guilty just about being. My first husband had left me some years earlier, just five weeks before the birth of our third child. So I was also traumatized by abandonment, which, on some level, I felt I deserved.*

*Here I was, pregnant, and he was with another woman. I felt powerless. I wondered what she had that I didn't. I felt terribly jealous. I found out who she was, got her phone number, called her, and my partner answered the telephone. The first thing he said was, "Nobody's here!" He'd been caught and was now stuck between two women. The other woman had the good sense and strength of character to tell my partner she didn't want to see him again. His pregnant mate was grieving while he was having an affair and she knew she would never be able to trust him in a committed relationship. If he did that to someone else, surely he could do it to her, too.*

*He came back to me as best he could—although that didn't end his extra-marital affairs, which persisted until shortly before I left him.*

*After our son was born, we were at a gala dinner for the opening of an art gallery. The other woman was at the dinner, too. I was very aware of her being there, and wondered if she knew who I was. I thought she probably did. At some point I got up, went over to the table, and introduced myself.*

*Now, more than forty years later, she and I are still friends! In fact, at some point, we realized we liked one another more than we liked the man between us. I often wished I had had her strength earlier—I admired her for that, and I told her so. Clearly, she taught me something very important. Once she saw who this guy was, that he had a wife who was pregnant, that he was a jerk and untrustworthy, she had the strength to say no to him. That was the end for her. It was until much later that I found the strength to say screw you and get out of there.*

Marilyn's stating that when she discovered her husband was having an affair, she *"didn't feel angry, just very sad,"* is not an unusual reaction to the discovery of a partner's unfaithfulness. It may be the result of her numbing herself to the pain, or on some level feeling that she deserved it—that she was not worthy of anything better. Or it may, as we saw earlier, simply be a matter of a woman's not knowing what she has a right to expect of her husband.

Whatever the reason, Marilyn came to realize that she could not let the betrayal pass unaddressed. Every woman will react differently to the thought of contacting the other woman, and it will not even occur to many to do so. How a woman reacts is shaped in part by her own psychological and emotional makeup, the support she has available to her, and her own past relationships. Through earlier life experiences, Marilyn had developed the courage, will and fierceness to take a stand for herself. That being said, those same abusive earlier life experiences may have rendered another woman beaten and submissive.

It is not unusual that it is the awesome force of the Mother Bear in a woman that will step forward as the Warrior Woman when needed to protect her children. Marilyn was pregnant with her fourth child, and it may have been this that pushed her over the threshold to where she knew she had had enough. She did what was needed to make contact with the other woman. Can you imagine how heartening the other woman's response—her telling Marilyn's partner she didn't want to see him again, —would have been to Marilyn? It is these kinds of actions that ignite the flame of hope in a woman, to keep moving forward through all manner of trials.

148

The other woman's strength to say no was a source of inspiration to Marilyn, awakening in her the possibility of doing likewise. Her stepping out to connect with this other woman initiated a friendship between them that continues even today. It is this kind of communication—seeking to connect rather than condemn—that begins to set in motion a change in the greater collective of women.

While some women will step out and contact or confront the other woman directly, as Marilyn did, most will turn their upset inward or dump their emotions indiscriminately on others. Others will philosophize their upset away, or—being more spiritual—"rise above it."

This spiritual bypassing—the use of spiritual practices and beliefs to avoid dealing with our painful feelings, unresolved wounds, and developmental needs—has become much more prevalent in our culture than is generally recognized. It is a strategy not only for avoiding pain, but also for legitimizing such repression.

What is true for every woman is that at some point, reclaiming her personal power and authentic presence will require she recognize not only her role in what led to the infidelity, but also what she is projecting onto both the other woman, and the man who betrayed her. How might this look? In Chapter 10: *Projections—What We Resist, Persists*, we will look at one woman's initial efforts to do just this.

# CHAPTER 10

## Projections—What We Resist, Persists

### GAIL: *"I was not ready to forgive"*

*The hatred, the anger, the disgust that I felt for the other woman was still with me, over a year later. The intensity had perhaps dissipated some, but it was still there … even the wish that she was dead. I had the insight to see that the purpose of my holding these feelings was wanting payback; a sense of power. I knew it was not good for me to be holding onto this, but I seemed unable to shift it. I wasn't even sure I wanted to.*

*I knew about projections—how we project disowned parts of ourselves onto others rather than owning them in ourselves. But I had not been able, or willing, to see how this disgust and hatred I felt for her could live inside me. One day I decided that, with the support of a skilled friend, I would do what I needed to do to look more deeply into how these emotions lived in me, and were being triggered by this woman.*

*My friend asked me, What was it that disgusted me about this other woman? What disgusted me was that while knowing my husband was married and had children, she still chose to enter into a sexual relationship with him. I am disgusted that a woman would stoop so low. What she did was so cruel—it hurt me so very, very badly. Yes, I wished her dead.*

*What was my role in allowing this infidelity to happen? What is it about what I've allowed to happen that disgusts me? What do I hate about what I've done? My husband had called me to tell me that he wanted to explore the "sexual magnetism" between himself and this woman. He told me that they both wanted to know how I would feel about this. Of course, I was shocked. I didn't believe it would really happen. I spoke at length about it being impossible for us to know the ramifications of this, what it would mean for us and for our family; that he was playing with fire. I said, "I can't stop you, but please don't do this."*

*Why did I say that?! Why didn't I say, "NO! Do not do this!"? There had been similar situations, though not this major, where he had ignored my requests he not share a bed—even if there was, as he said, no physical attraction—with the other women. While I believed he was not being sexual with these women, it repelled me. He couldn't accept that as reasonable or rational. I am sure his feelings were compounded by the fact that in the area where we lived there was a lot of permission given to the right of the individual to get his or her sexual passions met. Polygamy was an accepted practice in some circles, though not in those I personally knew. It was only much later that I heard of his involvement with others to whom monogamy was considered "archaic."*

*And so I wanted to be reasonable, understanding ... not a controlling or demanding wife. There was something else here, too, that I did not recognize until much later: my not knowing where to go within myself to set firm boundaries in this situation. I didn't know I had a right to assert he not do this; that it was a reasonable demand to make of my husband. It did not occur to me to demand her phone number and contact her immediately. In essence, I did not take a strong stand for myself, and he chose to take this as my giving him permission to do what he did. In these ways, at the very least, I had a role in how this unfolded.*

*Had I been much firmer in my communication with him, and contacted the other woman directly, things may have unfolded differently. It may have been that my husband did not convey my distress to the other woman. How naïve of me to believe that he would! She may have thought it was okay with me—as difficult as it is for me to imagine that. And even if he did mislead her initially, he himself told me as the weeks went on that she was "really upset" that I was so upset!*

*Seeing so clearly my role in what had happened changed my feelings toward her a little, but they were still there. I found myself feeling very, very sad. Sad that I was so stupid. Sad that I had not set stronger boundaries. Earlier, in several similar but different situations, I had insisted that we see a counselor. He had maintained his right to his values and to getting his needs met. I had considered expressing my concerns in a small group of friends that we met with monthly. I didn't do this because, although personal sharing was a norm in this group, to speak about this felt too personal, and I did not want to embarrass him. Upon reflection, that was ridiculous. If I had done that, everything would have come out into the open and been addressed so much earlier. I did not do this, and as a consequence my marriage ended in a hurtful, humiliating way.*

*I can feel compassion for myself, for my knowing no better at the time, but the sadness is overwhelming and does not fully allow me to release the disgust ... whether it be for myself or for this other woman. I can still feel the hatred; hatred for that part of me that was so weak so as to not stand up for not only myself— but the children. What kind of mother does that?! Oh, there are so many layers to this, beneath the hatred, the disappointment ... it runs so deep.*

*So yes, I could see that I was projecting onto her the intensity of the disgust I felt towards myself for not standing up for myself. She did not say no, I did not say no. And yes, I feel disgusted by what I've allowed to happen, for all those years, in his relationships with the other women. But I felt too beaten by the whole situation, too exhausted, even now, to take any action to shift it. It was clear I was not ready to forgive. I didn't want to. I had not yet forgiven myself.*

To recognize what it is in her that she is projecting onto the other person, requires a woman be willing to consider the possibility that whatever shows up in her relationship with another person is not only about the other—it may also be about her. Whether it is that someone is disrespecting her, or has betrayed her, resolution begins with her enquiring how she is not respecting herself, or how she has betrayed herself. Usually it will have to do with her in some way not being aware of her own needs and rights, not respecting herself, or not setting and enforcing healthy boundaries.

Once again we see the naïveté, the lack of wisdom or experience, in a woman's simply not recognizing her right and her need to take a stand for her herself in the face of her partner's disrespect and dismissal of her requests. And once again, we see how these acts can be clouded in cultural values that condone an individual's right to get his own needs met, even at the cost of choosing to hurt or harm another.

Exhausted, believing she needs to *do* something to shift her feelings toward the other woman, Gail is thinking from within the realm of the masculine. Breathing into her belly, opening her heart, can allow her to access the self-compassion that will ease her exhaustion, enfold her in self-forgiveness, and begin to restore her energy. Moving her attention into the body carries her into the receptivity of the feminine realm, of simply *being,* and will shift her feelings—and her experience.

It may not be until she has had *absolutely enough* of experiencing these debilitating emotions—the disgust, the hatred—that a woman will be able to work directly with them. Doing this will demand that, every time she finds herself feeling that disgust or hatred, she calls the courage to be present to the energy of these feelings in her body. This cannot be done through the conceptual mind. The emotions want to be experienced, and only when she is fully present to them will they move of their own accord through her body.

She will need to do this again and again. What is being released is not only the feelings and emotions activated by this infidelity, but all the other times when she has compromised her values, her integrity, her truth. As long as she projects all of her anger on *her* or *him*, she continues to disempower herself. She needs to connect with that same energy in her that she is projecting onto another, to experience it as it lives within her—without becoming victim to it.

In those moments when this seems impossible—and there may be many of them—stating with absolute resolve, *"I have had* enough *of these debilitating thoughts and feelings,"* and bringing compassion to herself is itself an act of the Warrior. This resolve in itself initiates a change in her relationship to the situation she finds herself in. And yes, she is wise to recognize that before she can forgive the other woman, she will need to forgive herself.

It's not easy and it doesn't happen overnight. Again and again, the debilitating emotions will return. If need be, she calls herself back one thousand times a day.

One day, she will realize, to her surprise, that there is no longer any blame, no *"because of you I ... "* Instead, she stands centered in her own wisdom, strength and equanimity.

While the intensity of Gail's hostility and desire for retaliation is understandable, as long as she carries these feelings she is giving the other woman and the situation power over her. As long as she remains at the effect of these debilitating emotions, she not only perpetuates her own suffering but is releasing these energies—the hatred, hostility, even violence—into the collective. Further incentive for a woman to reach that point of having had *enough* of these disempowering feelings can emerge from her recognition of the hatred and the deep mistrust that gets perpetuated, woman to woman, through her rage and condemnation.

In time, Gail could set in motion a level of healing within the Sisterhood by opening a line of communication with the other woman. This need not be with any intention to be friends, but rather for her to hear Gail's voice, her broken-heartedness at what had happened.

Now, to turn to an earlier journal entry from Gail, in which she had allowed herself to explore how the rage that she had been projecting on her husband, lived in her.

*I struggled with how I could begin to communicate across the immense chasm that my husband's affair had put between him and myself. Only months ago I would have said this was the person I was closest to and knew better that anyone else in the world. But now, I didn't know who he was. I didn't know how to reach him through the feelings of grief, anger, shame and rage that had become my constant companions.*

*I began to question the real issue underneath all this rage. And, I came to experience not only the depth of the grief and rage I felt—but also the liberation I experienced when I allowed myself to feel all that I had been projecting onto Mark.*

*I had believed I needed Mark to understand that how he went about this affair was unbearably cruel and horribly dismissing of me and the relationship we had shared. What kind of man can just walk away like that? It was so incomprehensible that after all these years, so suddenly I didn't matter. Our family didn't matter. Not only that, but the fact that he was setting an example for betrayal to be okay was absolutely—absolutely—devastating to me. His doing this would lead to others thinking, "If he did it, why can't I?"*

*Now, with the support of my friend, I moved into the heartbreak and the rage as it lived in my body. I embodied the depth of those emotions. I sobbed and sobbed as it passed before my eyes how every act of betrayal—whether it be the betrayal of a partner, of other human beings, even of a nation—sets the stage for more acts of abuse, disrespect and violation. I viscerally felt the horror and distress of this in the very fiber of my being.*

*I sobbed until there were no more tears. I felt cleansed, purified, as I moved more deeply into a place of calm, inner strength, and clarity. I knew now that in aligning with this place in me, I was aligning with the Warrior in me. And that speaking from this place in me, he could, perhaps, hear me. Whether or not he did, was no longer as important to me. I knew now where my strength was.*

*While I had wanted him to wake up to be accountable for what he had done, I now recognized that all I could do was articulate my distress, my horror, my heartbreak at what I saw was happening, with every act of betrayal normalizing another. I came to understand and accept that he seemed, at least at this time, to be incapable of recognizing the depth of the harm he has caused.*

*I wondered, was this side of him that is so self-centered and self-serving always there? Was I blind, stupid, not to have seen this before? A wise friend had often told me he didn't see me for who I was—he only saw me through the filter of his own needs. I only now saw what she was saying. I saw, too, how his inability to acknowledge the harm he caused, and the stories he told to justify his behavior, was typical of his personality type and pattern of needing to be right, to look good. I could even recognize that this was sourced, as he would be the first to say, in the unmet needs of his own childhood.*

*I wondered, was I stupid to stay in this relationship for so very long? No! I would not invalidate the good that we did share, who I was, who he was, who we were together. We were both where we needed to be and doing what we needed to do, and seeing the other as we needed to see them—for that period in our lives—to learn what each needed to learn, to see what we needed to see.*

*Just as this whole experience has revealed to me these parts in him that I'm sad about and disappointed in, there is nothing in what he did or in what he has done since, that leads me to feel that I want to continue a relationship of any kind with this man.*

Again, here we see that typically when we feel anger, we project it at someone or something else. However, the experience of these emotions—whether it be anger, or rage, or despair—lives in us. Initially Gail was projecting her anger onto Mark. When instead she recognized how and why it lived in her, she was able to choose to use it wisely.

What we resist, persists. Energy follows attention, in other words energy flows where attention goes. Every time a woman places attention on what she doesn't like in the other, or on the energy of the problem, she is feeding that negative quality. Changing the dynamic requires she recognize that she is in some way accountable for whatever is showing up in her relationship, and to bring the focus of her attention back from the other, and onto herself.

A woman does not need to know what's going on with the other person, only what's going on in her own experience. She focuses not on what *he* needs to do, but what she needs to do. She puts her attention on herself—and the quality or state of being that she wants to experience. She puts her attention onto giving and receiving this for herself, rather than on what it is that she does not want to experience.

It may not be easy for a woman to identify where she is not respecting herself. One of the reasons this can be difficult is in the simple fact that she does not *want* to recognize how that quality she is projecting on the other, lives in her. It truly takes the courage of the Warrior to be willing to inquire as to how it expresses in her own words and actions—towards herself, towards others. It requires a genuine willingness to be transparent and vulnerable. It demands courage and commitment to plummet into those depths that she would rather turn a blind eye to. Yet once seen, the seeing and owning of that quality or energy as it lives in her, can change everything in a split second … *"Oh my goodness, now I see!"* At very least, it begins unraveling the pattern, and with the intention set and sustained, in time, it will unravel.

Seeing and accepting that at this time, Mark was incapable of recognizing how his choices harmed others, was liberating for Gail. She now saw who this man was, outside of the projections and beliefs she had carried. She realized that seeing this didn't take away from the fact that she had loved him, that they had shared many wonderful experiences together—but the curtain had been parted, and with what she has now seen and understood, she wants nothing further from the relationship. There is wisdom in her allowing herself to recognize that even now, there is something that must be honored about what she and Mark have shared, *and* that it is time to recognize it is done—it's time for her to move on.

In Chapter 14: *Once Friends—Colluding in Our Silence*, we see how projections shape not only a woman's experience of the "other woman" and of her own partner's infidelity, but also other women's responses to the infidelity that may hurt and confound her. Firstly, let's look more closely at this lofty ideal of forgiveness.

# CHAPTER 11

## Forgiveness—As the Wound of Infidelity Heals

*"Many people have trouble with forgiveness because they have been taught that it is a singular act to be completed in one sitting. That is not so. Forgiveness has many layers, many seasons … The important part of forgiveness is to begin and to continue. The finishing of it all is a life work."*

—Clarissa Pinkola Estés, *Women Who Run With the Wolves*

To forgive may seem an impossible ideal as a woman grapples with the crushing pain of betrayal. Suggesting forgiveness of the one who has been unfaithful while a woman is still stinging from the aftermath of the betrayal, is to be out of touch with the reality of the depth of her hurt and heartbreak. Blaming or judging herself, or allowing herself to be admonished or judged by others for not forgiving, will exacerbate her shame and anguish .

*"In the best of circumstances, a genuine forgiveness takes time and emerges gradually as the wound of infidelity heals."*

—Dennis Ortman, Ph.D., *Transcending Post-Infidelity Stress Disorder*

A woman may rush to forgive, in order to avoid the work of trying to understand what happened and to avoid feeling the depths of her pain, her anger, and her grief. She may rush to forgive because she thinks she "should." This kind of pseudo forgiveness offers no resolution and leaves lingering and deeply embedded resentment. Residing in the physical body, this in time may manifest in illness.

*"In a great injury, something is broken, psychologically or spiritually. The break not only erodes our sense of living in a fair world, it corrupts our experience of our own worth, and fragments our control over our own lives and emotions; it also fundamentally damages our faith in the worthiness of others. It is that loss of the other that we absorb, and somehow transform, in forgiveness."*

—Molly Layton, psychologist, *The Long Road to Forgiveness*

Whether in the role of the betrayer or the betrayed, forgiveness is something a woman may struggle with for years after the infidelity—and most often for a lifetime. The struggle will be compounded when there is an absence of clarity as to what constitutes forgiveness.

## What Forgiveness Is—And Is Not

Shirley P. Glass Ph.D., *Not "Just Friends,"* states clearly what forgiveness is *not*:

- *Forgetting or pretending the infidelity didn't happen.* The lessons learned are an essential part of the remainder of a woman's life journey.

- *Excusing or condoning the behaviour.* The necessity of forgiving an act means that a grievous injury has occurred.

- *Reconciliation.* You can forgive without wishing to reconcile.

- *Giving permission to continue the behavior.* Forgiveness requires you be safe from further hurt.

*"In our culture there is a notion that forgiveness is a one hundred percent proposition. All or nothing. It is also taught that forgiveness means to overlook, to act as though a thing has not occurred. That is not true either."*

—Clarissa Pinkola Estés, *Women Who Run With the Wolves*

Forgiveness *is*:

- *A gift you give to yourself.* Forgiveness allows a woman who has been betrayed to free herself from continual suffering, without minimizing the injury.

158

- *A choice.* Authentic forgiveness acknowledges the wound and is the result of conscious effort.

- *Letting go of revenge and the need to punish.* A decision to seek solutions rather than blame.

*"Forgiveness is not surrender, it is a conscious decision to cease to harbor resentment, which includes forgiving a debt and giving up one's resolve to retaliate."*

—Clarissa Pinkola Estés, *Women Who Run With the Wolves*

## Dignity and Self-Respect Come First

### DEE:

*I was so glad to read in Chapter 4: In the Aftermath of Infidelity—The First Year, where Kate Rutherford, Ph.D., said, "Forgiveness is not always the answer—dignity and self-respect come first." I wanted to shout out loud when I read that. That's it exactly. I loved that she told counselors to "encourage unforgiveness (of the unfaithful partner) to keep her safe at first."*

*And she said, "Let her anger be her strength." Anger is necessary to counterbalance the collapse and pain of sadness and loss. That's what needs to happen for a good long time, anger turning to sadness turning to anger … until there's an internal core structure of dignity and self-respect rebuilt. Self-forgiveness is so very important, too.*

A woman who has been betrayed often blames herself. She may not like—she may even fear—who she has become since the discovery of the infidelity. A woman may need to forgive herself for the wrathful, grieving, unstable, insecure person she now appears to be. It demands humility and courage for a woman to recognize both her strengths and her weaknesses, and to see herself in the *entirety* of who she is—and not as she imagined she was or as she would like herself to be.

*"To truly heal, we must say our truth, and not only our regret and pain but also what harm was caused, what anger, what disgust, and also what desire for self-punishment or vengeance was evoked in us. The psyche understands human nature with all*

*its foibles and gives pardon based on the telling of the naked truth.* "

—Clarissa Pinkola Estés, *Women Who Run With the Wolves*

A woman may blame herself for being too gullible and trusting. She may believe she could have done something to prevent the infidelity. She may blame herself for not seeing the clues, for ignoring the clues—for not being a good enough wife. She may blame herself for not holding the family together, not being able to prevent the subsequent separation or divorce, for not "getting over it" sooner. She may be disappointed and judge herself harshly for not being able to control the outbursts of anger, fury and suspicion that emerge with such vengeance. She needs to understand that any and all of these reactions are normal and best met with compassion for herself and her predicament.

## Practices for Self-Forgiveness

*"We ask for forgiveness and offer forgiveness not because of some imagined wrongdoing but because we no longer wish to carry the load of our resentments and guilt. We allow the mind to sink into the heart."*

—Stephen Levine, *Healing Into Life and Death*

Self-forgiveness requires a woman feel acknowledged—at very least by herself—for all the ways she feels she has been wronged by her partner's infidelity. It requires she acknowledge all that she wanted from the relationship that she didn't get, and how she felt as a result of this. Next is her naming all that she herself wishes to be forgiven for—all the ways in which she failed to protect the relationship, herself, and her family. This process is best done in writing, and may be helpful to do in the company of a trusted other.

When a woman follows this process through to the point of genuinely feeling acknowledged for *all* of this, she has opened that window into forgiving herself for simply not knowing how to do it differently at the time. Recognizing herself as human, as imperfect, she can begin to accept and forgive herself.

*"I am embarrassed to admit that, over a decade since his cheating on me, and after being divorced for four years, going through counseling, and 'putting it all behind me,' I still haven't*

*fully processed the anger, sadness, frustration, embarrassment, shame, and mourning .... Your book is giving voice to many of the inner whispers I have silenced and ignored. I truly have felt lighter—uplifted, even—after reading this. It is like the dialogue that was nebulously swimming around in my head for years has been articulated on paper. I recognize now that I didn't feel heard or validated—by my former spouse, the counselor, or my parents/friends. And I recognize now that I never heard or validated myself. I wasn't honest with how I was feeling, thinking, and experiencing everything."*

—Early reviewer

By inviting in self-forgiveness, a woman can access the tenderness and compassion that resides in her heart. Forgiveness has the power to dissipate self-condemnation, and begins to establish an inner environment of self-acceptance and compassion. This is the first and vital step in forgiving the other.

*"Forgiveness, it seems, cannot be forced. When we are brave enough to open our hearts to ourselves, however, forgiveness will emerge."*

—Pema Chödrön, *The Places That Scare You*

A woman may forgive herself with her mind, from some conceptual place, but deep, authentic forgiveness is sourced in the heart. While in the shock and trauma of the infidelity, it is easy for a woman to close her heart not only to others, but also to herself. When she closes her heart because it hurts too much to keep it open, she closes herself to the loving kindness and self-compassion that is there for her, regardless of what she has done, or not done. Authentic forgiveness rarely happens in one sitting, or in one process.

*"Whenever we get caught, whenever we get 'hooked' by (negative) emotions, it's helpful to remember the teaching that suffering is the result of an aggressive mind. Even slight irritation can cause us pain when we indulge in it. This is the time to ask, 'Why am I doing this to myself again?' Contemplating the causes of our suffering, right on the spot, empowers us. We begin to recognize that we have what it takes to cut through our habit of eating poison.*

*"When we find ourselves caught in reactions, strategies, storylines ('He's a bastard,' 'I'm not good enough') ... Then,*

*right on the spot, we can go beneath the words to the nonverbal experiences of the emotion. What's happening in our hearts, our shoulders, our gut? Abiding with the physical sensation is radically different from sticking to the story line. It requires appreciation for this very moment. It is a way of relaxing, a way to train in softening rather than hardening ..."*

—Pema Chödrön, *The Places That Scare You*

Then rather than indulging the pain, we return to our own heart. We recognize that we don't have to carry the burden, the suffering, anymore. We can forgive ourselves and begin again.

Eventually, we will find our capacity to forgive those who have done us harm. As Pema Chödrön writes, *"We will discover forgiveness as a natural expression of the open heart, an expression of our basic goodness."*

This process is hugely facilitated when there has been a sincere expression of remorse, and a request for forgiveness from the unfaithful partner.

## Sincere Remorse

Each moment is an opportunity to make a fresh start. However, until a woman sees that her pain has been truly recognized, it will be very difficult—if not impossible—for her to move on. Sometimes people try to handle relationship injuries by ignoring them, but unresolved traumas do not heal. For the man who betrayed her to take ownership of the injury he inflicted, and express regret and remorse, he will need to listen to and engage with his partner's pain, showing it has an impact on him.

### DEE: *"Most men would try to get away from the pain"*

*When he told me he had been with this other woman, I felt like I was caught in an earthquake and the ground under my feet was falling away. I literally got dizzy. When I regained some presence, I asked him if it was just sex. He said no, that he felt an emotional connection with her too. I went ballistic. I never get angry enough to get destructive, I like my things too much, but in this case I needed to smash something. I actually smashed things I really liked. I was hurting so bad that I needed to express my pain physically.*

*I began hitting him. He didn't defend himself, he just asked me to stop and I did. But I wanted him to hurt. He was baffled by this reaction because he thought it would be better for me if it was an emotional attraction, but for me that was far worse than if it were just physical. It wasn't just the sexual act, it was the betrayal—the fact that he cared for her so much he was willing to betray me. It felt like both my very survival and my connection with him, were severely threatened. It was a survival assault.*

*When I could express myself with words, I was very open about how I was hurting. I wanted him to know how much this hurt me; to even experience, himself, the hurt I felt. But when I think about it, a lot of our communication at the time was nonverbal. There were many moments of caring and reassuring conversation, of his extending kindnesses, and comforting but not sexual touch.*

*He assured me he wanted to spend his life with me, not with her. I told him it would take time to trust him again, I didn't know how long it would take, and I couldn't promise that I would trust him again. He said he understood and that he was in it for the long haul, however long it took. His reassurance that he loved me and his willingness and ability to connect with me empathically, helped me get through it faster.*

*He didn't once try to defend himself. When he first saw my pain, the full force of what he had done really crashed down on him. I literally saw the pain and remorse on his face. I wanted him to feel it. I didn't try to soften it, but at the same time I wasn't trying to make him hurt. I just wanted him to really feel my pain. That was enough.*

*It helped so much that he was able to take it on, to share my pain with me. He didn't know what to do, but one of his personal gifts was that he did his best to live in the moment without pushing the experience of the moment away. He was able to embrace the fullness of life, whatever it was. And so he sat in the experience of my pain with me. We sat in the fire of it together.*

*Most men would try to get away from the pain, to deflect both the pain and their responsibility in causing it. I think that's what hurts women the most. The underlying message is that her pain, her experience, isn't valid. The underlying message is that she doesn't get to feel what she feels. That's what makes people crazy enough to do desperate things.*

*T this deep, shared experience actually deepened our relationship and fairly soon afterward we got married. Looking back, I have nothing but gratitude and respect for him, and how he really did his best to do me right in all aspects of our relationship.*

To feel remorse when one has betrayed another doesn't mean crawling on one's knees, begging forgiveness. It is not about shame. It's about feeling the feeling that enables the person who has been hurt to feel "seen" and "felt."

> *"Remorse goes beyond accepting responsibility for hurting someone. It is to feel deep sadness, mourning, even pain for the pain you've brought to another person."*
>
> —Shirley P. Glass. Ph.D., *Not "Just Friends"*

Healing is so much easier when there is a sincere request for forgiveness from the unfaithful partner, and an inquiry into what can be done to set things right. Along with words of remorse for their transgressions, an offering to make amends, to inquire sincerely of the other, *"Is there anything I can do to right this?"* enhances the betrayed partner's ability to trust the sincerity of the request for forgiveness. It also allows her to participate rather than only be the receiver of *"I'm sorry."* She now has the opening to say, *"Yes, this is what I want you to do to set this right,"* or she may simply respond with, *"Thank you for your sincere apology."*

## Sincere Apology

Sincere apology will always necessitate the unfaithful partner staying emotionally present and acknowledging the wounded partner's pain, as well as their own part in it. There is no room here for defensiveness or justifications. While forgiveness is often spoken of as a moral decision, and letting go of resentment as being the right and good thing to do, the decision to forgive will not alone restore faith in the person who has been betrayed, or in the relationship. What is needed is a healing conversation that fosters not just forgiveness, but also the willingness to trust again.

Dr. Sue Johnson, *Hold Me Tight*, identifies common "token apologies:"

1. The four-second *"where is the exit"* apology: *"Yes, well. Sorry 'bout that. What shall we have for dinner?"*

2. The minimizing responsibility apology: *"Well, maybe I did that, but ..."*

3. The forced apology: *"I guess I am supposed to say ..."*

4. The instrumental apology: *"Nothing is going to work till I say this, so ..."*

These token apologies can sometimes work for very small hurts, but otherwise they only increase the wounded partner's pain.

Johnson names the elements of a sincere and genuine apology as:

1) the injuring partner making it clear to his partner that he feels and cares about her pain;

2) his explicitly telling her that her hurt and her anger are legitimate;

3) his owning up to exactly what he did that was so hurtful;

4) his expressing shame. He tells his partner that he, too, feels dismayed and disappointed by his behavior; and

5) his reassuring her that he will now be there to help her heal.

Sincere apology, says Johnson, *"is not just a statement of contrition, it is an invitation to reconnect."*

## No Guilt, No Remorse?

What can it mean when a person feels little or no guilt over his behaviour, no remorse for breaking the covenant of trust? What can it mean when someone hurts another person, acknowledges what he has done, recognizes the pain it has caused, says he accepts responsibility for his actions—but expresses no feelings of remorse for what he did? Expressing and evidencing remorse are ways of saying, *"It hurts me to know I've put you through such pain. I now share your distress, most especially as it was me who caused you to hurt."*

Janis Abrahms Spring, Ph.D., in *After the Affair: Healing the Pain and Rebuilding Trust When a Partner Has Been Unfaithful*, identifies five common reasons why a person may feel no guilt or need to apologize:

1) He has written off the relationship and is using the affair to expedite his exit.

2) He has a characterological disorder. This makes him incapable of experiencing compassion or remorse.

3) He is angry at his partner, and euphoric about his lover. Transported by an intense sexual or emotional connection to his lover, removed from the mundane obligations of an enduring relationship, he may not care about or even question how the

affair affects others. *"I feel so supremely happy ..."* may signal to him that he is experiencing true love at last, and leaves no room for guilt.

4) He holds certain core assumptions that justify adulterous behaviour. Some reflect long-held ideas about love and commitment. Others may be rationalizations, conjured up to protect his self-esteem, suppress his guilt, and grant him permission to stray: *"My affair is permissible as long as I love the other person." "My affair is permissible as long as I don't love the other person." "A one-night stand, a fling, doesn't change our relationship." "My affair has made me a happier and therefore a better partner." "People aren't meant to be monogamous." "I shouldn't have to sacrifice my needs to make my partner feel secure or happy."*

5) The blind spot of romantic love. Romantic love is an intense attachment toward his lover that is likely to make him want to leave his partner, no matter how their life together has been. *"My love for her must be real or I wouldn't feel such high chemistry."* The blind spot is that this passion may have more to do with his unmet childhood needs than with who this other person really is. How do you distinguish between a torrid but temporary attachment and an enduring covenant of love? Why turn away from romance when it feels so wonderful, or stay with your partner when your gut instinct is to run? When emotionally entangled with their lover, a person is not interested in asking these questions.

It may also be that it is simply too threatening for the unfaithful person to face the reality of the pain he has caused others. Sincere apology requires empathy. While some people are incapable of empathy, others simply lack the willingness, courage, or moral fiber to experience it. To empathize and apologize would not only mean acknowledging and feeling the other's pain, but also bring crashing to the ground the whole story they have built to justify their actions, and the "new life" they have built based on those actions.

Perhaps what is essential is not so much that one experience regret or remorse, but that one is able to recognize the harm their actions have wrought, i.e. what they have set in motion, and the consequences of these actions on others. What is essential is to bring oneself into the experience of compassion and empathy for the one who has been hurt.

Compassion and empathy are generated and experienced in the heart and when in heart, there is no shame, no guilt, only a deep feeling of connection with another. It is from here that a person can recognize that their actions, even if unintentionally, have harmed another. Then inevitably, there will be a sincere request for forgiveness. *"Please forgive me. What can I do to make this right?"*

## Healing Alone

*"I sat in my chair and cried after reading these pages. So much of the closure I wanted and needed from my former husband could have been achieved with what is written here. To this day, I have yet to receive a single apology or recognition in any way of how his behavior affected me, or our marriage. In fact, I doubt he has any remorse—I think he truly felt like he deserved to do what he did, and I deserved what pain, negativity, and hurt was associated with his actions."*

—Early reviewer

In the absence of a request for forgiveness, a woman is left to heal alone. To do so requires her cultivating that courage that allows her to keep her heart open in hell. This is the *"hell of her own frustration ... discouragement, anger, resentment"* that Chogyam Trungpa writes of. In time she will recognize that, more helpful than condemnation of the unfaithful is for her to turn her attention to self-inquiry, and to attend to her part in what led to the infidelity.

She may ask, *What is it that I may have done to set this up, what situations have I perpetuated that could have led to this? Where have I not stood up for myself, where have I remained silent, and where have I just not known any better? Where have I felt something was wrong in the communications between us, with certain of his behaviors, that I let pass? Where was my fear, naïveté, my denial, my gullibility?*

Even when, in her pain, a woman believes the man who has betrayed her deserves condemnation, it's not for the man but for herself that she needs to forgive. At some point, she may discover this need to forgive, for her own sake. She recognizes the personal cost of anger, and the need to decide whether she wants to live with hate or love.

An essential part of the process, especially for the woman left to heal alone, will be identifying all that she wanted from her partner that she did not receive; and naming how she felt when she didn't receive this. This means everything, from examples evidencing his absence of respect to the apology that was never given—and how this left her feeling. It is this that can be a key to a woman opening her heart—to herself. The anguish and the broken heart may still be there, but she can discover that wonderful place of equilibrium within that is balanced and whole.

While with time the intensity of the feelings and memories fade, they never disappear altogether ... grieving for all that has been lost, for her relationship, her family, likely her home and financial security, her way of life, dreams and expectations she had held for her future—with her partner. In the early years, being alone after years of being coupled may color every moment of a woman's daily life because she is dealing with so many losses.

The process of forgiving reduces stress, anger, depression, and the significant risk factors for heart disease, stroke, and other serious illnesses. Forgiveness expands our capacity for feelings of connection and trust, and our capacity to live, love, and laugh again.

## Toward Forgiving the Other

> *"There is nothing about genuine forgiveness that preludes holding people accountable if we have that power. Nor does forgiveness necessarily include restoration of the perpetrator to a place in our daily life. I'd be highly suspicious of a marital partner who rushed to forgive an infidelity without wanting to understand both partners accountability for the breach. Forgiveness is not about being blind or stupid."*
>
> —Molly Layton, psychologist, *The Long Road to Forgiveness*

A woman may be disappointed in herself because of the unexpected outbursts of anger and suspicion that emerge with force even after she believes she has forgiven her partner. These are normal and natural feelings, given what she has experienced. Indeed, virtually all women will always carry the scars and a deep sense of loss and grief from the betrayal. Whether a woman has stayed, left, or been left, it must be remembered that time is the salve on this journey towards forgiveness and healing, because it is also a process of grieving.

Authentic compassion and empathy for the unfaithful are what make forgiveness possible, and will come only with time—and intention.

> *"Some people, by innate temperament, are more easily able to forgive than others. You are not bad if you do not forgive easily.*

*You are not a saint if you do. Each to her own, and all in due time ...*

*"Once you've reached a bit more than halfway, the rest will come in time, usually in small increments. The important part of forgiveness is to begin and to continue. The finishing of it all is a life work."*

—Clarissa Pinkola Estés, *Women Who Run With the Wolves*

When a woman moves from rage and pain to the compassionate acceptance that engenders detachment, she finds she is no longer harboring judgment or resentment, and no longer at the effect of the one who has betrayed her. She has set herself free. Ultimately, of course, her freedom requires not only forgiving the man who betrayed her, but also his lover.

As we will see in the next chapter, the other woman's greatest struggle is often to forgive herself.

# CHAPTER 12

# *Bad Girls—Looking for Love In All the Wrong Places*

The chapter title, *Bad Girls,* came from two of the women who shared their stories of being the unfaithful partner. They both referred to themselves as bad girls: *"I was one of the bad girls,"* and, *"Am I the only bad girl?"* Of course there are *many* bad girls, and as we will see, they are far from *all* bad. To a degree, healing requires some understanding of the "other woman"—who she is, and why she did what she did. It is important to understand that the journey may, for these women, not be altogether unlike that of the women they betrayed.

While not for a moment attempting to represent all those women who engage in an affair, the stories shared here will offer some insights and perspectives—and hopefully engender some of the understanding that is essential to a woman's recognizing that which is endemic in the feminine collective.

That said, as we will see in the following chapters, understanding is one thing—forgiveness another entirely. Firstly, let's look at infidelity from the perspective of the "bad girls" themselves.

### KRISTI: *"I didn't feel safe without a man"*

*I was sexually abused as a child, and so I came from a place of deep mistrust of self and of men when it came to sexual relations. I was fine being a buddy, little sister, peer, friend; but never a spouse, girlfriend, or lover.*

*I was violently raped at eighteen. I met the man who was to become my husband the following year. I chose to marry before I understood what marriage or a lifelong commitment meant. Up until I was twenty-seven, I put up with what I thought was normal guy behavior—he does what he wants, when he wants. We fight. I cry about it, but then I deal with it and just go on. Then, I found he had been cheating on me with another woman. It's crushing when someone takes your trust in them—your honor—and throws that out the window and you don't have a choice in it. It leaves you in a very disempowered and dark place.*

*At twenty-six, I was depressed. I felt things were broken between us, and asked my husband to go to counseling with me. He flatly denied. A year later I said I was done, I wanted out. He then said he would go to marriage counseling. It was in the course of counseling that I met someone else, and I cheated on my husband.*

*I could justify it on all manner of grounds—most especially because it had been done to me so many times, it was about time I got to do it. This guy was brilliant; he knew everything to say and do to draw me in. And so I divorced my first husband and married my affair partner.*

*I can say—and I truly believe—that at the time I met him I wasn't looking for a man, but I also have to own that he wasn't the one who had taken a marriage vow. I was. And in marrying him, I didn't trade up. I just escaped. He was the epitome of how I felt about myself at the time—he was mean. I was with him for three years.*

*Through a series of bad relationships, I came to see that we are the company we keep. I saw that I chose people who were really crappy, so I must be someone who really sucked. That was the wake up call for me. It was then I found that my own happiness was to be found in me.*

*I decided I wouldn't date, wouldn't partner with a man again, until I felt good about myself and knew I could trust that I would never cheat again. It was a huge step for me to decide not to have a boyfriend. Because of the way I was raised, I felt men were the dominant ones. I finally came to see that on some level I had decided that if I couldn't beat them, I'd join them.*

*I came to realize that part of why I attracted the kind of men I was with, and part of my not trusting men, was because I had been sexually abused as a child; and yet at the same time, I didn't feel safe without a man. I know now that I need to learn how to feel safe by myself before I can feel safe with someone else.*

*Today I recognize that I betrayed myself by choosing infidelity. I feel sick about the fact that I, too, wound up betraying my partner. I didn't realize how damaging it was to me as a person—to my heart, to my spirit. I did not trust myself not to do this again.*

*Part of what I have learned and hope to teach my daughter is that none of that stuff comes from the outside. While I could say that men treated me horribly, in reality, it was because I allowed myself to be treated that way. What scared me more than any other piece of this was the fact that not only had I allowed myself to be treated this way, but that I myself betrayed my husband. Now, in my early forties, when I look back over the past twenty years, what I haven't been able to let go of is my own shame and guilt that I also betrayed. That still haunts me.*

Early abuse destroys the core of the basic trust that is the earliest developmental stage in the life of every human being. In the absence of this basic trust, a child learns that the world is unpredictable and unsafe. Both compounding and inseparable from this is the shame that thrives in an environment of abuse. This was the only environment Kristi knew as a child. Shame is horribly painful for children because it is inseparable from the fear of being unlovable. It is experienced as a threat to the very survival of a young child who is still dependent on her parents for food, shelter and safety. A child learns to do whatever she needs to in order to survive. Shame and fear of survival drive her to betray her instincts and intuitions.

Kristi felt like most any woman would feel—that she had no choice in the matter when her partner betrayed her. However, in every moment, a choice is made. In this situation, the choice rests in how she interprets and reacts or responds to the betrayal. The choice that will be most supportive of her wellbeing may sometimes seem to be awful, even frightening. It may mean leaving the relationship and stepping out into the world alone, or having to fight for the custody of her children. However, the consequences of not owning that choice will impact how she thinks and feels about herself.

Buying into the illusion that she is trapped will usually be far worse than choosing otherwise. Whenever a woman does not own her choices, she is—most often unconsciously—choosing to be a victim. At the time of the betrayal Kristi had, at very least, the choice to inquire into how she could empower herself in this relationship. At that point in her life, as is true for so many a woman, there was no awareness of that choice.

As Kristi came to understand, we teach people how to treat us. When a woman does not respect herself, when she is not aware of her right to be treated with care and respect, when she accepts the disrespectful or abusive behaviour of others, others will see this as a guiding light on how to treat her. Kristi's childhood gave her no clue as to her right to say *Enough. No more.* It was years before she understood that she was deserving of love and respect ... and years before she understood that setting boundaries is an expression of self-love and self-respect, and an essential element in any healthy relationship.

As life would have it, Kristi did choose to make that journey towards self-love and personal empowerment. She has come a very, very long way from those abusive years of her childhood and from her unhealthy relationships with men. The burden of shame that she still carries for how she participated—albeit unwittingly—in those betrayals prevents her from recognizing the distance she has travelled, diminishes the experience and presence of herself as an empowered woman.

How a woman is able to respond to the shame that wells up in her depends in part on her awareness of the dynamic—what triggers the shame in her, and how it disempowers her. With awareness there is the possibility of her witnessing the shame, rather than being totally consumed by it. Naming what thoughts and feelings are triggered in her and what the shame tells her about who she is or who she is not as a woman, and challenging the value system that holds these thoughts and feelings in place, will call her out of shame's all consuming grip. It will begin to open insight toward healing the wound that underlies the shame, and with that the receptivity to embody more of her authentic self.

> *"Meeting our pain with compassion and awareness instead of fear and judgment, what we call guilt does not harden into shame, but instead softens into remorse. And a sense of being able to do it better next time."*
>
> —Stephen Levine, *Turning Toward the Mystery*

A host of rationalizations and justifications will arise. The inner voices saying, *"It's too difficult,"* and *"It's too much to deal with,"* or *"I'll do it later,"* can lull a woman back into her habitual and disempowering ways of acting and reacting. Moving her body into the stance of the Warrior, taking a deep breath, feeling herself connected to the earth through the soles of her feet, she grounds herself in her body. Grounded, centered, a woman can call up gratitude for her being able to see this pattern of shame and self-betrayal so very clearly. *Nothing* can be changed until it is recognized, acknowledged and named.

Kristi's commitment not to date another man until she felt good about herself and could trust she would never cheat again is a strong proclamation of intent. However it can be easy for a woman to be seduced into feeling good about herself because of what a man says and does, rather than because she does, indeed, feel good about herself. Her resolve to never cheat again will also demand that she recognizes and names exactly what hooks her, what gets triggered in her that has drawn her so habitually back into unhealthy relationships with men.

Kristi said that she needed to learn how to feel safe by herself, before she could feel safe with someone else. More accurately, it is only when a woman is able to stand on the ground of her own self-love and self-worth that she can truly feel safe. She will need to persist in questioning all the values and beliefs she has bought into, that define her as anything less than good and worthy of love. In time, she will recognize that through these experiences—unwanted and uninvited though they may be—she cultivates the compassion and wisdom that has brought her to where she is today, and that will ultimately bring her home to herself.

Kristi's willingness to forgive herself for simply not knowing any better at the time, will begin to dissipate the burden of shame and guilt that she carries, even today. Her awareness of the importance of not passing unhealthy patterns on to her daughter is a huge element in what it takes to effect change in the feminine collective. The fact that any emotional trauma which remains unacknowledged is not healed but rather held in the body and passed on to the children—verbally or nonverbally—highlights the significance of Kristi's own determination to heal herself.

Children learn through our actions more than our words; through our example more than our advice. What Kristi teaches her daughter will be conveyed primarily through the woman she has become—the strength she has cultivated, along with her integrity and commitment to right action—more than through any verbal teaching.

Note: There is a tendency for many women when speaking of their own experiences, to use the word "you" in referring to themselves rather than the word "I." When a woman engages in this mode of communication with others, she energetically removes herself from being fully present within her own physical and emotional body, and thus separated from being present in her experience with those to whom she is speaking.

### SUSAN: *"Infidelity is what I grew up knowing"*

*My mom always dated married men—infidelity is what I grew up knowing. By the time I was sixteen, I was doing the same. I remember feeling a lot of conflict about my choices ... I didn't understand why I kept getting myself into unhealthy relationships. I felt frustrated with this, and yet I wouldn't date men who could show me something different. I can see now that I was attracting older married men because I was uncomfortable dating men my own age—men who could partner with me or marry me, and do something healthy.*

*I'm forty-four now. I want to share my understanding of why I did what I did. My behavior damaged at least three marriages. What I know now is that I repeated the pattern of dating married men and breaking up marriages I had learned from my mom. She had a deep hatred of men. She didn't trust them, and she didn't believe in herself. I watched her and I took on those same beliefs. I didn't trust men; I just looked to them to take care of me. Married men did that. They took care of me financially, but not in the way I needed most. The emotional support I needed was never available.*

*I learned that the unconscious, deep-seated pattern of infidelity is so strong that if we are not aware of what's playing out, we will just repeat the pattern. As much as I didn't want to do that, I did. Even now, twenty years later, as I'm telling you this, tears fill my eyes and I feel in my throat and in my chest the shame and guilt I still carry for being so unconscious ... the shame and guilt I still feel for making choices that were devastating to me and to other people. I gave away my power, my body; I just handed it over. Through acting out that way, I never got what I needed. It was a huge journey taking my power back, working through my beliefs about men, and recognizing my self-worth. The big thing was learning to feel safe. I never felt safe with a man.*

*When I was young, I was sexually abused by my half-sister's father. Even now, I am crying as I recall this. It was so very horrible. My mom was also sexually abused by her dad, my granddad. There was so much distrust. It almost seems a natural fit, when you are looking for approval and love and security from men, yet scared because you don't trust them, to be with someone who's married. You can be with them but not fully committed. It takes tremendous conscious intention to break the pattern. It's so deeply ingrained, so unconscious, that when you get stressed, you go right back to that place; you just play it out.*

*I think the first step in my breaking the pattern was when, at twenty, I met Don. He was married, of course. We were dating. He told me he wanted to get divorced. When I realized how much I cared about him, something inside me said that if I kept dating him, waiting and waiting until he got a divorce, he'd never want to be with me. Why would he want to be with me, if I didn't have any sense of self-worth?*

*I don't know what got me to this awareness. I had started a class in psychology—maybe something there clicked, some insight I needed to do something different. I made the decision that I would no longer partner with married men. I moved to Oregon. A little later, Don got divorced. We got together again, and married. I was now twenty-five.*

*I didn't date married men again, although there was period when I started looking to do this. It was when Don and I had been married ten years, that we started having problems. I wasn't feeling good about myself, and I almost went right back into that pattern of dating married men because I wanted to change the way I was feeling. You get that with a married man ... you get that false sense of worthiness, the sense that you're important. I'd done a lot of personal growth by this time, but I saw myself going back into that pattern. I could've ruined my awesome marriage. The only thing that stopped me was that I was conscious of it, and I had learned to be able to witness my behavior. I had learned to step outside of it and acknowledge that I was feeling bad about myself, and ask what was I going to do about it.*

*What got me to the point of being able to stop the pattern? Don was also struggling at the time ... then we both sought help. Don got treatment for misuse of prescription drugs. I was introduced to Al-Anon. That was it for me. Once I started on that road of recovery and looking at co-dependence, it changed my life. I knew I'd never ever date married men again. I was on a path of self-empowerment, and along with that, looking at all I had wronged. I became so aware of my own pain and disempowerment, and the pain my actions were causing to others. I knew I never wanted to feel this way again.*

*When I was in a relationship with a married man, I felt powerful. It was like wow, they're so interested in me, this is so fun, they really desire me. Then the minute it's over, I wasn't getting the attention or connection I wanted, and I would be left feeling like a loser. I felt so much shame. I felt dirty, yucky, slutty, weak.*

*I can see it so clearly now, but at the time it was so confusing—I was trying to get approval; a sense of self-worth. I was seeking connection, but to get to that place, I did things that left me full*

176

*of shame and countered my being able to experience any self-worth or connection. One of the married men I dated was the husband of a friend of mine. This is the one I feel the most shame about. I was so narcissistic, so desperate to get my needs met, that though we were friends I literally didn't see or think of her. I am so sad to admit to this. It is such a narcissistic thing to cut oneself off from any empathy.*

*Al Anon was my first wake up call to recognizing that we are one hundred percent responsible for our own behavior. With Al Anon, I made amends with my friend. I told her I didn't expect her to forgive me, but I was sorry. I told her that I hadn't even seen what this would be like for her. I admitted my unconsciousness. I told her I was so, so sorry for what I did. I owned my own part of it.*

*She asked me why I thought it had happened, because her husband had had affairs before. I told her that I knew now I had done wrong, and I knew that she blamed me. And I also told her that as long as she kept blaming others and saying she was a victim, as long as she kept accepting his behavior, she was allowing the pattern to continue. She kind of heard me, but she said, basically, that she felt stuck. And to this day, she and her partner are still together and he is still doing the same thing.*

*Don was married for the first three years of the time we were together, and his wife tried to overlook it. She allowed it to happen, even though she knew. I think it was because she didn't want to deal with the consequences of divorce. I didn't think about his wife, about what my being with her husband might mean to her. I don't recall a single time when I sat down and thought about her—it was all about me. To the extent I did think about her, I thought she was stupid—stupid because she was denying what was happening, and she wasn't taking care of the marriage.*

*The biggest insight I've had is how, when acting out in that way, you are so self-consumed with trying to get your needs met that you don't even consider how this might hurt anyone else. It's sad, really sad.*

*I viewed the wives of the men I dated as weak and undeserving of empathy from me. I was able to go on with this behavior because I saw them as weak—and that was one thing I was never going to be.*

*My dad had always cheated on my mom. My mom took it. I viewed her as really weak—I see now that I was projecting my anger at my mom onto these other women. I projected all of this anger onto them, and that gave me permission to do what I did.*

The seeds of self-betrayal are planted in childhood; but the story does not end there. Susan's sharing illustrates how those early experiences are carried and reinforced again and again in later life experiences that a woman draws to her through her own absence of awareness. Her story illustrates the insight and courage and perseverance needed to change these patterns.

Susan is not alone in *"looking for love in all the wrong places."* This was the direct modeling she had from both her mother and father, as they looked beyond the vows of their marriage to find the fulfillment and connection that every human craves. In the absence of healthy role models, Susan knew no better. Even when this isn't as blatantly modeled in childhood as it was for Susan, women are in both subtle and not so subtle ways led to believe that it is through the men in their life that they will find both security and fulfillment as women. Yes, even today.

As Susan came to recognize, to sustain her own autonomy and a healthy relationship with her partner requires a woman do her own individual work outside of the relationship. The relationship can magnify and reflect what needs to be brought to conscious awareness, so that it may be addressed. This is not to say that deep healing experiences do not occur between two people in a relationship, but when a woman enters a relationship, she brings her own family history, her own unresolved issues and unmet needs from her childhood and earlier relationships, and her own karma. It is her responsibility to wake up to all the ways in which she habitually acts and reacts, that harm rather than heal.

The resurgence of Susan's need to be with a married man in order to feel good about herself, even after having successfully stepped outside of this pattern for ten years, reflects how deeply embedded these patterns are. Her willingness and courage to recognize that what she was dealing with was no less than an addiction, and to participate in a Twelve-Step program, was an expression of her again reaching the point of *Enough, no more*, and standing again on the ground of the Warrior Woman. Her recognition that it takes tremendous conscious intention to break the pattern, and her determination to engage the mindfulness, discipline and persistence needed to change these patterns, was a crucial factor in her empowerment.

Susan's offering a sincere apology to the wife of her ex-lover is quite remarkable, and a significant step in healing the mistrust that is so prevalent among women. It is also remarkable that a woman who has been betrayed inquire of the one who partnered with her husband, why she thought the affair had happened. Susan's response offered genuine insights that could have truly shifted her friend's life, had she taken them on. That she did not, does not diminish the intentions of the two women to communicate openly and honestly with each other, in order to understand their part in the infidelity.

In making any such apology and offering insights to the woman she has wronged, a woman needs to be very clear that her sincere intention is to protect her friend from further hurt, and that she is not seeking—even unconsciously—to justify or defend her own role. Well intentioned though such a sharing may be, to inquire whether any semblance of *"if only you hadn't ... this affair would not have happened"* will diminish the heart and authenticity of the apology.

The Twelve-Step programs ask that a woman not only apologize to those she has wronged, but that she also make amends. To make amends means, as much as possible, restoring justice. It does not require a woman clear her conscience at the expense of offending or hurting someone else—most especially the person she has wronged.

Is it the responsibility of a woman who has betrayed another woman, as Susan had, to open her friend's eyes? Perhaps of more relevance, is she the best person to do this? As we saw in Chapter 9: *The Other Woman*, given the hatred and distrust that a woman feels towards the woman who has partnered with her husband, perhaps not. Is it helpful for her to attempt to do this? This will depend in part on their relationship. If she is indeed a friend, it will be important to consider whether she has the capacity to receive this communication. Perhaps it would be best delivered at another time, and not immediately following the apology. It may be that it would be especially difficult for her friend to receive this communication from someone she knows has betrayed her—even if she is just now apologizing. It may be that there is someone else better suited to open this woman's eyes than the woman who had been her husband's lover.

Beyond a simple, *"I am so sorry for what I have done,"* it may be best that she simply ask, *"How can I make amends for this?"* Perhaps the other woman, having received what she felt to be a genuine apology, may say the apology itself was enough. Regardless, the woman who has been unfaithful has then fulfilled her responsibility to, as much as possible, restore justice.

I do not mean to imply that there is anything black and white with respect to what may constitute taking responsibility and right action in making amends. Here, though, is an example of what this might mean. Always, discretion is warranted. Every situation is unique.

Sometimes people talk about "living" amends—this means that they choose to live differently; they make a genuine change in their behaviour, beyond what might be the Band-Aid of an apology. This, Susan has certainly done.

Making amends, if a woman has been having an affair, may or may not mean her telling her marital partner of this affair. It will, *without question*, mean ending the affair and bringing her heart and attention back to her spouse. It may or may not mean staying in that marital relationship. It *will* mean that in the event of her not doing so, she does everything within her power to come to full and respectful resolve with her partner before leaving the relationship.

Susan's never thinking of how the wives of the men she illicitly partnered with might feel, and her viewing these women as weak and stupid, perpetuates the distrust and competition that is endemic amongst women. The beliefs and attitudes we as women hold about ourselves, and about women in general, are passed—often silently—from grandmother to mother to daughter. Knowing this, we have the opportunity—and the responsibility—to recognize what has been so damaged, to recognize how these qualities live in us, and to do what we can to ensure this legacy will not be passed to our daughters, and to our daughters' daughters.

There are many points in Susan's story that illustrate the stance of the Warrior Woman. The distance she has travelled over the years is huge. This began with her questioning why a decent man would want to be with her, if she had no sense of her own self-worth. It is also apparent in her resolve to never again enter a relationship with a married man. Then there is that moment when she is so mindful as to observe herself falling back into an old pattern—she witnesses herself, questions what she is going to do about it, and recognizes the consequences of her choices.

Mindfulness is a crucial element in this process. It is the practice of observing what is, without getting caught up and swept away with judgments, aversions, or reactivity. It takes resolve and mindfulness to catch that space between stimulus and response in which a woman is able to witness herself rather than succumbing to her habitual reaction—and to choose wisely. Her sincere questioning of herself and her actions ultimately empowered her ability to discern integrous action—and to choose it.

To break this down a little further, we can outline here a process that can be very helpful in moving from first becoming conscious of a pattern, all the way through to its resolution.

### Step 1: Becoming conscious of the pattern

*"I wasn't feeling good about myself, and I almost went right back into that pattern of dating married men because I was wanting to feel good about myself ... I saw myself going back into that pattern. The only thing that stopped me was that I was conscious of it."*

### Step 2: Witnessing

*"I had learned to be able to witness my behavior, to step outside of it and acknowledge I was feeling bad about myself ..."*

### Step 3: The inquiry

*"... and to ask what was I going to do about it."*

### Step 4: Recognizing consequences

*"I could've ruined my awesome marriage. I became so aware of my own pain and disempowerment, and the pain my actions were causing to others, I knew I never wanted to feel this way again."*

### Step 5: Conscious choice of course of action

*"I had started a class in psychology. Maybe something there clicked, some insight I needed to do something different."*

### Step 6: Commitment and discipline to act on that choice

*"I made the decision that I would no longer partner with married men."*

### Step 7: Finding the support to carry you through

*"I didn't date married men again, although there was period when I started looking to do this. Don was also struggling ... then we both sought help."*

Susan is determined to change these habitual patterns not because she feels worthless or unacceptable as she is, but because she cares about herself and knows that by making these changes, she will be happier and healthier.

It may be helpful for a woman in any kind of disempowering situation to explore this process. Self-forgiveness and self-compassion will inevitably be two very potent components. In the absence of self-compassion, a woman will view any personal failings or imperfections through the eyes of the Inner Critic. Self-compassion allows for more accurate perceptions and self-concepts.

### AMY: *"Looking for an exciting summer tryst"*

*We met in New Mexico on a week-long hiking vacation. I did not have a partner at the time. He did. Had I had a partner, I believe I would have resisted this, unless my current relationship was nearly dead anyway. I was looking for an exciting summer tryst. Had I known what was to come of it, I would have been more cautious. After the time in New Mexico, we met once at a motel for a few hours. We were very deeply connected and though we didn't often see each other, the intimacy was sustained through our phone calls with each other.*

*I sleepwalked through my life for that first year. I had never experienced this before—it was almost completely overwhelming emotionally. I had no interest in anything other than being with this man. Everything else in my life was just ashes. I was running a business and had plenty of family responsibilities, so I put one foot in front of the other and did what needed to be done.*

*The sexual fire never really did die down, but without a willingness to leave his marriage, there was nowhere for our connection to go. We couldn't come apart and we couldn't come together—he wasn't able to leave her. After that year, I started to date online and began to move on, even though it took several more years to completely disengage from him.*

*If I had known that my actions would traumatize another woman, would I have cared? Would I have done something different? Maybe—but truthfully, I doubt it. The attraction was just overwhelming. I did care in as much as I certainly had no interest in traumatizing anyone; I would never have done it if it was someone I knew. But I didn't know her, so I had no claim to her affections. He had told me that she was furious. There was a lot of upset between them because of this. I just helped him deal with his end. It looked like they might separate, and I made a serious attempt not to be involved or take sides. It was his decision as to whether he left her.*

*I never got any sense that she was honestly trying to make the marriage work. If I had, it would have been difficult for me to be with him. I feel sure I wouldn't have liked her. Bill never badmouthed her, but I knew he was deeply unhappy with the marriage. The efforts he had made to improve the relationship had borne no results. Maybe I was thinking this as a way of making it okay for me to be with him, but I didn't think this woman cared about him—I felt this from the very beginning.*

*I can't think of anything I could have done differently at the time. After that initial connection was made, the die was cast. As I said to my own sister when discussing this experience: Sisterhood is powerful but not powerful enough to keep me away from this man. Of course, now I know that these kinds of connections generally end badly with the emotional angst pretty much more than the whole situation is worth. I think when you've done it once, you're going to be wised up to that. Presented with a similar opportunity, I wouldn't do it at all.*

Without question, romantic love is a natural high. The intense, all consuming passion is sourced in the biology of the body, which is literally flooded with amphetamine-like chemicals such as dopamine, norepinephrine, and phenylethylamine. It feels nothing short of compelling, magnetic … euphoric, even.

Without fear of conceiving a child, a woman is free—and tempted—to pursue this natural high like never before. However, when a person is in a committed partnership, this amounts to infidelity. Most women have no idea of the devastation the wife of her affair partner will experience, and the ways in which this will reverberate through their family and their community.

Amy seems unaware of the fact that when there are problems in a marriage—and what marriage doesn't have them—an affair can only exacerbate them. She does not know that affairs can happen in happy marriages. She does not know that if a man was happy in his marriage before an affair, he will not be when he has engaged in one. She believes that, even knowing her actions would traumatize another woman, at the time she would not have done any differently.

Amy was unaware that a lover will tell her partner whatever she needs to hear to give her permission to do what they both want. Under the intoxication of sexual passion, a person is driven to get what they want and to say and do what is needed in order to get that desire met … *now*.

*"There is a sense of intoxication that comes along with a love affair that keeps those involved from thinking rationally. Affairs are as addictive as alcohol or drugs; the 'in love' feeling gives a sort of chemical high. So, they return as often as possible for that short-term hormonal feeling of infatuation ..."*

— Dr. Jay Kent-Ferraro, Ph.D., *Affair Love vs. Authentic Love*

The fact that her lover is engaging in this infidelity does not speak well of his efforts to improve his relationship with his wife. Just as he is going to tell Amy exactly what he wants her to hear about his marriage, Amy is going to think what she needs to think in order to justify this betrayal. She is likely right in considering that her conviction she would not like her lover's wife—and that his wife didn't care about him—were convenient ways for her to justify being with him.

More often than not a woman will dismiss her lover's partner as demanding, submissive, stupid, or frigid. Feeling no sense of sisterhood with the other woman, she may view her as a rival or undeserving of the marriage. She may believe that monogamy is outdated, in which case she absolves herself of any accountability to those who will be hurt as a result of her choices. She will put the existence of her lover's wife and family out of her mind. She may perceive herself as a good person who offers advice to her lover on how to improve his communications with his wife. In other words, she may use all manner of rationalizations to avoid feeling guilty and justify her actions.

It's likely Amy's belief that she attempted not to be involved in whatever was happening between her lover and his wife similarly reflected her need to justify her actions. The fact is that she was involved in the marriage— and in the state of the marriage, due to her sexually partnering with this man. Helping him deal with his end more responsibly would have demanded she get herself out of the threesome that she had formed, and refuse to see him until he and his wife had received counseling to clarify what they wanted. As to her statement, *"the die was cast,"* every moment we have the opportunity to choose differently. Amy does not even think to question her role in perpetuating the condemnation, mistrust and betrayal that exists between women.

She is right to respect, in hindsight, the disruptive power of passion.

Shirley P. Glass, Ph.D., reports that most surveys of attitudes simply ask people whether they approve of extramarital sex. 85 to 90% of people say no. But asking more specific questions—such as, *Do you think it's okay to have an affair for sexual excitement, or to get understanding or affection?*—greatly discriminates the conditions under which affairs are justified. While some people do not think an affair is justified for *any* reason, others think it's okay if you're not "getting enough" with your spouse, or if you fall in love with someone else—most especially if they are your "soul mate." For women, the highest justification is for love; emotional intimacy comes next. Sex is last on their list of justifications. It's the opposite for men: sex scores the highest.

There are some women today who seem to be treating sex in the same casual way and exploiting power in the same way as male philanderers. Nevertheless, in our culture there is a sense of male privilege that not only condones but even encourages affairs.

### HANNAH: *"I hadn't been in love with my husband for years"*

*After sixteen years in a marriage that I entered only because I was young and pregnant and that's what young and pregnant girls in Wisconsin did back then, I fell in love with another man. I was thirty-two years old. I lied, I cheated, I behaved terribly. This being in love state literally doesn't have a brain. I did stupid stuff. He was married. I knew he was married. I was married too. There's no integrity in such a liaison if either is in a committed relationship; it's an illicit affair. But I only knew what I knew at the time, and that was it.*

*It started innocently. We went for a coffee. Three hours later he walked me to my car, there was a kiss, and that was it. I was ripe, given the deadness of my marriage. I had never experienced anything like it before. The sexual energy was incredible. This was for me a real sexual awakening, as well as love. I could talk with him on a deep intimate level. I knew I had to get out of the marriage I was in, where there was none of that. I had no hope of ever ending up with my affair partner, but I did it and it caused a leap for me—I got a divorce from an abusive marriage to an alcoholic. I hadn't been in love with my husband for years and years, and had never had an orgasm.*

*What in my mind gave me permission to enter this relationship? A deep, primal longing for real intimacy, and I felt I could find that with this man. A primal longing that was mainly sexual, but even more important to me was that I could communicate with him on a deep and intimate level. Even at the initial encounter, I felt that.*

*After the divorce I was trying to handle both kids, working, and flying around the country to spend weekends with him. I was physically and emotionally exhausted, getting little rest, but I couldn't stop myself. Once I found myself literally waking up, drugged, in a mental hospital. I didn't have a brain in what I did. I was swept up. I lied. It was incredibly sexual as well as real love ... it was really powerful, something I will never forget. But that said, I betrayed.*

*Today, I believe that when we betray, there has to be an underlying guilt connected with our actions—a healthy or appropriate guilt because there is a loss of integrity. We turn into naughty little kids who stole a toy from the local dime store. It's a simultaneous exciting/horrid feeling. I know, from the time I betrayed my partner. Jeepers, what does one do with that feeling? Remember the emotional sick gut feeling and never do it again, I hope.*

*So all this mess creates the deeply embedded shame that follows betrayal. But I bet it hides for a while because of the euphoria, the cloud nine, the feeling of floating, suspension, like a magic act when the magician makes someone levitate.*

While this kind of sexual and romantic passion feels wonderful, magical, out of this world ... as Hannah recognized: *"There's no integrity in such a liaison if either is in a committed relationship. It's an illicit affair."*

*"Love, here, is a personally constructed narrative—a story—which we vehemently adhere to because we need it to be true. After all, so much depends upon it being real. The possibility of 'true love', the confirmation that 'soul mates' exist, the justification for destroying families, leaving spouses, children, jobs and friends—all must be justified with legitimacy and purpose. Otherwise, those of us in affairs are nothing but hedonistic idiots ...*

*"You confuse an emotional experience, i.e. the affair, with the person who you are having the affair with and believe you 'need' that person to keep and preserve that experience. Willing to risk almost anything to legitimize the affair, you call it 'love.'... The stage is set for grandiosity and narcissistic self-indulgence. On this platform, all manner of illogical and nonsensical choices are made. We are in pursuit of a valid human need—deep intimacy and belonging. Yet, we are moving toward our fated demise. Authentic love, based on friendship, history and seasoned emotionality, can never result from affair love, which is grounded in escape, deception and illicit illusions. Anything*

*based upon deception is destined to fail. Period. Without integrity, life simply doesn't work."*

—Dr. Jay Kent-Ferraro, Ph.D., *Affair Love vs. Authentic Love*

Hannah's hope that she would never do it again is, in itself, but a hope. Her recognition of the illicit nature of her affair and the repercussions of what she did are a healthy and essential element in her never doing it again. She is right, recalling the *"emotional sick gut feeling"* can be helpful in resisting any temptation. Hannah talks about a *"healthy or appropriate guilt."* If guilt is to be healthy or appropriate—if it is to serve as an element in her never doing this again—she will need to remain mindful of the seductive power of that energy and make an authentic declaration of *Enough. No more.*

You may recall my saying that I have both betrayed and been betrayed. Here, I share my life as a "Bad Girl."

I was twenty-four years old. Unlike the other women here, I hadn't been abused or neglected as a child—in fact, to the contrary. I had returned to university for a post-graduate degree in social work, and had my own home (and mortgage) near the university. I had a brand new car, healthy friendships, money to enjoy good restaurants and theater. I went to the gym. I meditated. I was happy, independent. I wasn't looking for a boyfriend—or feeling the need for one.

I had two spare bedrooms in my home: one was occupied by my girlfriend, the other was rented at this time to a university student. One night when I was heading out for the evening, I went into his bedroom to ask if he needed anything—he was in bed with a migraine. He pulled me down to him and kissed me.

That night when I returned, he moved into my bed. It didn't ever—ever—occur to me that I was doing anything wrong. He was a gorgeous looking guy. Supple, healthy body; beautiful, shoulder length blond curly hair; and a great grin. It wasn't a wildly passionate relationship, but we were having a great time. It's hard for me, now, to understand how it could be that I didn't give his wife a second's thought. He went home on the weekends to be with her—and his early adolescent daughter. I had the weekends to pursue other interests.

Perhaps six months later, he came back one weekend and said he couldn't do it anymore. *"Couldn't do what?"* I asked. He said that he couldn't sleep with me during the week and go home to her weekends. I was perplexed—I couldn't understand why he was saying this. I asked him if we could sleep together this one last night. He said no, and went to his room.

I wasn't devastated, in that I'd never seen us getting married—we were just having a good time. I was disappointed and perplexed as to why we couldn't continue as we had been.

What fascinates me—in fact, absolutely astounds me—is that it was not until well into the second and final year of writing this book that I saw it—I had betrayed. Or, to be more precise, I had colluded in his betraying his own wife, which to me at least, is one and the same thing.

Today, I deeply regret what I did. I am thankful that my lover had the integrity and decency to end our relationship. I simply didn't know any better, at the time. I certainly do now.

# CHAPTER 13

## *The Drug that Masquerades as Love*

Hannah spoke of the *"deep, primal longing for real intimacy"* that in her mind gave her permission to engage sexually with another man, even though she herself was married. The sexual impulse is the animal drive in humankind, the deep primal longing that serves to perpetuate the species. When a woman is in a monogamous relationship, satisfying that deep, primal longing with someone outside of that relationship equals infidelity—and people *will* be hurt.

### AMY:

*What did I learn? Well, there's sex and then there's passion. On a scale of one to ten, this was about a twelve. I would say that this experience gave me a tremendous amount of respect for the disruptive power of passion. Sex doesn't generally trash your life in my experience, but passion sure can do it. Watch out!*

This passion, and the impulse that propels it, is innate in the physiology of the human body. The disruptive power of that impulse, indiscriminately pursued, warrants it be treated with the respect and discretion demanded when considering the use of any mind-altering drug.

Before going further into the ramifications of the indiscriminate use of sexual energy as it relates to infidelity per se, let's look briefly at some fascinating findings from biological anthropologist Helen Fisher, author of *Why We Love: The Nature and Chemistry of Romantic Love.*

### Lust, Attraction and Attachment

Fisher believes that love is not an emotion, it's *"a motivation system ... a drive ... part of the reward system of the brain."* Sexual desires,

189

romantic longings, and feelings of long-term emotional union are running on different brain circuits. Fisher identifies lust, attraction, and attachment as three distinct, but interrelated emotional systems in the brain that mediate mating, reproduction, and the rearing of young.

**The sex drive** (lust or libido) is characterized by the craving for sexual gratification. While it doubtless evolved to initiate the mating process, Fisher believes it contributes to many cases of date rape and other forms of inappropriate human sexual conduct—not least among them, infidelity. Lust is driven by the hormones—the estrogens and the androgens.

**The attraction system** (passionate love, romantic love, or infatuation) is characterized by increased energy, focused attention on the beloved, obsessive thinking and intense craving for the beloved, euphoria when things are going well and terrible mood swings when they're not. As an emotion system, it evolved to support essential functions in the mating process—such as selection between potential partners, and maintaining the focus of mating energy until insemination occurs. It is driven by high levels of dopamine and norepinephrine and low levels of serotonin.

**The attachment system** is characterized by feelings of calm, security, peace, and the social comfort experienced in the company of a long-term partner. Attachment behaviors include maintaining proximity and displaying separation anxiety when apart. This emotion system evolved in part to motivate individuals to sustain their bonding long enough to complete their parental duties. It is associated in the brain primarily with the neuropeptides, oxytocin and vasopressin.

Fisher points to the countless human habits, traditions, and artifacts that stem from the evolution of these three emotion systems: lust, attraction, and attachment. These include the nuclear family, customs for courtship and for marriage, terms for kin, and *"the plots of many great operas, novels, plays, films, songs, and poems."*

Fisher proposes that while these emotional systems served our ancestors well in matters of mating, reproduction, and rearing of the young, these distinct brain circuits contribute hugely to today's worldwide patterns of sexual jealousy, rape, stalking, spouse battery, adultery, divorce, homicide, suicide, and the clinical depression associated with romantic rejection. However, far from despairing about these escalating patterns of

190

behavior, Fisher states, *"Evolution has brought us to a point with a neural system that enables us to rise above our inappropriate or inconvenient mating tendencies."*

Central to this system is the prefrontal cortex. Fisher believes biology and culture—nature and nurture—are but two of the major forces shaping human behavior. The third is our psyche—our capacity for reason, choice, and self-directed action.

She suggests that biology plays a less consequential role in, for example, inappropriate sexual yearnings, the "roving eye," and the restlessness in long relationships that threatens to destroy family lives.

The prefrontal cortex, the area of the brain that lies directly behind the forehead, expanded dramatically during human prehistory. Referred to as the "central executive" of the mind, it has connections to many sections of the brain and body, and is responsible for the active processing of information. We use the prefrontal cortex to organize the myriad bits of data that register in our brains, reason hypothetically, consider options, plan for the future, and make decisions.

While biology predisposes us to love in general ways, cultural experiences modify those predispositions, overcoming some and heightening others. Yet each of us assimilates the forces of biology and culture in our own way. We are capable of monitoring and, at times, overcoming the power of lust, attraction, attachment, and detachment. As Fisher concludes, *"Most of us are, in large, responsible for how we love."*

The implications of these discoveries, as yet in their infancy, are far-reaching. For example, as scientists discover more about the pivotal role of the psyche in directing human action, those in the medical and legal communities will learn that most people have the physiological capacity to overcome their restlessness in long-term relationships, to say no to adultery and divorce, and to refrain from stalking a rejecting partner.

## Choosing How to Love

The strength of that surge of sexual energy can feel overpowering. To resist it requires the integrity and maturity to recognize the initial sexual stirrings in the body, and to choose to simply—but by no means easily—not buy into that energy. It's human nature to have such physiological reactions ignited. Between the stimulus and the impulse that drives it to find fulfillment there is a moment of time, a space in which a woman has the power to choose how to respond to that stimulus. Whenever sexual feelings arise, there is always a choice as to whether or not to act on them. It is natural, human, and healthy to have these feelings. There is nothing wrong with these feelings, per se. However, not every sexual feeling needs to be, or should be, followed or expressed—no matter how consuming it may be.

What might it demand of a woman to not succumb to this impulse? Firstly, she needs to know that she does indeed have the capacity to say no. This may require that she remove herself from the situation. It *will* require not spending time with a man when her heart is racing and she feels the heat rising in her body. She can move away. Breathe. Bring to mind the fact that people are going to be hurt—deeply hurt—if this surge of passion is acted on. What about when *"I can't stop"*? Then, a woman might ask, if her partner were to walk in the door—would she be able to say no?

It takes not only integrity but also a Warrior's will and a certain fierceness to say, *Enough. No more.* In this situation choices and actions are often driven by the impulse for immediate gratification rather than from the cultivated values and integrity of a fully awake and aware woman.


## Is It Infidelity?

Questions a woman may ask when unsure if she is stepping over the line into infidelity include:

- *Am I in control of what I am doing?*

- *Am I honoring my vows to my partner?*

- *Would I do this if my partner were here?*

- *Am I stepping outside of my relationship to meet a need that should be met inside the relationship?*

Integrity requires a woman ask if this man is married or in a committed monogamous relationship. *Has his partner given her consent? How would she feel if she knew we were having sex? Are there children involved?* The fact that a man will tell her what he wants her to believe further necessitates her summoning the courage to contact the man's partner herself, and ask her if she consents.

Integrity demands a woman:

- keep her vows, her commitments, and her agreements

- when needed, renegotiate her commitments and agreements

- when she has broken an agreement or commitment, acknowledge it, acknowledge the impact it has had, apologize, ask how she may make amends, and create a new agreement and commitment.

Integrity demands she inquire of herself, *Does partnering with a man in a sexual relationship counter my professed values? What would—or does—it say about me to choose to do this? Who might be hurt? What would my actions be teaching the children?*

Sadly, many women just won't care.

## Who Cares?

Shirley P. Glass, Ph.D., *Not "Just Friends,"* reports a magazine survey of 4,700 single women involved with married men revealed that 84% knew that their lovers were married. Although very few of them had reservations about sharing a man with his wife, 61% said they would break off the relationship if he had another lover besides them. 30% said they felt no guilt, 32% had very little guilt.

### SHIRLEY:

*I had two lovers, both married. I cared about the wife of my lover who was my friend, but not about the other one. How mean. I had met her sixteen years before, and yet I felt rather cold toward her. He messed around … she must have known. I disengaged from any responsibility. Not very pretty.*

For some single women, a relationship with a married man is what they prefer. A woman is not accountable to him if she wants to see a past lover or on occasion date another good-looking guy. Plus, the sex itself is likely more thrilling, and more passionate, because it is clandestine.

Glass notes that although many women have no guilt about being involved with a married man, few survive with no regret. As we've seen, connecting with a married man may be a one-time deviation, or it may be a lifelong pattern that a woman carries from her own childhood experiences or family constellation.

Does either situation justify her choices and actions?

Perhaps more pertinent to the woman betrayed is whether the stories in this preceding chapter from the "bad girls" open a door, even a *little*, for her own sake, into forgiveness of the other. A little, at this point, is very good. Not at all, at this point, is understandable.

*"To everything, there is a season."*

—Ecclesiastes 3:1

In Chapter 8: *Choosing to Stay*, you read of Sarah's struggles with that sexual impulse as she sought to discover "true love." In Chapter 19: *Coming Apart, with Care and Compassion*, you will read of others who, rather than impulsively giving into the lust of that sexual impulse, chose otherwise.

# CHAPTER 14

# Once Friends—Colluding in Our Silence

Many women spoke of how painful it was to find that friends and people they had thought cared for them withdrew contact after their partner's affair. Some women found this to be as bewildering and hurtful as their partner's betrayal itself. With time, each of these women came to recognize the need to let those who so chose, to simply fade away. Some asked friends who wanted to remain "neutral" to choose *"either him or me."*

Here we focus on the experiences of women whose relationships ended with the infidelity, though—as we saw in Chapter 8: *Choosing to Stay*—even couples who chose to stay and work on their relationship faced similar issues. As Melissa said, the loss of friends was a *"double whammy."* The sadness, the pain of this, remains with these women even to this day.

### LINDA:

*In therapy, over a decade later, I was reminded that infidelity isn't a single-layered trauma, but multi-layered and ongoing for years. One layer was the number of people who confessed to me in the beginning that they had had affairs and couldn't be my friend anymore because it was too painful to watch me suffer.*

## *"Choose Him ... Or Me"*

### GAIL: *"I felt powerless to stop my mind agonizing over the possibilities"*

*I was deeply saddened and surprised to find that women who I thought were my friends, aligned more strongly with him than with me. I found it really hard knowing that my friends were seeing both of us. What had he said to them, how had they responded, what did that mean? I had only my imagination to inform me as to what he had said and regardless, I knew that they viewed me differently because of whatever it was that he told them. Of course, he would distort the truth to look good and be right.*

*I was careful in my communications with them not to get into stories about him. I didn't want to get into, "What did he say to you?" "Oh, but that's not true…" or, "And did you know that he …?" kinds of conversations, but at times I felt powerless to stop my mind agonizing over the possibilities. On one level I felt that they had a right to see him and to be friends with both of us, but I also felt betrayed by their decision to remain friends with him. I felt they were condoning what he had done by letting their relationship with him continue. I found myself withdrawing from them because of this, but that only left me feeling lonely.*

*I didn't want to inflict my values on others. I wanted to be fair. Caught in shame, and not recognizing the need or having the strength to set boundaries that would support my healing, I did not take a stand for what I needed. It was not until eighteen months after the affair when a highly distressing incident, emerging out of a well-intended but disastrous break in confidentiality between myself and a friend, illuminated the untenability of such a triangle. She had broken her confidentiality with me, to tell him I was suicidal. This led to all manner of outcries.*

*I decided to email several of the women I really wanted to remain friends with, but whom I knew were seeing both my ex and myself. I requested that they choose to associate with either him or me. Their desire to be friends with both had been a source of torment for me for such a long time. I wish I had done this so much earlier.*

Many women commented on having variations of Gail's experience. While most understood why their friends wanted to remain friends with both, they felt betrayed by them. Virtually all found that to remain in a friendship with anyone who aligned with their spouse, or attempted to remain friends with both, was untenable. Some chose not to speak of this directly to their friends, but instead to cease reaching out to them and let them simply fade away. Others made it known that there was a choice to be made.

One woman was hurt when hearing that her friend had chosen to align with her ex because she could not afford not to, professionally. Another decided that her friends could reach out to her if they wanted to hear her side and be there for her. If they didn't, or if they were also keeping contact with him, she ignored them, being civil if she saw them in public, and moving on. These women felt that it was clear where these "friends'" allegiances lay, and it was not in favor of their healing.

Some women found friends were "unfriending" them on Facebook and other social media sites. As one commented, *"It's hard to be treated as the bad one when your partner has betrayed you."* It was especially hurtful when "no contact" also involved children they had felt a special connection with. They were left to wonder what these children were being told.

Other women themselves removed those who were choosing to be friends with both, from their contact lists. Many worked hard to cultivate new friendships. They found not having to wonder what was being said about them by their ex-partner, was very important for their healing.

### REBECCA:

*It would make a difference to me in being asked to choose, whether the unfaithful person had sincerely apologized. If he had, then I would have trouble choosing, and resent having to. He had made a mistake and he had done what he could to set things right. If he had not, then on principle, because of the values that I hold and because of my own experience of the pain of betrayal, I would choose not to be friends with him—and tell him why.*

In being asked to choose, a woman may feel offended that she isn't being trusted with the ability to discern what is true and what is not of the stories she is being told. She may think it unreasonable that her friend is dragging her into her drama with this man, or feel resentful or uncomfortable being asked to choose between two people she cares for. She simply may not share the values that would ignite in her any impulse to take this stand against infidelity.

Melissa and her partner, having decided to do what was needed to reconcile their relationship, found it was important to only remain friends with those who wanted to support them in the healing process. Many friendships were severed. As Melissa says, it was so hard both *"being betrayed by my partner and also losing so many other friendships."*

# Through the Filters of Her Own Experience

## GAIL:

*He and I shared a Skype account. A week or so after learning of my husband's infidelity, I went to Skype a friend. There was a "chat" on the screen, staring out at me. I read it—stunned. The chat between my husband Mark, and "our" friend Jen, went something like this:*

*Jen: "Hi Mark, how you doing, how is the hot romance?"*

*Mark: "Deep, really deep. Just keeps going deeper and deeper."*

*Jen: "Sounds good, really good."*

*Mark: "Yes. Awesome. I've never felt so alive before. I don't know what to do about my wife though."*

*Jen: "Maybe you don't need to do anything about her."*

*Even now, as I recall those words, I feel the shock, the hurt, the bewilderment.*

*A week or so later, Jen—who would have had no idea I had seen this—emailed me to say that she was there if I needed a friend. Again, I reeled with hurt and bewilderment! I responded with a few lines, copying her the exact message in the body of my email, and saying, "I guess we have a very different idea of what friendship is." Period.*

*I think I had hoped that she would send an, "Oh, I am so, so sorry." Instead I got a defensive, angry email to the effect that she had been through this experience herself, and had spent years feeling a victim about it, and admonishing me for "being a victim." She said that I should "get on with my life." It still hurts, so much, thinking about that.*

When a woman has not resolved her own past experiences of infidelity, another woman's betrayal will be the screen onto which she will project her own unfinished business. She will not see this betrayal for what it is, but through the filters of how her past experience still lives in her.

Jen's initial flippancy in response to the infidelity, her inability to meet the reality of Gail's pain, her reactivity and defensiveness as evidenced in her retort to Gail, is likely a sign of what is triggered in her as a result of her own unresolved business with infidelity. It may be that this degree of defensiveness is the strategy she has developed for dealing—or not dealing—with the painful experiences in her life.

When a woman feels good about who she is and what she has done, she can simply respond to a disturbing or confronting situation from the anchor of her integrity; her authentic presence. She has no need to react in a defensive way as Jen did.

Even while thinking Jen's response was unreasonable, Gail felt hurt by it. This too, is to some degree an issue of self-worth, of her own shame, and also of her not being well grounded and therefore indiscriminately at the effect of whatever another says about her. When a woman is not grounded, she tends to take on whatever someone says about her as true—even if this is done unconsciously. On one level Gail knew that Jen's response was reactive, but even so, she was unable to find that place in herself from where she could put up her boundaries to say—at least to herself—*Not true*.

When someone accuses or judges a woman, rather than automatically buying into that accusation, she can breathe, ground herself, and ask, *Do I believe that this is true of me? How much of this is true of me? How much of this is about the other person? What can I do to stand up for myself, and to empower myself in this situation?*

If the shoe doesn't fit, don't wear it! Instead, a woman can say something akin to, *"You may believe that, but I don't believe it to be true."* Period.

When the communication from the other person is not made in a respectful way, it may not be worth even attending to.

## Wanting to Remain "Neutral"

### MAGGIE:

*I didn't directly ask people to choose, but over the years I've been clear to cut people out of my life who condone my ex's behavior by their friendship with him. At the time of the recurring betrayals, I was in a spiritual community where it was said that everything is part of God's plan and as it should be. I didn't see how to set boundaries in the face of that, but it always felt really wrong to me. I needed people to be clearer in their stances of what behaviors they accepted and endorsed and what they did not, but I didn't know how to ask for this.*

*Some people will say that they want to be "neutral." I think it is cowardice, criminal, to be "neutral" when people are being hurt and suffering. That said, "taking sides" makes the whole matter of choice sound very cheap. A woman's decision as to who to remain friends with and who to move away from, is a matter of her heart and the kind of company she needs.*

What anyone says and does is justified internally by who they are—their values, their consciousness, and their courage. While many of these women had expected their friends would align with them on principle, they felt they had instead chosen to take "the easy road"—walking the fence and not siding with or choosing one or the other.

However, it may be that it does not even enter their awareness that, for their friend, there is a principle involved. Or, perhaps they are aware but believe they understand why her husband did what he did—it does not necessarily mean that they do not care about her. Perhaps they are seduced by or living vicariously off of the drama or passion of the unfaithful partner's hot romance.

## Friendships that Nourish

It is important for a woman in the very vulnerable place that she is in after the discovery of her partner's infidelity, to choose *"the kind of company she needs."* It is for each woman to determine what is true for her, and not to question or judge herself harshly for the decisions she feels she needs to make, in the interest of her own healing.

As long as she believes that she is being betrayed by those aligning with her ex, she remains at the effect of this belief. When she has had *enough* of the suffering this belief brings her, when she recognizes each woman's right to choose according to her own values, and when she at last comes to a place of relative neutrality to the emotions that arise in her with respect to this, she will be able to rest in that place in her heart where she can accept that her friend loves and cares for both—and has a right to do so.

Only then is she able to choose friendships that nourish her. She may find she can accept that one friend loves and cares for both equally, or she may trust one woman's ability to not be seduced by what she believes to be the "lies" of her ex—and find that she is unable to accept this as true of another woman. She may be right, in both cases. It is for her to discern and decide.

# "Had She Told Me ..."

### SHIRLEY: *"I knew what I had done was wrong"*

*One day Tony appeared in my office. I had been attracted to him but had never acted on it because he was the husband of a good friend. He asked me to go for a picnic lunch with him. I thought nothing of it. My husband and I had gone out with Tony and his wife, Della, many times. So he drove me up to Courtney Park.*

*We had lunch and then he started kissing me. It was only for five minutes or so and I felt horrible afterwards. I said to him that this didn't feel right. I said I wanted to go back to work. I didn't say anything more. When he dropped me off at work, I said goodbye. I pretended everything was okay. I think I was shocked. I didn't know what to do. I never wanted to see him again after that. I hated him. I adored Della, and yet I didn't stop kissing him right away. I knew what I had done was wrong. I was so sorry and wanted to apologize to her. I went home and wrote her a note. I said something like I wanted her to know that I had met Tony that we had gone on a picnic, and things got carried away. I alluded to what had happened without being too specific. Why did I send a note and not make direct contact? I was really ashamed. It felt safest to send a note.*

To be able to establish and call personal boundaries into action in the face of temptation demands a level of consciousness and commitment that few women have ever contemplated. A woman's articulating and sharing her boundaries with others invites in both a deeper commitment and a more meaningful level of accountability. Yet such conversations about boundaries are rare. And so, even with Shirley's concern for her friend, and even though she felt horrible for kissing Tony, she didn't know that place in her that she needed to access in order to enforce a boundary on a second's notice. Being very clear of the values reflected in the boundaries she has chosen can be a factor in a woman's ability to access the strength to do this. In this case that may have surfaced as a strong physical reaction that makes her position clear, and a strong verbal, *"No!"*

At this time, Shirley was unaware that the hatred and disgust she was projecting onto Tony was very like that which she holds onto herself for going along with this. A helpful inquiry could begin with her asking what she needed to address within herself, so that she was not projecting her hatred onto him. Yes, he may be—correction, he *was*—a creep to do this, but while not questioning her right to disapprove of what he did, he is not accountable for her response to his advances. The truth is she didn't make a stand for herself with him.

At the time, Shirley simply didn't know how to handle the situation any better. Like most women, she didn't know where to go within herself, to enforce the boundaries that needed to be enforced. This is also apparent in her pretending everything was okay when Tony dropped her off at work. Had Tony seen and heard Shirley's outrage, rather than her complicity, he may have thought twice before coming on to another woman. Then again he may not, but at least Shirley would have acted in a way that left her feeling very differently than she does now.

Shirley later commented that she was more concerned about how this would hurt Della, than about how it would hurt her own husband—and what it might mean to him. Now she saw that while she had, on some level, known at the time that her relationship with her husband was on the rocks, she hadn't yet been clear with herself about this. That, however, is another story.

### SHIRLEY:

*Della made mention of it a year or so afterward. We were doing something together, and she thanked me for the note. She alluded to the fact that he had done this before, but we didn't really discuss is any further. Some years later, Tony left her suddenly, for another woman.*

*The following year, Della and I met for dinner—she had moved to another state and we had less contact. This time she said that she had been used to him straying. I was totally aghast that she would have stayed with Tony, knowing that he was straying. I'd not perceived Della as someone who would do that.*

A woman with instincts and boundaries intact may have reacted immediately to Shirley's note. She may have contacted Shirley right then and there and told her she appreciated that she had let her know something had happened. She may have told Shirley how she felt on hearing this, and asked her what she meant by *"things got carried away."* She may have then taken a stand that was respectful of her own wellbeing, perhaps by speaking directly to Tony about it. She may have ended the relationship then and there.

Every woman, even with instincts intact, may very well respond differently. A woman may discern it best to be silent, for the time. This may be so for any number of reasons. She may need time to collect herself and consider how best to respond, or she may want to seek counsel with a trusted other. Then again, it may that something in a woman's history, in her psyche, prevents her from even considering taking a stand for herself.

Now I personally know these women, although this story was new to me. I realized I needed to check, with Shirley's permission, that Della was okay with her story being printed in this book. Della's responses to reading what Shirley had said, brought additional and revealing angles to light. Firstly, the awareness that Della and Shirley had different definitions of "straying." To Della, straying had more to do with a wandering eye than anything as explicit as kissing.

### DELLA:

*Shirley's comments were a revelation to me. I had no idea that kissing was involved … that might have been a deal breaker for me with Tony. I had perceived a flirtatious quality about him that I thought was inappropriate. I got feedback from some women that they were uncomfortable with it, though as long as I felt secure I didn't mind.*

*I thought it was just his bad judgment about who would be offended, and that he was picking women who were offended. I also knew of several instances of women who had been sexually abused in past relationships who got plugged in by his sex jokes or innuendoes.*

*I never knew there was any kissing. Had Shirley told me that had happened, I'm sure it would have led to a confrontation, ultimatum, demand for counseling, or us splitting, or something. That is over the line.*

What about Shirley's comment that she had not perceived Della as someone who would stay with a straying husband? Della had long admired her husband's extremely unusual devotion to *"telling the truth."*

### DELLA:

*He would share vulnerable stories about himself with others. He would come home from business trips and tell me about his infatuations and how hard it was not to act on them—for example to resist getting in the elevator with a woman who had attended his seminar and invited him up to her room after they had dinner together. He would tell me how, despite the temptations, he would say no. I would say, "Oh, great." I thought he was showing willpower and discipline by being so honest.*

203

*Of course women wanted to get in his pants. He was this successful guy, he had just led this great seminar they loved, he was male gold dust. So I was all understanding because it made sense to me, and I never considered there was anything wrong with this. His honesty talk really deluded me, seduced me. When he said it was "so hard to resist," my intuition told me there was a glitch there, but I didn't listen well enough to hear what needed to be heard. I didn't wake up to the bizarreness of his telling me how it was hard for him to resist, rather than "I love you so much, it was easy for me to resist them."*

*I see now that it was sick. He would tell me how hard it was, how he had been victorious, and I praised him for that. It didn't occur to me to question him: "If you love me so much, maybe you shouldn't be putting yourself in these situations. If you don't want to return to your room alone after you have done these big testosterone presentations, I can understand that. So to protect our marriage, perhaps I should go on the road with you, or you not make these trips." None of that occurred to me.*

*I was deluded by the idea that anyone who was so honest— sometimes painfully so—to me about his attractions to other women, and who was making such a point of being excruciatingly honest about them, could not possibly be having affairs, having sex, dating, kissing or straying. A counselor later wisely remarked to me, "Don't pay as much attention to what he says, as to what he does."*

Brené Brown, in *Daring Greatly*, writes, *"Vulnerability without boundaries leads to disconnection, distrust, and disengagement. In fact … boundaryless disclosure is one way we protect ourselves from real vulnerability … vulnerability is bankrupt on its own terms when people move from being vulnerable to using vulnerability to deal with unmet needs, get attention, or engage in the shock-and-awe behaviors that are so commonplace in today's culture … Vulnerability is not a secret-sharing free-for-all."*

Was Tony's pushing the boundaries of what most people would think of as appropriate with his "excruciating honesty" more accurately "boundaryless disclosure"? Was his seeming vulnerability in so openly telling Della of his attractions to other women in fact a smoke screen that distracted her, and shielded him, from the need to tell the real truth?

Shirley commented that on two later occasions, mention had been made of what had happened between Tony and herself. Here was a further opportunity to clear the air. Why didn't they pursue this?

204

Here is Della's response:

> *I remember a year or so later, when we met for dinner, Shirley said something about being sorry she and Tony "went over the line." I didn't really pay any attention as Tony was doing that all the time. I probably said something like, "Oh yes, Tony has a wandering eye and is often flirting." I didn't pursue it, because I thought that it was resolved—there was nothing to really pursue.*
>
> *Now I know that "crossing the line," or "a wandering eye" meant different things to us. At the time, it didn't occur to me to question that. If I had known there was any kissing, if she had been more explicit ... The honesty thing had really thrown me off.*

Credit is due to Shirley for pulling herself back rather than fully succumbing to the seduction of the moment. However, had she spoken to Della directly, and not simply sent a note or spoken vaguely of what had happened when the two met for dinner, this story may have ended very differently. Della was left to figure out what had happened alone, and to interpret the situation very differently to how it actually was. Had Shirley had some awareness of what that might have meant for her friend—or a stronger sense of self—she may have found the courage to speak more truthfully. And had Della been more in touch with her instincts, more astute and discerning, she may have not been so easily misled by her husband.

While Della appreciated Shirley's telling the truth, another woman may very well be furious. Always, discernment is needed.

As emphasized in Chapter 7: *Unraveling the Patterns of Self-Betrayal,* boundary agreements must be articulated and clear. What "trustworthy" means to one person may not be what it means to another. Assuming a shared understanding of what constitutes a breach of trust, or of what "being faithful" means, is inviting disaster.

### SHIRLEY:

> *Today I have a stronger sense of myself—the result of a number of relationships over the years, all of which I ended. Today I know I can live on my own and survive. As a child I grew up without a strong sense of myself, my abilities and skills, and at that point in time getting attention from a man and making him happy was more important to me than getting what I wanted for myself. Having a man was more important to me at the time than*

*sticking to my own ethical constructs. Today, I would not hurt someone I knew and loved.*

## Friends: Going Silent, Disappearing

GAIL: *"I asked him, pleaded with him, to stop"*

*He was in the heat of the affair and sharing it with everyone, telling them that he hadn't experienced this passion with me for years—if ever. I asked him, pleaded with him, to stop. He insisted that he wanted to be transparent, honest. He told me people were happy for him, told him how great he looked! I felt really bewildered, sad, hurt, that not even "our" women friends he was sharing this with—whom I considered to be my friends—reached out to me. Not even an email that said, "Sorry you and Mark are having a hard time. I am not available to offer you support, but I wish you well." Not a single one of them reached out to ask how this was for me, or how I felt about what Mark was saying and doing.*

*Was it that it was too embarrassing or awkward for them? Did they feel it would be inappropriate to get involved, to "interfere?" From what I had heard, they were "involved." Mark had initiated that possibility, and their concurrence in hearing "his story" ensured that. Don't people feel any responsibility to call him to some level of awakening or accountability for what he is doing?*

*I couldn't understand what was happening. Are people not calling him out on it, or reaching out to me, because this kind of betrayal freaks them out? Does this trigger something so deep and fearful in people that they are unable to be present to the reality of what is happening?*

*Did anyone ask him if he had my permission to share this highly sensitive personal information, with them? Did anyone have even a momentary tweak of conscience that something may not be caring/respectful/honorable in Mark's words or actions, or through their engagement with him as he told "his story?" And if they did, or did not, what might this mean?*

Firstly, with respect to people not reaching out, most people simply don't know what to say or how to begin. Even a funeral has familiar protocols for expressing condolences and offers of support, but at the news of a

206

partner's infidelity even a woman's close friends may have no idea how to offer support. In their own discomfort at not knowing what to say or do, they may avoid her. They may be looking for cues from her that she doesn't want to be left alone in her anguish, or that she wants company. Their staying away may be driven by respect for what they believe is her desire for privacy.

The difficulty is that many women who have been betrayed are in such a state of shock, or so consumed by grief or by shame, that they do not feel able to reach out. The brain processes shame or social rejection in the exact same way it processes physical pain—emotions both hurt and cause pain. At the same time, as we will see, often what is happening is that her friends' own past experiences of infidelity have reactivated the humiliation, shame, and grief they experienced.

Many friends disappear or go silent because they can't face or deal with the enormity of what the betrayed woman is experiencing. The emotions of a woman in the throes of infidelity are intense, erratic and unpredictable. One moment she will be in tears and the next spewing forth all the venom of the dark goddess. It is very difficult for most people to be present to these emotions. Most women simply don't have the grounded presence and personal boundaries to enable them to stay present in such an uncomfortable situation.

Whether the unfaithful partner is caught in the ecstasy of the romance of the affair, or whether he has found confirmation of his masculinity and is presenting as an accomplished and satisfied stud, most people will find it easier to align with him than with the woman he has betrayed. Why? As we will see, the reasons are many and complex. To begin with, culturally people are much more comfortable aligning with the rational, linear thinking of the masculine and turn away from the instinctual, non-linear nature of the feminine. The unfaithful will inevitably have a "good, rational story" to justify what he did. Then, there is also truth in the refrain, *"Everybody loves a lover."* Who *wouldn't* want to be around that energy? It can be extremely seductive and tantalizing to those looking in on it.

Few are those who, through their own life experiences, have developed the wisdom to be able to recognize not only the insanity, but also the heartless disregard in dismissing another's pain.

## Shame Thrives in Secrecy

There are many who fear adultery is a contagious disease that might spread to their own relationships if they get too close to a woman who is in the throes of it. They may be threatened by what they don't understand, or fear their own relationships are more vulnerable than they want to admit.

### SUZANNE: *"Today I understand what I did not recognize then"*

*People want you to get over it, but these emotions need their own time. Today I understand what I did not recognize then: anger, rage, and grief are very uncomfortable emotions for most people to be around. I read of a woman who had experienced betrayal and wore a Band-Aid over her heart when she went to work because she wanted people to ask her what had happened. That kind of symbolic gesture is very significant.*

*The risk is not just about women getting lost in their emotions, but about their acknowledging them at all. So many people don't want to tell anyone because of the shame. It is very important that the truth be told. A woman may need to be encouraged to stay with the simplicity of the feelings ... rage, hopelessness ... and know that in the midst of this, a level of healing is happening simply in being present to what is.*

*There is too much emphasis on saving face and looking good in this culture. That's why the Band-Aid over the heart seems beautiful to me. I think it's also important to be in the company of other people, but in situations that are tolerable ... perhaps preparing a meal together, something where the hands are occupied. It can be difficult to reach out at this time, but it can be very helpful to be with others.*

Shame thrives in secrecy and silence and depends on a woman's belief that *"I am alone."* Now, there is certainly nothing wrong with being alone. However, here the reference is to a woman being alone in her shame. In this state, unchallenged, the *"I am alone"* reinforces her belief that she is flawed, not good enough, unworthy of love.

Suzanne spoke of a woman who went to work with a Band-Aid over her heart as if to say, *"In the face of my husband's infidelity, even while broken-hearted, here I am."* Wearing a Band-Aid over her heart, this woman reached out to be seen and acknowledged. While not denying her heartbreak, she refused to succumb to the voice of shame, refused to feed any feelings of victimization.

It is best that whenever possible, a woman speak—and act—so her words are congruent with what she is feeling. If asked, *"How are you?"* and she

208

responds with, *"Fine,"* when she is in fact filled with rage, or on the verge of tears, this sets up a dissonance between body and emotions. It won't always be appropriate to speak honestly, but whenever possible, it is best to get in touch with her emotions and speak authentically about what is so. It need not be anything more than, *"I am feeling really devastated about how our relationship ended,"* or, *"I am really disgusted at what he has done."* Period.

### VALERIE: *"I felt like it was totally my fault"*

*When Dan left, I didn't want people to know we had separated because of an affair. When I needed to say something, I would just say we were separating. I was always so ashamed—I felt like it was totally my fault.*

*I had earlier planned and paid to go to a professional training a month after he left. At every break between sessions, I would go lie on my bed and sleep. People would ask me if I was okay. I didn't tell a soul my husband had had an affair, not even that we had separated. I felt it to be such a huge failure and embarrassment. If there had been anything mutual about it, it would have been different. I might have been more willing. Then there was also the fact that I feared if I said anything, I would burst into tears.*

*My reaction was very different to that of a friend whose husband had had an affair some years earlier. When she heard of her husband's affair, she called everybody—his parents, neighbors, friends, people at work. She told them, "This bastard has had an affair. I want you to know who you are dealing with." When I asked how she could do that—publicizing he had an affair—she replied, "It's clear he's a jerk. Breaking his vows ... why would that reflect badly on me?"*

*And these people rallied around her. She was indignant, she was angry, and she was right. The extreme to which she took it astounded me, like saying to his parents, "I want you to know what your son just did."*

*Now of course, there is also the woman who would say, "Oh yeah, I'm with another cheater. They're all the same." This wasn't like that.*

What's important is that a woman respect what she herself needs to do, and doesn't judge or compare herself to anyone else. Valerie, even while knowing how her friend had reacted some years earlier, simply saw her reaction was very different, and accepted that she was doing the best she could in the predicament she found herself in.

A woman's not speaking out may not only be about what people will think of her—it may also be that she doesn't know how she will react herself if she says out loud that her husband has betrayed her.

### REBECCA:

*Many times, when I needed to be able to control myself enough to manage a transaction or communication with someone, I would say—if something needed to be said—that he had died. I feared I would break down if I told the truth—my husband had left me for another woman. I was afraid I would lose it, and I didn't want to be more embarrassed about the whole thing than I already was. To tell the truth brings up the whole horrible nightmare in my face again. Even now, my body still reacts.*

A woman's not openly speaking of her husband's infidelity does not necessarily mean that she is repressing or avoiding the pain. It is for each woman to discern, moment to moment, how she can best do what she needs to do—which is not to say that she must face this alone.

*"The poet Rumi saw clearly the relationship between our wounds and our awakening. He counseled, 'Don't turn away. Keep your eye on the bandaged place. That's where the light enters you.' When we look directly at that bandaged place without denying or avoiding it, we become tender toward our human vulnerability. Our attention allows the light of wisdom and compassion ..."*

—Tara Brach, *Radical Acceptance*

## Their Silence: How It Hurts

### GAIL: *"I was consumed with grief, with shame"*

*It seemed all the world went quiet. A silence descended. This was in the early weeks after he told me he was with this other woman. I knew that he was traveling around the state with her, showing off his new love, sharing openly with the people who I had believed to be my friends as well as his ... and yet, not one of them reached out to me. Not a word. Silence. My whole world was silent. I couldn't go out. I couldn't face people. I cloistered myself in my rooms. I talked—I cried, I sobbed—on the phone with the women I had called out to, in my shock, when I first learned of his betrayal. And still, they were there for me, whenever I called them. But otherwise—silence. And in that silence, I was consumed with grief, with shame. I felt so abandoned.*

*Some ten months had passed since my husband had met his "soul mate" and announced, soon after, his sudden and unilateral decision to leave me, for her. Just like that. He and I were talking in the usual strained way over Skype—as we had to, on occasion. He was calling from a friend's place where he was staying. I— we—had spent many vacations at their home.*

*Now, I heard them walk into the room my husband was Skyping from, laughing. They heard my voice, and called out, sounding so happy. "Hi Gail! How are you doing?" I was stunned. What was I to say to that? They had not contacted me in all these months, and now they were acting like nothing had happened. I said, "This isn't a good time to talk."*

*A few months later, I ran into a similar situation. Different couple, exactly the same thing. Again, entering the room, the laughter, the happy "Oh, that's Gail? Hi Gail, how are you?" It hurt so much.*

It was some twelve months later when Gail had a work-related need to email a friend whom she had not heard from since her partner's infidelity. Gail took the risk to ask her friend why she had not contacted her. Her friend's response offered her a wholly new insight into what had been happening. Here is her friend's response:

### ELIZABETH:

*When I got this email from Mark, broadcasting this new love he had found to a whole bunch of his friends, I had to walk away from the computer. I would have thrown up on the keyboard. I couldn't believe it, this was so insensitive. What are you doing, I thought, broadcasting this to the world, like you are proud of it? How does Gail feel? I'm sorry I didn't reach out to you. I was lost, absolutely lost in the humiliation of the memory of my own experience of being betrayed.*

Other women offered additional insights into why they did not reach out to their friend, and also into their seeming collusion with the betrayal, by not calling the unfaithful partner to accountability. Here is one such story:

**CHRIS:**

*It was over a year after I heard of my husband's affair, when I had need to communicate with a woman who I had been surprised had not contacted me. By this time, I could find it within myself to ask her why. She replied:*

*"When I met James and he started telling me about his pole dancer girlfriend, it triggered my own humiliation and embarrassment from when I learned my husband was cheating on me. I was immediately back in that experience, of someone telling me my husband was fucking around. I went into such humiliation and embarrassment with that memory, that I could not even call you, his wife—my friend!*

*"I was rolling in my own shit. It restimulated all this embarrassment and humiliation, and why should I be embarrassed when it was my husband that had the affair?! It's that poisoning that happens when you've been cuckolded. I went into such deep embarrassment and humiliation—I am very sad I didn't reach out to say to you that I was so sorry."*

## There's No One Home

And then, yet another reason why people stay silent:

**DIANNE:**

*I had heard he was having an affair, and sure enough, a few months later when I saw him, he went right into telling me about this new woman in his life. When I asked, "How did your wife feel, it must be hard for her," he just went into this whole litany … "I want passion, I need passion. It's been so long without passion. I don't want to go to my death without passion. I was drying up. I was drying up, now I feel passion again. I didn't think I'd be able to feel this way again."*

*He was totally self-referential. He was in that ungrounded, rapturous state that I've been in before. I don't think it has anything to do with the other person, but everything to do with tapping into your own unfulfilled potential, unmet needs, and all the demons that run you and warp your life. It's depressing.*

*I listened to him and I thought, I don't know how to respond to you. You are so wrapped up in this passion, I can't relate to you right now. There is nothing to say. There is no point of connection. I was just watching him. I wasn't even witnessing him like a caring person would; I was just observing him.*

*The room could have been littered with bodies; he was in such a self-delusional state that he wouldn't have noticed. As high as we fly to touch the sun, we fall as quickly.*

It takes a great deal of skill to be able to relate to this level of self-referencing. Energetically, it is as if "no one is home." It may be impossible to connect with a person in this state. Their energy is so strong that the listener may find herself swept up into it and stunned, unable to even consider what, if anything, can be said. This is further complicated by the fact that the listener will be hearing what is said through the filters of her own experiences—or absence thereof—with infidelity.

When the person listening can remain grounded and centered they can consider asking questions along the lines of, *"Have you considered that your family will be devastated by this? That people you love will be hurt?"* Or simply, *"Don't do this. People will be hurt. I don't want to hear any more about it."* It just might make a difference. At least, with time, if enough people—or the "right" people—were to say this, it may put some cracks in the massive wall of denial the unfaithful partner has built around himself.

## The Disease to Please

**HANNAH:** *"Silence gives us an excuse to be dishonest and an opportunity to avoid speaking our truth."*

*I realized that I felt uncomfortable when Pete was sharing the story of his affair, but I didn't think to say that I was feeling that way, nor did I think to confront him. Why? In retrospect, I see that I was in shock. Embarrassed. I was embarrassed that I was behaving the way I was behaving—relapsing and regressing into the cultural norms of "be nice" that I grew up with.*

*Later, I was alone with Pete. I told him how I felt about his wife … my love and admiration for her. Here I recall getting very emotional, and I am getting very emotional now, choking up as I say this … I was thinking, How could you just leave her like this?! I chose not to confront him, but rather to talk about my love for him and for his wife. It is only now I see that the "be nice" script that I learned so well as a girl, had stopped me from directly confronting him.*

213

*I felt horrible when he started showing me photos of his new lover. I didn't want to see her. I felt disgusted by the whole situation. In my mind, I went back to when I was betrayed ... to how many times my first husband fucked other women, including my best friends.*

*I regressed, responded how I was taught to in the first fifty years of my life. It's not the first time I've done it and it won't be the last. It's so goddamn easy to do that. It's so ingrained, it's cellular ... to be nice, be nice ...*

*It's true that I love Pete, that he is like a brother to me; and it's also true that it's never easy for me to confront someone ... but such facts don't usually stop me.*

*I don't like admitting it, but liking Pete made it harder for me to confront him. I didn't want to risk losing his friendship. I just wanted to make our time together pleasant ... So I became a quiet observer, seeing but not speaking out. It hurt too much. When Pete showed me that picture, I just ran from all of this ... I didn't want to know about the other woman, about what was going on.*

*I didn't contact my friend—his wife—for months. It's hard for me to realize I didn't do that. Why didn't I? I went into hiding ... I think I started to grieve right then and there when Pete showed me the photo of the other woman. I should have said, "You fucking asshole, what the hell are you doing?" And I wonder whether Pete himself had a more profound effect on me than I realized—he can be so charismatic, so charming. I wonder, because what otherwise could have kept me from reaching out to Amelia, of all people—it blows me away.*

*I must have known how much she would be hurting. I was seeing the end of a relationship between two people who meant so much to me—who have both figured so significantly in my life. There's him and there's her and there's their relationship, which is an entity of its own. It was just too hard to contact her sooner because it was hurting so much. That's why it took me so long ... I had to move through it before I could finally contact her.*

*I see now how we are led astray by our silence. Silence gives us an excuse to be dishonest and an opportunity to avoid speaking our truth.*

This "being nice," this "disease to please," is understandable given our culture and what has been passed on to us as women through millennia—

but it comes at great cost to a woman, and to her children, and the Sisterhood. It demands she sacrifice her instincts and her integrity.

By not stepping up and speaking what we know to be true, such acts of infidelity are legitimized and perpetuated—through our silence. Often, as with Hannah, it may only be on later reflection that a woman is aware that she has made a decision to collude in her silence. She has succumbed to the familiar, *"Be nice, be quiet."* When a woman is willing to reflect on her actions, the question becomes, *How do I keep myself awake?* It's not easy. It's as if a veil descends—the veil of our own self-betraying patterns.

How does a woman keep herself awake and courageous? One way is to keep the company of women who are willing to speak what is true. Whenever a woman steps out and speaks her truth, this can ignite in another woman the possibility to do likewise. It demands courage, resolve, and commitment. We need each other to remember and to hold us accountable.

Hannah's recognition of, and self-inquiry into, the nature of her silence was in itself a step towards reclaiming her integrity. To step still further and reclaim her voice, she could communicate to Pete what—in retrospect—she now recognizes as a more authentic response. The physiological and energetic shift activated by such an action cannot be underestimated. The instincts are innate, and a response such as this snaps the instincts back into the consciousness, back into the body, and begins forging those different pathways to the brain. This is how we change the neurological and cellular patterning of the voices of patriarchy that are so ingrained in us.

In closing, Hannah says, *"I see now how we are led astray by our silence. Silence gives us an excuse to be dishonest and an opportunity to avoid speaking our truth."* We are not in fact led astray by our silence, but by all that which leads us to be nice—and in so doing, perpetuates our silence. Self-betrayal is the epidemic that both makes it possible and perpetuates it. Silence gives us the excuse not to speak what our instincts would have us speak whenever we are afraid—for whatever reason—to say what is true for us.

The question is, how uncomfortable are we as individuals, and as a collective, with these many expressions of betrayal—and to what extent will we allow this discomfort to keep us numbed and silenced?

# CHAPTER 15

## *Weathering The Tsunami*

The discovery of a partner's infidelity hits so suddenly, so hard, so deep; and in its aftermath a woman's life is changed, irrevocably, forever. Having somehow survived that initial shock, the reverberations of the devastation continue to surge and materialize through a woman's life. Will it never end? Painstakingly, heavy of heart, gutted, she finds herself day after day swept off her feet by what appears to be an unrelenting succession of waves of anger, grief, despair, and fear crashing over and through her.

She has known nothing like this ever before. Even if she has known others who have been betrayed, nothing in her life has prepared her for this. *How can it hurt so much?* She knows, deep in her being, that even when the initial shock of the tsunami has passed, life will never be the same again. For now, through the first year, two, three ... she does whatever it takes to get through each day and, whenever possible, cultivate a sense of hope and possibility for the future.

Here, women share how they supported themselves in weathering these early years.

### MARILYN:

*What helped, what got me through it? No one can take away the pain. No one can do it for you. It is hell but you have to walk that walk. Having children, you need to be strong for them. And my women friends being there, with me. You just have to keep on breathing, putting one foot in front of the other. My mother used to say to me, "This too shall pass. This too shall pass." And that was always helpful.*

As simple as it sounds, one cannot overestimate the value of breathing, centering in the present moment, putting one foot in front of the other, and cultivating hope and possibility even when it feels that there is none.

### AMELIA:

*I was so depressed. I learned the only way to keep going was not by living day-to-day, but breath-by-breath. I had to do this, for my children. I kept reminding myself that every breath I took was one more breath towards getting through this, and sometimes that was all that kept me going. That and learning the importance of focusing on myself, and staying away from my ex and my past with him. It took a long, long time, but I lived to discover that I could laugh and love again.*

Here is a woman's recognition that her point of power is to keep her attention on herself, what she can and must do to support and empower herself—not on what *he did* or what she wants or wanted *from* him.

### REBECCA:

*It was only my love and concern for my daughter that kept me going. I felt sick at the thought that she would live her life knowing she had a father who had left her and a mother who couldn't take care of herself. This pulled me through periods when I wanted nothing but to end my life.*

*Days when I felt devoid of hope and of strength, it was that love I felt for her, and my wanting to do the very best I could for her, that got me through the day. As an adult, my parents now deceased, I still draw on the ever present love and support they offered me. I wanted at least some of that, for her.*

*And so I learned to endure, to find the strength and courage in me to lift up my head and open my heart and take the next step … and the next. And that strength and courage and endurance, I know I have that in myself now, to call on whenever I may need it.*

Always, for the love of the children, woman after woman through millennia has kept going.

*When I heard of my partner's infidelity, I didn't know what was happening to me. I had no tools to cope. I didn't know how to ask for help. I felt incredible shame on one hand, and on the other I thought that I didn't deserve any better. Looking back now, I am amazed that I really didn't know what I needed or wanted. I was already in therapy, and that helped. My work was my refuge. I tried to be present with my kids as much as possible. We split the kids 50/50 and that was the beginning of my healing. I felt so lonely much of the time and began to work on healing myself. In retrospect, I had a lot of healing to do as a human being—and I am still working at it!*

Be it thanks to work, children, or the support of friends or therapy, a woman opens a window into a whole new realm of possibilities whenever she recognizes infidelity as an uninvited invitation to heal.

## Connecting with the Inner Child

### REBECCA: *"I didn't 'fit' and I didn't know why"*

*One minute I would be feeling really strong and confident, and then he would say something like, "So-and-so said you're acting like a victim," and in an instant I would find myself flooded with shame. I came to realize that I was hooking right into some childhood shame and with time, I could deny it no more. I needed to connect with my Inner Child—something I had not done in many years. This is how it was, for me, as it appears in my journal entry:*

*I lie down, hands over my heart chakra, and call her in, ever so gently. Ahh, there she is. I see her in my mind's eye. I feel so much love for her. I radiate this love to her. I take the time to simply be in that field of energy with her, connecting. I tell her how much I love her. I am so sad to see her hurting so much. I ask her how she feels. I find that she is feeling humiliated. So humiliated. And she is feeling very little, wanting to hide, not wanting to be seen. And then, there is also grief. Oh, so much grief ... I am right there with her, validating her feelings. "Yes, I see you. Yes, no wonder you feel that way."*

*When I look at what is beneath that grief, it is her believing others are seeing her as being pathetic, over-emotional,*

218

*overreacting, needing therapy. And that she feels powerless to do anything about it. She wants to run away and hide. Again, I validate her feelings and radiate love to her. As I do, she softens, she smiles. The distress, for now, has dissipated.*

*Of course I understand exactly how she feels. These experiences of feeling humiliated, powerless, unfairly judged, have occurred before many times—even as an adult in situations where I've done something and felt misunderstood, misinterpreted, or disregarded. At these times I have seen or imagined that they were saying something awful to others about what I did. Or it might have been that I was trying to connect with them and they were walking away like they were disinterested. I would feel so awful, so alone, as if I simply didn't belong. I didn't "fit" and I didn't know why.*

*Because these experiences first occurred in my childhood, my Inner Child can easily get hooked into shame today when I, as the adult, am not in the place of clarity and strength in myself to be able to take care of her by witnessing, rather than buying into this pattern.*

Connecting with that Inner Child can open a new window into what is needed for a woman to heal from her experience of infidelity. She may connect with her through journaling, or in a guided imagery or meditation, and then radiate love from her heart to this Inner Child. The more she does this, of course, the easier it becomes. With time she can connect with her in moments, and give her the love and reassurance she needs.

There is an additional step that a woman may take with this process. When she has connected with her Inner Child and what she may be feeling—in this case with her shame—she can ask herself, *How do I want to feel?* It may be, *I want to feel strong and centered. I want to stand in my own truth of who I am, who I know myself to be, despite what they say … I want to stand in my goodness, courage, and integrity.* It is important that she name the qualities she wants to feel. And now, using her breath, she can ignite those qualities in her emotional and physical body.

When it's courage she wants to ignite, she can recall an experience when she has felt courageous. If she cannot recall one, she can imagine one. She can call to mind a character from a movie or a book … someone who exemplifies courage. Recalling or imagining as best she can how that energy would feel in her body, she calls the energy in slowly, steadily. Using her breath, her will, *and* her imagination, she infuses her whole being with it. Whenever her mind takes her away from experiencing this, she uses her will to bring it back into her consciousness and into her body.

When she wants to feel strong and centered, she recalls a time when she has experienced that energy. If need be, she recalls a character who exemplifies these energies. And now, breathing in that energy, breathing out any residual shame, she can allow these qualities to infuse her whole being.

It takes will to remain there, to continue to receive the experience of strength and centeredness. Some women need to be especially alert to remaining in the body—in the receptive—rather than drifting into the head. When a woman notices this has happened, she simply calls herself back so that she may once again receive that experience of courage in her body.

A woman can draw on this process of using her breath, her will, and her imagination to ignite the desired quality in herself at any time. The more she is able to develop an understanding and experience of how that quality lives in her and translates into her everyday life, the more deeply she becomes that which she aspires to be.

Accessing this quality, grounding it in her body, practicing this over and over again, will begin to reset the frequency of energy in the body, and her nervous system will be more and more likely to remember the pathway to it. In time it will become a state she will find herself accessing more and more readily, until at last she will realize, with gratitude and wonder, that it has become her natural way of being.

# Gratitude

**MARILYN:**

*My world was falling apart—I had a husband who was leaving me, my two little sons, and a baby growing in my belly. The therapist told me to be strong and be thankful for what I had. He ignored the horror of what this man was doing to me and his children. It took me years to sort it all out ... and to recognize my own strength—the strength of a woman who knows she must survive and be strong for her children.*

Gratitude is *not* a cure-all for every bad feeling. Gratitude can be helpful to a woman in shifting from the energy of victim, but when a woman is experiencing grief, she is not "playing victim." She is in the process of experiencing a deep loss. Her grief is a normal and healthy human reaction. She needs to know this, because Western culture will not condone this view.

When a woman has experienced a great loss, it may be very difficult for her to feel any kind of gratitude. Loss engenders grief, and this grief needs to be respected. However, it is also true that experiencing gratitude may be difficult for a woman because she *does* blame the world. If she is not in grief and is still unable to come up with anything to be grateful for because, day in and day out, *"Nothing good happened today. I cannot think of a single thing to feel thankful for,"* she is probably blaming the world. This may be so especially if she has a chronic pattern of blaming other people, or things, or situations. Her choice, then, is whether to remain in that familiar role of victim, or to explore gratitude as a path toward breaking this pattern.

In the aftermath of infidelity, the grief can be so overwhelming that a woman may find it impossible to access any desire or energy to experience gratitude—even while knowing it would be good for her. When this is so, it may be best she simply give herself a break and, accepting where she is in this moment, surrender to the grief with tenderness and compassion.

When a woman wants to see more possibilities all around her, to feel the freedom to be able to laugh and to love again, gratitude can be the path through to this world. It may require courage and will to consciously bring to mind loved ones and experiences that she is grateful for having in her life—be it her children, caring friends, her home, or the way in which she is heartened by nature or objects of beauty.

Gratitude opens the heart and infuses the mental, physical and emotional body with tenderness, patience and peace—and in time, even joy. In a state of gratitude, anger and bitterness fade away. But to reach this state from a place of grief cannot be hurried. It will take the time it will take. A butterfly cannot be forced out of the cocoon. Surrendering to the loss and grief—for as long as it takes these emotions to move through her—she will wake one morning to find she has wings. She is ready, again, to take flight.

## Tuning into Your Body

### REBECCA:

*I would set my alarm or phone to ding every hour or two. When it went off, I would notice how I was feeling, and think of how I could lovingly respond to my body, in that moment. I might simply stretch, take a few deep breaths, take a walk, or even meditate.*

Kind, reassuring physical touch also has an immediate effect on our bodies, activating the soothing parasympathetic system. Physical touch can move a woman's attention from the habitual storylines running in her head, into the feelings and sensations in her body. Any form of reassuring touch will do, even something as simple as placing a hand over her heart or belly, and taking some deep, gentle breaths.

It can be helpful, with each breath, to breathe in through the nose with the intention, *All that I need, I inhale*, and to breathe out through the mouth with the intention, *All that I don't need, I release.* Centered in the present, she is no longer at the effect of all the stories about what has been or what may be, and is best able to discern the best course of action.

When she is angry, taking deep breaths moves that energy through her body. Doing this mindfully, with her will and intention, activates the quiet strength of the Warrior Woman.

## *"I Am Not My Emotions"*

### SUZANNE: *"I had known so much betrayal"*

*When I was twenty-eight years old, and my daughter was eighteen months, her father abandoned us. I went into "little girl" state. What I needed to do was find my core self, but I had known so much betrayal in childhood, that it was very hard for me to find who I was. I knew myself only in relationship to this man who I was totally in love with and the father of my child, so I had to embark on a lot of deep therapy, and found my way into deep meditation practices. I had been doing yoga for years, but I had never made the connection that I was not my emotions. My emotions were so strong, I thought I was my emotions. I was a victim of them.*

*In Western culture we identify so strongly with the ego, we tend to take things so very personally. At the time of my first experience of betrayal by my partner, I was totally at the effect of my emotions. I was depressed, incapacitated, for several years. Over time, I have explored various processes to learn there is something deeper in me than my emotions. Some people refer to it as the essential self or core self; that place where I am not at the effect of my emotions. It was astounding to me to discover that I could feel my emotions. I learned that it was in fact really important for me to feel them, in order for me to know what was going on—but I didn't have to assume that they were the truth. I'm still working on that.*

222

*It's been a long journey learning the skills that allow me to feel my emotions—even my "negative" emotions—but not to the point that they become disenabling. I'm still learning how to regulate my emotions and let them go up and down without falling apart and getting caught in hysteria. For much of my life, I was very prone to just falling apart. It has helped to be around people who modeled what I didn't get. When I find myself feeling anxious, I remember to breathe ... to take a breath, then consciously slow down, breathe, and talk more slowly."*

It is true that in Western culture we tend to take things so very personally, and it is literally transformative to learn not to be at the disempowering effect of the emotions, and to deepen contact with that core self. As Suzanne has learned, her "negative" emotions are not in themselves disenabling; a woman can learn to be with them in ways that do not disempower her. In fact, these emotions often carry the very energy and momentum she needs to break through many of the illusions she carries about herself and the world around her.

Once again we see mention of the breath, and the value of mindful breathing for body, mind, and spirit. A woman may dissipate disempowering emotions by simply being aware of her breathing, and bringing the breath to a slow, calm, rhythmical cadence. As she does this, the energy settles and her whole body returns to a place of calm, balance, and strength. With time and practice, this place of coherence can become the default position a woman moves into whenever she becomes stressed.

## Pulling Oneself Back from the Abyss

### SUZANNE:

*When I start to spiral out, and betrayal can do that, it's like suddenly the ground is taken away from under my feet and I lose my bearings totally. There is no sense of being able to find the ground to stand on. One therapist told me that I had to make sure I felt the ground beneath my feet—to go outside, stamp on the earth, feel the earth beneath me and then realize I had choices. I could choose if I was going to allow myself to go down that path into an emotional spiral, which is really an emotional indulgence, or if I was going to catch myself and pull myself back from the abyss.*

*On the other hand, if I try to suppress my feelings completely that doesn't help. And if I'm lost in them, at some point it becomes indulgence. I don't mean that I'm intending to "indulge"—I'm not. It's simply that it's all I know, it's what I've learned, and I need to find my way out.*

Suzanne recognizes the power she has in that moment, to either allow herself to fall into an emotional spiral, or to catch herself and ground back in her body. While Suzanne may do this by going out and stamping on the earth, another woman may—in the middle of that hell—ground herself by calling a friend who understands, who has been on that journey and can be present to the depths of her emotions and validate her feelings.

### SUZANNE:

*At what point does it become indulgence? It's very hard to say. When we're in the early stages of grief, there is no ground under our feet. It's an insane time—that's why traditional cultures are very careful in how they structure time for people going through grief so they can find their way out. I think if, as time passes, we cannot find our way back to feeling the gift of being in a body ... to feeling a sense of gratitude for being alive ... it's likely we've gone too far. If the debilitating state persists for months and months on end without relenting—if it's unremitting pain—then probably I'm lost in it.*

Feminine collapse or descent into that place of total blackness where it is impossible to see any light at the end of the tunnel—that time outside of time where a woman feels like she has no choice but to surrender to it—has been recognized in other times and cultures as a sacred initiation. It takes skilled support, both to be there without getting lost and also to inquire when—and how—to work with this descent.

## One Foot in Front of the Other

### DEE: *"I felt so ashamed"*

*When he left I was so scared. I couldn't eat, couldn't sleep. I lost about twenty pounds. I was rail thin and looked like hell. Friends were scared for me. I got an awful job at an import place ... I felt so ashamed, it was so beneath me, but that's what I had to do to keep moving forward. The owner was kind. I had a little office room to myself, and he allowed me to just do my work.*

*During the first six months I spent a lot of time sitting at the desk, crying while I was working. He would walk in, see my tears, ask me to let him know when I could talk to him, and then leave. I was a trooper. I refused to be a victim. I just kept on going, day after day.*

*It was so good to have that space to feel sad and not to have to feel ashamed about it. He also held the expectation that I would get the job done—maybe because I held that expectation of myself. I earned his respect. It was awful, but I did it. He was impressed. That combination—the space to be sad and work that I was invested in doing well, was a healing combination for me.*

*It's good for me to reflect back on this. It's good to remember that I survived this hellhole, and how I did it, because there are losses in life, and sometimes I find myself fearing potential losses. This reminds me I have a game plan—something I know works—to get up in the morning and put one foot in front of the other and keep on going.*

*There are no quick fixes; you keep going until it stops hurting. I think you stop hurting when you find some meaning in your life. I think wellbeing is a lot about your ability to make sense of your life. With an extreme loss, that's what we struggle with … finding meaning to what's happening.*

*I learned that for me this comes with time, as I keep moving forward, step by step, with as much integrity as I can muster. Slowly, I begin to get moments of clarity where I get a glimpse of meaning, and slowly these glimpses of meaning come more and more frequently. There's more of an ease in my belly, and a sense of being able to breathe. I got through it one breath at a time, one day at a time.*

*I loved the movie "Castaway" with Tom Hanks when he was telling a friend how he got through his ordeal and he said, "When it gets down to it, all we can do is just keep breathing because we never know what the next tide will bring in." For him, the next tide brought in the material to build the raft that allowed him to leave the island.*

*I recognize now that the fear I went through is part of the deal. I just kept putting one foot in front of the other. With time I slowly pulled myself up and moved up in the business. My boss and I became friends and I put together many systems for him before I finally moved on to something more of my liking.*

This is a woman intent on doing what needs to be done on the physical plane, but not at the expense of her broken heart. She uses the otherwise debilitating emotions as skillful means for healing. Neither the heartbreak nor the healing is to the exclusion of the other. She now recognizes that the fear she went through is a part of the deal. She recognizes that by acknowledging and accepting all that has been uninvited and unwanted, she finds the pathway home.

This pathway will never be an easy one to follow. However, for some women it will be more difficult than for others.

## The Damage is Real

**LINDA:**

*I was medically diagnosed with severe, complex post-traumatic stress disorder. My hair fell out, and I stopped getting periods (never the option of having another child). I didn't even remember how to cook, or that I used to love to cook. That is just how my body reacted. And it still reacts—a decade later. I continue to get help, but I also continue to get sicker. Last year I was diagnosed with an immunodeficiency (CVID), which is probably just from pushing myself to carry on while in shock for years. I still have to work with myself, just as if I were a war veteran.*

*Middle-schoolers have broken hearts. Women who devoted their lives to men and bearing and raising children, creating a home and family, and then being blind-sided by the person closest to them in the most intimate way possible, don't have broken hearts. They have a lifetime of trauma recovery to face.*

In the opening chapter I asked the question, How does a woman heal a broken heart? Linda expresses so well the fact that the term "healing a broken heart" is a gross underestimation of the work that is to be done to fully remove all traces of trauma from a woman's body and psyche.

Linda's comments do not appear in those early chapters because of my concern that a woman who is in the early throes of hearing of her partner's infidelity, would likely be harmed rather than encouraged or supported by this. However, it is my belief that many women reading this who have made it through that early period of discovery, will resonate strongly with the substance of what Linda is saying.

Linda's story is not as unusual as might be thought. Often the damage will not show up for many years, and the correlation between the impact of the trauma on the physical body and the current physical ailment, will not be recognized. The toll of stress on the body is huge. It is inevitably greater when the heartbreak, the trauma, is suppressed rather than directly addressed. That said, no woman should be judged—or judge herself—for how "quickly" or how "well" she appears to resolve the trauma. No one can know how deeply infidelity impacts any particular woman, nor the path she will need to take in order to heal.

## A Treasure Chest of Processes and Practices

I believe every woman should have her very own treasure chest of practices that she can draw on in time of need. She will find that different times call for different practices. Below is one such practice that I found really helpful. It is called the Mirror Process, adapted from an exercise by Lisa Nicholls.

### GAIL:

*There were many, many times when I felt so discouraged, so defeated, so full of shame, that I viscerally recoiled from the thought of standing before the mirror. Every time I summoned the courage and will to do just that, I walked away from that mirror only minutes later, with humility, gratitude, and newfound strength to step into another day.*

Here is the process:

*1. (Your name), I am proud that you ...*

Stand about eighteen inches away from a mirror, and look at yourself in the reflection. When you are ready, name seven things that you're proud of yourself for. Each day you may repeat something of the day before, but say seven different things each day. And begin each with stating your name, as in ...

*"Gail, I'm proud of you for mustering the strength to do this process. (Already, my tears are coming). Gail, I'm proud of you for doing your best to be with all this grief and fear. Gail, I'm proud of you for taking actions to move forward. Gail, I'm proud of you for staying with this even through your fears and sobbing and resistance. Gail, I'm proud of you for remembering to breathe ..."*

Remember to maintain eye contact with your reflection throughout this process.

*2. (Your name), I forgive you for …*

Name seven things you forgive yourself for, from yesterday, today, last week, twenty years ago. Begin each with stating your name.

> *This one shocked me, hit me right in the gut. Tears began pouring down my face before I even began naming them. I wanted to quit at this point, turn and walk away from the mirror. I kept going …*
>
> *"Gail, I forgive you for fucking up your marriage. Gail, I forgive you for letting your daughters down. Gail, I forgive you for not keeping the family together. Gail, I forgive you for not being stronger. Gail, I forgive you for feeling like a victim."*
>
> *Until I did this process, I had no—no, no, no—idea of the depth of shame and grief I felt for letting my daughters down, and how much I blamed myself for "fucking up" the marriage.*

*3. (Your name), I commit to you that …*

Name seven things you will commit to doing, today.

> *At this point, the tears will still be coming, but no longer in racking sobs, as this final step in the process moves me into a place of deep self-acceptance.*
>
> *"Gail, I commit to being kind to you. Gail, I commit to being gentle with you. Gail, I commit to remembering that most days you are doing well. Gail, I commit to loving you just as you are, in the moment, now …"*
>
> *I feel emptied. I still I carry the heaviness, but now, with a level of acceptance and love, I move back into my day.*

This process enables a woman to acknowledge and validate feelings that she may have been unaware of holding, and the relief that comes with naming what has previously been repressed. This step can enable a woman to find the strength to face her predicament. Staying with this simple process can carry her through the guilt she feels to a place of acceptance, self-forgiveness, and self-love.

At first, doing this process can feel very awkward. This may be because a woman has had little or no experience of talking to herself this way. On top of that, it's tremendously difficult for many women to even stand in front of the mirror. However, when a woman can get through that barrier, this is a powerful process for emotional release—and healing.

It can be helpful to remember that her resistance—the part of her saying no to loving herself—is the part that most needs love. Even the deepest, darkest aspects of a woman deserve love.

When you find yourself with a negative thought, simply being aware of it, witnessing it, and shifting the position of the body can alone engender an energetic shift. Take a moment when feeling beaten and discouraged to stand tall and ground yourself ... feel the earth beneath your feet and breathe.

This is a simple and effective process a woman may use to change her mental and emotional state, in a moment. The power of mindfulness cannot be overestimated. By being aware when a disempowering thought or emotion enters the mind and, without judgment, simply shifting the position of the body, breathing, and grounding, a woman can return to a place of calmness and clarity.

### SUZANNE:

*A blessing of the modern world is that there are so many tools to support us in healing. This doesn't mean that the experience of betrayal, and the intensity of the emotional response, will be any less difficult. It's important that a woman learns what kind of person she is, and what can bring her to a place of calm—a place where she can open her heart to herself.*

*An extrovert may need to talk with people; an introvert may try to find it in solitude. Some women have never really thought about this, never developed an awareness of their gifts and shortcomings, of what inner strengths and resources they can draw on when they need.*

*There are so many tools to choose from—cranial sacral treatment, swimming in a warm pool, walking in nature. Playing soothing music really calms the nervous system, as can stroking a cat. Whatever it is, it's about finding your way back to solid ground, back to your own center. It might be focusing on the beat of your heart, putting one hand on your heart and another on your abdomen, it may be toning or chanting.*

We are body, mind, and spirit, and each of these dimensions of our being deserves our loving care and attention. Breathing, toning, bodywork, massage, prayer and interactions with animals—all these practices in themselves can be soothing. They can bring a woman to a place of deep inner calm and stillness. To reach this point is an accomplishment and, often times, enough for now. However, it is also important to recognize that whatever needs to be addressed and proclaimed, it is from this point of stillness in herself that she can access the clarity and compassion to be able to inquire more deeply—or simply to *know*—what is asked of her in any particular moment or situation. It may be to say, *"No, no more,"* to her partner. Or, *"Yes, I love you. Absolutely and unequivocally,"* to herself.

### GAIL:

*I discovered the deep peace, the expansiveness that came with allowing myself to simply be—without thought or judgment— fully present to the anger and the deep, deep sadness that lies beneath it. The grief and anguish that I feel in the presence of the devastation is inflicted and perpetuated with every act of betrayal. When I sit, fully present, holding these feelings in tenderness and compassion, my presence to the depth of these feelings in my body is in itself transformative. The energy moves to become an experience of profound compassion for all human beings. My feelings towards the man who betrayed me become irrelevant, inconsequential—inaccessible, in fact—from this place. Here there is no anger, no need for retribution.*

This is a woman who knows the depth of the journey through infidelity and its potential to ultimately deepen and empower a woman. She knows the value of compassionate witnessing—of it all.

In those moments when a woman is able to accept what has happened— which is very different from condoning what has happened—the ego is no longer deriving energy from it. In her acceptance of what is, all the feelings are simply allowed to arise and be felt through to completion— and with this, all the beliefs and fears and stories she has about them fall away. The internal conflict ends. The simple acceptance of what is ends the mental analysis, ends the resistance, and allows her to access what quantum physics calls coherence. This is that calm, still point where her reality is no longer victimizing her. The low, heavy vibrations of victim have moved to a higher frequency, allowing new ways of being and perceiving to emerge and begin to take up residence in her. The fear that she felt to be so real, has dissipated.

Often, the question, *What do I do with this, now?* may arise as a woman finds herself in the unrelenting grip of a debilitating feeling or emotion. Suppression is probably the most common response—and also the most dangerous. Some form of expression is definitely preferable to suppression—unless, of course, it could harm herself or another. Expression may be anything from screaming to simply crying, from throwing something or beating a pillow, to journaling or sharing her distress with a trusted friend.

The third response is simply remaining present to the feelings in the body, without trying to interpret or analyze who or what they might be about. By simply noticing the energy in her body without attaching anything to it, eventually it transforms into something else that brings deep resolution and healing. What makes this possible is a woman's awareness that she has some control and choice as to when and how she experiences her feelings and emotions. With patience and perseverance, she can to develop an ever-growing level of mastery in this practice.

Remember, the number one universal practice people have turned to throughout time in order to experience love and to heal, is to connect with the greater power in life—whether it be Goddess/Buddha/God/Spirit/ Nature. It is important that a woman be mindful of the ways she connects with the greater power—whether in nature, meditation, or prayer. By being aware of how it feels in her physical and emotional body, and remembering its essence, she can call it up in herself as needed. Over time, as she continues to practice returning to her heart, this will become her natural state—her resting place, home, still point, source of her being.

## CHAPTER 16

## *Reaching Out for Help—The Gift of Empathy*

And now, the importance of reaching out for support, and stories of the strength women found in the company of their women friends.

### MARILYN:

*My women friends were really important to me. Many of them had also suffered from abuse or abandonment. Just to have one woman share her experience and her ability to make it through that experience made a difference. To have several sisters share their experiences, helped me to realize I wasn't the cause of the pain and trauma. It was my husband's decision to betray me. Watching women rise to the occasion and outshine the men in their lives truly was inspirational. The Sisterhood is powerful when it consists of women we can trust.*

*I learned a lot from that experience and, ironically, if anything, now some thirty years later I'm grateful for it. I made it through those horrifically difficult and very sad times. I made it through the hardship and devastation of that period, and I am all the stronger for it today. I also learned that women are a lot stronger than men. They need to remember that.*

It can be helpful to remember, through this hell, that diamonds are formed under heat and pressure.

## Reaching Out for Help

### SUZANNE:

*I'm not usually a person who shuts down and withdraws. I reach out for help. Even when I look like a basket case, I can still reach out. When my ex left me for his affair partner, I immediately sought counseling. I have always been smart enough to get counseling, even when I had to go to free clinics. And I always found people who were compassionate and also deeply nurturing—both men and women. It's so very important to get feedback that you are not a terrible person.*

*We need to understand that betrayal demands care and attention, it's like everything inside us is screaming out for help, and if we don't have the resources within ourselves—and few do—we need to turn to others to learn what to do.*

At times, a woman may find herself in such a state of grief and depression that it is difficult for her to even get out of bed, shower, or feed herself. Reaching out for support—whether from friends, helping professionals, or trusted others—is then, in itself, a truly courageous action. Several women spoke of *SurvivingInfidelity.com*, where they could anonymously connect with others who were struggling to heal from infidelity, as being their lifeline.

Reaching out is crucial. The tendency can be to isolate. And, yes, to believe you are a terrible person. You are a failure, an embarrassment, a wrathful bitch, an incompetent—a disaster, really—as a human being. When others offer empathy and understanding, the brain releases natural opiates, or painkillers. Physical touch is known to release oxytocin and will be soothing to some women, but not to others.

### AMELIA:

*My women friends, they literally kept me alive. Even though they were miles away, they reached out to me through an email or a phone call. I felt the sincerity of their empathy and compassion. They shared their shock at the news of my husband's affair, and their empathy with what I was going through. One woman simply said, "I have no words of wisdom, but if there's anything I can do, I'm here."*

*Emails from others, though I knew them to be well meaning, were so hurtful. Comments like, "Many people are going through turmoil now. It is a call for big changes on the inner, whatever that might look like on the outer," and, "Anything that plays out between a couple is about both people, so there's no blame, only an opportunity to awaken ..."*

*These kinds of comments felt so condescending and patronizing, and left me feeling so alone and not understood.*

It can be difficult to listen to a woman's pain. The natural and well-meaning response is to offer reassurances: *"It happens to everyone these days,"* or *"Time heals all wounds."* This kind of reassurance does not feel like support to the woman in pain.

Support is communicated through empathy and compassion. Support is making the time to be with a woman in her pain, allowing her to share her true feelings. Support is being present to her distress without pretending everything is okay, without expecting her to "be positive" or "cheer up." Support is sharing one's own feelings: *"I'm so sorry,"* or, *"How could the bastard have done this,"* or, *"I don't know what to say, but I'm here for you."*

And here, the value of simply venting to another, in a safe, contained space:

### REBECCA: *"I was so afraid for myself"*

*Close friends and I have long had an agreement that when needed, we could call each other for a "negativity" or "dump" session. This night I felt I was losing my mind. I was so afraid for myself. It was the middle of night when I called Cheryl. She said, "I'm here for you. Tell me what's wrong." For maybe fifteen minutes, I sobbed my way through it: "I'm scared. I can't cope. I really can't do this. I can't ... I am so very scared ... I am so full of shame because ..." And when I paused, she would quietly and simply reflect back to me, in a sentence or two, what she had heard. "You are really scared that ... and is there anything more?"*

*The sobs subsided, slowly but surely. I just felt so empty. She asked, "Is there anything more?" "No. Thanks Cheryl." She reminded me that the feelings always hurt more if you try to push them away. She said something like this, which was lovely: "This is just your time to do this, to feel this feeling, and I'm just going to be with here with you in this shared space. This is what we are going to do together here."*

*She sat there on her end of the phone, and I sat here on my end of the phone, heart pounding more slowly now as we sat together in the silence of this shared space, breathing, for five or ten more minutes. Everything in me and around me felt so still, so calm. It was as if a storm that had been raging in me had passed through me, carrying everything in its wake. Nothing had really changed. I still didn't know how I would cope. I had no idea how I was going to do what I needed to do. She offered no advice, no opinions, no judgments. I said, "Thanks Cheryl, I feel calmer now. I'm going to sleep." And I did.*

It is important that a woman have the space to experience and express the depths of the emotions coursing through her. Premature attempts to "get over it and move on with her life" will only impede the natural passage of the emotions through her body and psyche.

A woman who can be present to the rawness and intensity of these emotions in another can do so because, through her own life experiences, she has met and accepted them within herself. She is aware of the healing and transformative potential inherent in these emotions. This allows her to be present to the entirety of her friend's experience, rather than prematurely encouraging her to forgive, to "just be thankful," and to move on.

## The Many Appeals to "Forgive"

What is underneath the countless appeals to "forgive," to "get over it"? In many cases it is about avoidance and shame—all the gyrations a woman goes through not to be aware of her own feelings and to instead project them onto another person so she doesn't have to feel them herself. More truthfully expressed, a woman would be saying, *"Please forgive him because it makes me uncomfortable that you have not,"* or, *"I don't feel comfortable knowing you're angry,"* or, *"I want you to conform so I'll feel better."* More directly, *"I will do what I can to manipulate you so that I don't have to feel my own shame."*

This discomfort or shame may be something a woman carries from her own past experience of infidelity, or even the unresolved feelings she carries towards a parent who was unfaithful, or the parent who never did forgive her spouse's betrayal. When a woman has not resolved her own past experience of infidelity, she cannot see another woman's betrayal for what it is. She sees it through the screen of her own wounding, and so has her own ideas about what needs to be done, and how.

A woman needs to make self-care a priority. Self-care includes her noticing people around whom she feels shamed or disempowered and, whenever possible, avoiding them. When they can't be avoided, a very helpful practice is to imagine a cocoon or bubble of protective energy surrounding her. By affirming that it is a space only love can enter, she can sense or feel or imagine the protection that space offers her, and she can get in touch with what she needs to to maintain that space. With persistence and practice, it will become second nature to be able to do this, and this field of protective energy will get stronger.

## GAIL:

*I am so grateful to those women who emerged as pillars of strength ... not for me to lean into, though I did that too, but for being there for me to stand with through the trauma of this experience. There was never so much as a shade of judgment or condescension from them, just an absolute acceptance of and empathy with where I was, in the moment. They held the light to me, because they knew that if I could be "over it," I would be. And they know that it's a process that takes its own time.*

# Not "Over It" Yet?

## AMELIA:

*I wanted to yell, "Fuck off!" to those women who judged me for not being over it, or not forgiving him. But the moment that I got those words or vibes from them, I went into shame. The shame depleted me, drained me ... before I could forgive him, I needed to forgive myself for this shame that I felt ... and that these women triggered in me.*

Here is how one woman responded to Amelia's email about the pressure she felt to get over it and move on with her life:

## MARILYN:

*This "over it by now" is an interesting concept. It just happens when it does. You were forced into a sudden and unexpected life-changing situation. It's going to take as long as it takes to recover from that, and each person in her own time. Allow yourself time to grieve. Had Graeme died, no one would say, "It's time you got over it." Graeme isn't dead but your relationship with him is, and that is experienced as a death.*

*You need to go through the stages of grieving ... and they don't come one at a time or first one, then two, then three ... each one comes unexpectedly and you have to face the emotion you're feeling when it comes up. That's the best any of us can do. And, one day, you will realize it is over and you're done. Until then, it's simply a process that needs to be honored.*

*There is no right or wrong here, so don't let anyone make you think there is. You will get yourself back but it takes time to re-collect and heal the threads of yourself that were severed somewhere between you and Graeme, and left dangling. You will wind them in because you are doing it mindfully. Be proud of yourself, dear heart!*

Marilyn is a friend who understands the importance of validating a woman's feelings and emotions, and when appropriate, taking the focus off of *him* and what *he* has done, and putting the focus back on *her*. She understands that this in itself can support a woman in coming into a different relationship both with the situation causing the suffering, and the suffering itself.

Marilyn knows that the practice of mindfulness allows a woman to enter that space where she has the power to witness herself, rather than succumb to the habitual and familiar, and to choose wisely. She trusts in the momentum of the process to, unimpeded, move through to its full completion—in it's own time. In her company, the fear a woman came with dissipates as she feels seen, validated, and safe.

Empathy communicates that incredibly healing message that *"I see you, I love you, and you are not alone."* This is perhaps the greatest gift a woman can give or receive, at this time.

## Retelling the Story

When a woman has experienced a trauma, part of the recovery is telling the story. The tsunami victim will go over and over the story—*"I was just about to call my daughter when the tsunami came …"* A woman's retelling the story is her trying to understand what happened, and how it happened. *"Didn't we see the black clouds? How did it appear so suddenly out of nowhere?"* In the same way, a woman who has been betrayed needs to tell her story. She will ask herself, again and again, *How could he have done this? How, how, how …* until the story, and the questions, no longer trigger a disruptive level of distress.

Traumatic reactions are normal and will diminish in time, but only gradually. First they decline in frequency, then in duration, and finally in intensity.

Until a woman feels heard and validated, it is difficult for her to move on. When she keeps telling the story again and again to anyone who will listen to her, it may be because she hasn't felt heard—heard by the person who betrayed her, or by others who have seen but not validated her distress.

# CHAPTER 17

## *Children of Infidelity—How They Hurt, and How They Heal*

**MARILYN:**

*If two people are in a committed relationship, they owe it to one another to be honest. If they cannot stay committed, they need to extricate themselves from the relationship before pursuing other relations. The consequences of acting otherwise are tremendous—especially when children are involved. When a man is unfaithful to his wife, he is being unfaithful to his children as well. How will the children ever trust again? What kinds of relationships will they have? Will they bring unfaithfulness into their own relationships because that's their experience in their own family and that's what they expect?*

Ana Nogales, Ph.D., author of *Parents Who Cheat: How Children and Adults Are Affected When Their Parents Are Unfaithful*, coined the term "children of infidelity" to identify children of any age whose parent or parents engage in one or more acts of infidelity. As permissive as society has become, most children are badly hurt by a parent's infidelity because, like the betrayed parent, they feel betrayed.

More than 800 grown children whose parents were unfaithful responded to Nogales's online *Parents Who Cheat* survey.

88.4% felt angry toward the cheating parent.

62.5% felt ashamed or embarrassed.

80.2% felt that it influenced their attitudes toward love and relationships.

70.5% said their ability to trust others had been affected.

83% stated that they feel people regularly lie.

86% reported they still believe in monogamy.

By and large, adult children of infidelity know, from experience, the extent to which a family suffers with a parent's betrayal, and so do not want to follow in their unfaithful parent's steps. A 2007 survey found 93% respondents rated faithfulness as the single most important component of a successful marriage.

Nogales's survey confirms that children feel betrayed when a parent betrays a spouse. While the betrayed parent may not expect anything from the cheating spouse, their child is left with hopeful expectations as well as a host of fears. Children often find themselves in a nightmare that offers few viable options. One option is to accept the unacceptable: that they have been betrayed by their parent, and hope that by doing this they will ensure their parent's love and attention. Another option is to express their outrage, and in doing so risk being abandoned by a person whose love they so desperately want and need. Whether six, sixteen, or twenty-six years of age at the time of a parent's infidelity, these children are left with psychological issues that—unresolved—can plague them throughout their life.

## Responses to Parental Infidelity

Regardless of their age, children whose parents have been unfaithful often react with intense feelings of anger, anxiety, guilt, shame, sadness, and confusion. They may act out, regress, or withdraw. They may feel pressured to win back the love of the unfaithful parent or to become the caretaker of the betrayed parent. The bottom line is that when parents are role models of infidelity, their children can't help but react—and they may have a particularly hard time finding their way through the challenging time of dating and marriage.

While every family is different, and each child is unique, Nogales identifies the following core responses experienced by children of all ages—from young children to adults—when they find that one or both of their parents has been unfaithful.

- **Loss of trust.** When a child learns of a parent's infidelity, they usually find it extremely difficult, if not impossible, to trust that someone they love will not lie to them, reject, or abandon them. They very often learn not to put their faith in love, and may also develop the belief that they are not worthy of receiving monogamous love.

- **Shame.** A child may feel as if the cheating parent's sexual transgression is a black mark against them and the rest of the immediate family. If the child has been pressured by the cheating parent to keep the secret of infidelity from the betrayed parent, the child is left with the added and unwarranted burden of guilt.

- **Confusion.** A child often draws the conclusion that marriage is a sham and love an illusion. Additionally, when parents stay married even while one or both continue having an affair, children are profoundly confused about the meaning of both love and marriage.

- **Anger and ambivalence toward the cheating parent.** When infidelity partially defines a parent's character, a child often feels torn between feelings of anger and yearning for their love.

- **Resentment toward the betrayed parent.** Some children resent the betrayed parent for requiring them to be their emotional caretaker, for under-parenting due to preoccupation with the drama of the infidelity, or for not preventing the infidelity in the first place.

- **Acting out.** Rather than confronting sad, angry, or confusing feelings directly, children may exhibit behavioral problems during childhood, sexual acting out during adolescence, and intimacy problems or sexual addiction during adult years. Issues of promiscuity may arise in an attempt to play out what a child perceived from their parents about the casualness of sex and the impermanence of love.

In an attempt to protect children from the realities of infidelity, a parent may fail to offer any explanation, minimize the situation by telling a half-truth, or simply lie—this then becomes a second betrayal. It is best when the parent discusses the infidelity in a way that is both honest and age appropriate.

The younger the children are, the less a parent needs to say about it. If the children have heard or suspect something is wrong, and are asking questions, then it is very important to recognize that a factual—rather than emotional—response is needed. It is worse for children to feel there are secrets being withheld from them, especially when these secrets are affecting them. When they have no idea about what has happened, it may not be necessary to tell them—even if they are adolescents. The caution here is that parents usually greatly underestimate what the child suspects or knows. It is best when parents who are separating agree what they will tell the children and then do this together, perhaps with the support of someone known and trusted by the family. It is easier on the children knowing that their intention is to continue to parent them together.

Nogales reports that when one parent betrays the other, a child's inner world and sense of the world at large are shattered. The personal environment in which a child lives and from which she draws her sense of safety and security—namely her family—is fundamentally changed because the most important people in that environment have become unrecognizable.

When children learn that the most important people in their world are untrustworthy, their ability to trust others can be seriously impaired. They may be overly suspicious, emotionally distant, or refrain from committing to a relationship because they can't trust the other person will act honorably and be there for them. Wanting to avoid being hurt in the same way they witnessed a parent being hurt, they may do whatever it takes to protect themselves from being emotionally vulnerable.

## Learning to Trust Again

Is it possible to relearn how to trust? Nogales believes that trust is a need and a feeling, but also a skill that can be learned. She outlines a process whereby even when a child has been subjected to infidelity, she can learn to trust again:

1) Acknowledge the need to trust. We all need to trust and to feel safe, to develop and express ourselves, and to give and receive love. A young child learns to trust when there is someone she can rely on to provide structure and be there for her unconditionally. Without that sense of security, she is afraid and tentative. An older child and young adult needs to be able to trust in order to develop healthy relationships and the sense of security that allows her to fulfill her goals. Admitting to herself that she needs to trust others in order to be emotionally healthy, paves the way for her being able to do so.

2) Each person goes through the process of developing trust at her own pace. With time, a person can learn to make wise choices about who she trusts, and to what degree. Trustworthiness is not black and white. While it is crucial to have people in our life that we can trust, we hurt ourselves if we allow ourselves to trust everyone unconditionally.

Each of us needs to remember that we always have the option to trust, even when that trust was shattered by a parent. We don't have to trust everyone, but we don't have to mistrust everyone either. A person can decide to be trusting of those who deserve her trust. Being aware of how others demonstrated or failed to demonstrate their ability to make her feel respected, listened to, and safe will help her hone her skill at choosing who to trust.

## Dealing with a Child's Anger and Ambivalence

Nogales offers guidelines for parents dealing with a young child's anger and ambivalence toward an unfaithful parent:

- Be willing to listen to what your child has to say, even if it's expressed with anger and hurt. Anger is a normal human reaction and, expressed appropriately, it is healthy.

- Listen to your child's angry feelings with respect, even if it means putting aside your own emotional distress.

- If you are the betrayed parent and your child expresses understanding or longing for the other parent, allow them to do so without interjecting your own bias.

- Listen to your child's questions and respond with the truth, even when it may not be pleasant. Lying perpetuates the lies of infidelity. Be up front and direct—usually, details are not necessary.

- There is no need to insist the child talk about what has happened, but being a good listener lays the foundation for your child's questions and venting of feelings.

### LINDA:

*What a horror it was for me to feel like I not only had to protect my son from the drama of my husband's betrayal, but from overwhelming him with my own grief and anger. I remember my anger just grew realizing how my relationship with my son had been broken and contaminated by the whole sordid nightmare.*

*I knew I protected him as a mother from the world, but it was a horrible feeling to realize I had to protect him from my own rage and sorrow. The only good news is that I did heal. My partner was deeply remorseful, and we were both committed to doing what we could to save our marriage.*

## Helping Adult Children of Infidelity Deal with Their Anger

It is important that adult children of infidelity feel able to share their thoughts and feelings with another person—be it a parent or trusted other—rather than hold onto any anger they feel towards the unfaithful parent.

Often, expressing anger or hatred leads to deeper feelings of sadness, hurt, and fear. Working to understand the main issues they are facing and the emotional impact of their parent's betrayal is an important part of the healing process.

A Native American story tells of a grandmother talking to her granddaughter. The grandmother said, *"I feel as if I have two wolves fighting in my heart. One wolf is the vengeful, angry, violent one. The other wolf is the loving, compassionate one."* The granddaughter asked her, *"Which wolf will win the fight in your heart?"* The grandmother answered, *"The one I feed."*

## Dealing with a Child's Sympathy for or Resentment Toward the Betrayed Parent

Nogales offers guidance for dealing with a child's sympathy for, or resentment toward, the betrayed parent. In summary:

- It is common for the betrayed spouse and children to stick together in the initial phase of the infidelity crisis. Once that time has passed, children need also to relate to their own support system—friends, and extended family.

- Both parent and child can benefit from counseling during the crisis. It is never the child's responsibility, regardless of age, to take care of their parent emotionally.

- Children of every age need to maintain a positive connection with both parents.

- Never encourage your child to "take sides" or feel animosity toward the cheating parent—even though you may feel it yourself.

- If you need to vent your feelings of anger and hostility toward your unfaithful spouse, do so with a trusted friend or therapist, not in the presence of your children.

**REBECCA:**

*I never thought that I would ever hate, or be disgusted by, the father of my children. But this is where I find myself. I am bewildered as to what to do. I can feel this way—my feelings are justified, but I don't want my children to grow into adulthood and their own relationships with men, hating their father, or knowing I hated him. Or, maybe it's healthy they do. Maybe it's healthy that they know men cannot be trusted. I don't know. I just know how I feel. I hate him.*

One side of a woman may say, *I hate him. I want to poison the children's relationship with him, and for them to refuse to have anything to do with him ever again. I'd love to get even.* The other side may know that the children need a dad, and that she does not want them to live with this bitterness in their hearts. And so she may worry, *Will they be afraid to commit to intimate relationships of their own? Will this turn them against the world? Will they blame themselves for what happened?*

In the face of a woman's hatred for her husband, for her to open her heart and find the courage to make the children's welfare—which includes supporting them in developing a healthy relationship with their father—the priority over her hurt, outrage, and desire for revenge, is no small thing. Questioning whether it's healthier her child grow up not trusting men, reflects both a level of self-absorption and also a truth in that it is appropriate her children learn all people cannot be blindly trusted—this, however, does not mean it serves to hate them.

It is important for a child—and woman—to be aware that because she loves someone, does not necessarily mean that person is worthy of her trust. It is neither safe nor wise to immediately give yourself over to what is in the moment seductive, especially when entering a sexual relationship. Trust is cultivated over time, and through self-inquiry. *Do I feel respected by this person? Are their words and actions congruent?*

## Advice for Older Children and Adult Children of Infidelity

Nogales advises older children and adult children of infidelity who are tempted to hold their betrayed parent responsible for the cheating parent's unfaithfulness, to remember that they don't know the whole story behind their parents' marriage and what may have led to the infidelity. It is also important that they be assured it is not their role to offer their parent ongoing emotional support. They may be sympathetic and comforting, but

244

an appropriate emotional boundary should always exist between parent and child, regardless of the child's age.

## Supporting Children in Facing the Impact of the Infidelity

What can parents do to open lines of communication with their children and help them face the painful truth of how a parent's infidelity is affecting them? Nogales asserts that the unfaithful parent must admit wrongdoing, if only to win back some of the respect from their child. When a parent refuses to offer any genuine apology—for the betrayal, for breaking up the marriage—and to acknowledge his child was profoundly affected by the infidelity, it makes it very difficult for the child to come to any kind of healthy resolution. When wrongdoing is admitted, this may encourage children to open up and talk about their feelings surrounding the infidelity.

> *"Most parents don't understand how severely their children are impacted by their infidelity."*
>
> —Ana Nogales, Ph.D., *Parents Who Cheat: How Children and Adults Are Affected When Their Parents Are Unfaithful*

Children need time alone to process what has happened, but also the opportunity to be together with a parent, even if the infidelity isn't brought up. When children finally do speak out, they need to be free to talk without an adult's commenting or judging what they say. Assure them that their feelings are valid, and that there is no such thing as a right or wrong feeling, and no shame in having emotions. When children bury their feelings, the rage, sadness, and confusion will spill over into other relationships without their being aware of it.

Jennifer Harley Chalmers, Ph.D., author of *Surviving an Affair,* likewise believes that when a cheating parent is able to end the affair and explain to their children how wrong they had been, as difficult and humbling as this may be, they are more likely to be able to alleviate to some extent the lessons they had taught their children.

## Adult Children of Infidelity Forgiving the Unfaithful Parent

It can be easier for children to think of forgiving the unfaithful parent when they understand that forgiveness does not mean ignoring or condoning what the parent did. It means coming to terms with what happened, and allowing themselves to move through the negative emotions that they find themselves in the grip of.

Forgiving is not condoning. Nor is it an agreement to ignore wrongdoing. Forgiving is about accepting human frailty—even that of a parent whom they looked to as their primary role model. Nogales emphasizes that to come to this place of acceptance as an older child requires going through a process of understanding, expressing, and letting go of their resentments. This includes understanding how they and their family were affected by the infidelity, working through and expressing their feelings about it, and finally relinquishing their anger and resentment.

This requires confronting difficult questions such as: *Can I accept that someone I love and trusted has breached my trust? Can I accept my parent failed to live up to his/her professed moral values? Can I accept that one parent deeply hurt the other?*

Counsel with a skilled professional or wise and trusted other can be very important, as can journaling, or some form of expressive arts therapy. To the degree a child of infidelity is able to come to a place of understanding and acceptance, they will be free of the weight and the shadow of all those unresolved feelings that otherwise follow them into their own intimate relationships with others.

## The *Parents Who Cheat* Survey

One of the most striking findings in Nogales's *Parents Who Cheat* survey of more than 800 grown children whose parents were unfaithful, is that while 87% of respondents said they still believed in monogamy, and 96% said they don't believe that cheating is okay even if one's partner doesn't find out, nearly half—44%—had been unfaithful themselves. Most of those who were unfaithful were so during the first stages of their relationship, after which time they realized that infidelity did not resolve their problems, nor did it fulfill their emotional needs.

Nogales is not alone in believing that the intense insecurity in children and adult children that being exposed to parental infidelity provokes, may create the need to resolve unfinished emotional business by engaging in the same pattern of behavior. Many adult children whose parents had been unfaithful repeated the same behavior as a way to act out, understand, and/or overcome what took place between their parents. So, although these particular statistics tend to indicate a contradiction between respondents' attitudes and their behavior, it may be that their unfaithfulness was an attempt to work through their feelings concerning their parent's infidelity.

Janis Abrahms Spring, Ph.D., in *After the Affair: Healing the Pain and Rebuilding Trust When a Partner Has Been Unfaithful,* proposes that adult children of infidelity may have an affair to create a safe distance between themselves and their partner, so as to protect themselves from being violated again.

## The Unacknowledged Legacy of Divorce—And of Infidelity

*The Unexpected Legacy of Divorce* by Wallerstein, et al., brings to light the largely unrecognized and unspoken reality that when children of divorce become adults, no less eager than their peers who grew up in intact families for love, sexual intimacy, and commitment, they are badly frightened that their relationships will fail—just as their parents' did. The strongest consequences of marital disruption do not appear until they confront the challenges of early adulthood. Now while Wallerstein is talking here of divorce, Nogales's study indicates that children of infidelity struggle with psychological problems similar to those of children whose parents have divorced. And of course, many of the parents of these children *will* separate or divorce.

Wallerstein writes that while the myths persist that children are resilient and resourceful—that *"most of the kids in their class are from broken homes, they'll get over it"*—the fact is that they perceive the world as a far less reliable and more dangerous place because the closest relationships in their lives can no longer be expected to hold firm. One might think that the grown children of older couples who experience infidelity or divorce would feel sad, but not devastated. After all, they're adults. But grown children, too, are profoundly distressed and suddenly propelled into examining their own relationships and worrying what and whom they can rely on and for how long.

### KRISTI:

*It's important our children see that while our marriage isn't perfect, that every relationship goes through its up and down periods, we can communicate and work on it together—even that we can get help when we need it.*

Wallerstein found that the contrast between children of divorce and children from even moderately unhappy intact homes as they reached adulthood and went in search of love, sexual intimacy, and commitment was striking. Now while it is true that Wallerstein is talking of children of divorce, not infidelity, the parallels are clear and surely few would argue that the implications similarly hold true for children of infidelity. The children from even moderately unhappy families, as young adults, had an understanding of the demands and sacrifices required in close relationships—and memories of how their parents struggled and overcame differences. Adults from divorced families were at a greater personal disadvantage. Anxiety about relationships was the *"bedrock of their personalities and endured even in happy marriages, as they lived in the shadows of their fears of disaster and sudden loss, of abandonment, betrayal, rejection."* Be they children of infidelity or of divorce, seeing the breakdown of one relationship after another intensifies the fear that their relationships will fall to a similar fate.

In Chapter 2: *The Nature of Infidelity*, we saw that young adults still expect fidelity and loyalty between their parents, and that adult children whose parents cheated still want monogamous relationships themselves. In fact, 93% of them believe marital fidelity is the most important element in a successful marriage. Wallerstein reports that despite their first-hand experience of seeing how marriage can fail, adult children of divorce sincerely want lasting, faithful relationships. They believe divorce in a family with children should be the absolute last resort.

### KRISTI:

*The frontal lobe region of the brain is not fully developed until twenty-five years of age, so much of our behavior before this age is driven by impulse. Children and young adults are constantly observing us, and learn so much from what we say and especially from what we do. Being healthy, positive role models is the best way we can support them in making healthy decisions.*

Again, this is not to say that anyone should remain in an unhappy, unhealthy relationship. Rather, it highlights the importance of a couple realistically looking at what divorce entails for the family, and the importance of exploring every possible avenue—including counseling—before making the decision to separate. And of course, with respect to infidelity, it highlights the importance of being aware of the repercussions on the family—and doing what's needed to protect the marriage.

We have seen, in many of the stories in this book, the struggles children of infidelity experience as adults in forming healthy and intimate relationships. The women here have emerged stronger for their struggles—but not without tremendous courage, pain, perseverance, and a willingness to learn from their own failed relationships. Many have gone on to form healthy relationships. Similarly, as reported in Wallerstein, many children of divorce have emerged eager to rewrite history, not repeat it. The women who have shared their stories of infidelity here would hope too, that their children may grow to rewrite, and not repeat, the past. They have chosen to do their very best to serve as healthy role models for their children.

# CHAPTER 18

## Fidelity—A Lie, a Bear Trap, or Whole-Hearted Commitment?

**LINDA:**

*The word fidelity is a lie, it's a bear trap—you walk up to it and step in believing that it's real and going to happen. Standing in church all dressed up in a white satin dress with the idea that I have some control over my life and how this is going to play out ... it's fantasy land. So we're going to be true to each other?*

*Standing up in front of a whole bunch of people to do this whole marriage vow thing is such a cute, innocent, childlike act—and those who have been there are looking on saying aren't they sweet, aren't they cute, aren't they crazy kids, what the hell do they know, they'll find out.*

*And it's expensive to do this, to go through all these vows. I lost my voice during my vows ... I had to kind of whisper. I threw up for three days afterwards. All these omens ... helloo.*

*I had learned as a child that betrayal of self is the name of the game. I had no clue about what served me and what didn't. There was this whole paradigm of traditions defining my every move. Here is what you do: you go to college, get married, create a home, have a family ... Here is what you do, this is it, it's a prescription. It's a prescription you will accept unless you look closely and ask if this is serving you.*

Fidelity is a bear trap when a woman naïvely, unconsciously takes on the collective assumptions and understanding of what it means. It's a fantasy when entered into in that nebulous, innocent way where there is no substance to it. The word fidelity is a cultural construct; an outgrowth of the patriarchal and religious structures that have dominated our consciousness for millennia. It is each and every one of us who continue to give permission for it to be what it is—and is not.

There is nothing in this prevailing paradigm of traditions that supports a woman questioning, *What is true for me? What do I need and want?* There is nothing that encourages her to examine her beliefs and her choices and determine what is serving her and what is not. So many women live their lives, as Linda has, believing self-betrayal to be *"the name of the game."*

Unlike Linda, most women do not have a clue that they are doing this, that they have a choice—that something else is possible. There is not even a crack to be found within the confines of this paradigm for a woman to question, *Is this what I really want for myself?* While this is changing, slowly, this paradigm dominates the consciousness of the great majority of women today—even in the Western world, and even amongst those who believe themselves to be "liberated."

### DELLA:

*George and I had an open sexual relationship. I didn't allow myself to feel jealous. I acted like I wasn't. Like, well this is what you do in this day of sexual liberation. I thought it was horrible, but I didn't realize I had a choice. I wanted to be cool. Jealous people were backward, unevolved, stuck in their egos. There were only negative descriptions of jealous people. They were bad people and a guy certainly didn't want a jealous girlfriend.*

Fidelity is not a bear trap to the degree that:

- a woman defines what she needs and wants in the relationship, what the parameters of fidelity are for her, and what kind of thoughts and actions overstep the bounds

- both partners articulate what constitutes faithfulness and fidelity, and what does not, so that the boundaries they are each agreeing to are clear

- both partners commit to being respectful of the agreements or vows they have shared, of the entity they form in partnering in this way, and of who they are as both independent and interdependent human beings.

This minimizes the likelihood of assumptions and misunderstandings, and lays the ground for a meaningful commitment—a commitment that is an expression of each partner's love and respect for themself, for the other, and for the entity that is their marriage.

Any guarantees? No. But being aware of what it takes is a great step in the right direction.

A woman's faithfulness and integrity then demands she be:

- true to herself and to the promises she made

- true to the person to whom these promises were made

- true to the energy and intention of the commitment she and her partner entered into, together.

Integrity supports her in doing what is needed to reconcile the struggles that inevitably arise. It supports her in respectfully dissolving the relationship, if this is what is needed. While this will not ensure that there will not be grief in the coming apart, it lays healthy foundations for any new relationship that may come into being; as well as the best possible foundations for the children—who carry the modeling of their parents' relationship into their own future.

This is not to suggest that a woman remain in an unhappy relationship. Rather, integrity with the vows exchanged requires she then:

- engage in a process to identify the source of her unhappiness

- share her concerns with her partner, not from a place of blame or defensiveness, but as a means of respecting the vows they made, and the love that brought them together

- along with her partner, review and renegotiate agreements as needed

- seek counsel at what may be a pivotal point in her life—and in the lives of her children.

Even today most couples vow, *"until death do us part."* These are the vows spoken, in that sacred moment. If it becomes clear that these vows need to be changed, then they can be rewritten. But to simply walk away without rewriting the agreement, and releasing the vows? Little wonder infidelity—and divorce—is so terribly painful.

## For Romantic Love to Turn into Committed Love

Dennis Ortman, Ph.D., *Transcending Post-Infidelity Stress Disorder,* states what is needed for romantic love to turn into committed love:

- an understanding of what commitment means,

- sensitivity to your partner's feelings,

- a generous heart, willing to give to your spouse even when it means doing without yourself,

- the ability to take into consideration the needs of your spouse,

- a willingness to be honest, dependable and trustworthy,

- most of all resilience, acceptance, and forgiveness.

## *"The White Knight story ... is a bunch of crap"*

Sustaining a committed relationship is a day-to-day process that requires a couple find a balance between their needs and desires as individuals, and their responsibilities as adults, committed partners, and often as parents. Careers, schooling, finances, children, teenagers, aging parents, healthcare, can all exert tremendous pressure on the relationship. On top of this, the seduction of the fantasy of the perfect romance that leads to the perfect marriage and forever after happiness holds all but the seasoned and very wise in its grip. Many people experience one disappointment after another—infidelity after infidelity or divorce after divorce—both because they continue to look to another to give them the deep love and acceptance they first need to give themselves, and because nobody will ever live up to their fantasy of "the one."

According to CDC's National Center for Health Statistics, approximately:

- 3,000 couples in the U.S. get divorced each day—well over one million per year;

- 20 to 25% of these individuals are divorcing for the second or third time;

- Second marriages will end 23% sooner than first marriages, and third marriages will end 43% sooner than first marriages;

- 80% of couples who divorce as the result of an affair later regret their decision to divorce;

- Fewer than 10% of all extramarital affair relationships result in a marriage between the two affair partners; and

- If an affair-born relationship does result in a marriage, three out of four of those couples can expect their new marriage to also end in divorce.

## EVA:

*The whole White Knight/Princess Cinderella story is a bunch of crap. It is disrespectful of women and their inner strength and power and equally unfair for men (or any gay partner) to have to bear the burden of being the stronger one who fixes everything while letting the weaker one fall fainting on a couch. The only person who can rescue us, is ourselves.*

As we have seen again and again, the belief that as women, it is through the man that we will somehow find our worth and fulfillment, is huge. The fact is that the more fulfilled a woman is within herself, the more of her true self she can bring to the relationship. To the degree she is aligned with her authentic self, she is able to meet the authentic self of her partner, rather than her projections of who she needs them to be. She no longer has the expectation that the other is responsible for making her whole and happy.

## Best Friends, Lovers, and Soul Mates

Not only are partners today expected to be best friends, advisors, confidants, and lovers—they are to be "soul mates." Unrealistic expectations inevitably lead to dissatisfaction. Yet these expectations plague the unconscious of most individuals: *I shouldn't have to work for love. My partner and I should feel a deep connection at all times. My partner should be able to anticipate my needs. A good marriage is free of conflict. When passion dies, so does the relationship.* Assessing how much unhappiness is due to a person's unrealistic expectations and how much to the partner's inability to satisfy that person's needs, requires a willingness to be ruthlessly honest with one's self.

*"Soul mates are created, not found. True love exists but not for the faint of heart or narcissistically challenged. Success has requirements. So does real love. It requires you to know yourself intimately, all of you—how you've been wounded by life and how to evolve as a person capable of loving another. It requires you to be transparent, authentically asking for what you want and being willing to enthusiastically give back. It requires you to grow up. Groveling when things go wrong is out. Keeping your integrity and standing firm on your commitment is in. It requires you to stand for what you know is possible, despite terrible circumstances, and demonstrate the courage of a warrior, even when you don't feel like it, even when you've lost that loving*

*feeling, even when you aren't getting your needs met on a regular basis."*

—Dr. Jay Kent-Ferraro, Ph.D., *Affair Love vs. Authentic Love*

## Sustaining a Committed Relationship and Love that Lasts

Very little today supports families, commitment, and intimacy. In the words of Dennis Ortman, Ph.D., *"It is a demanding, complicated process to love and be loved."*

Ortman states that to sustain a committed relationship requires:

- maturity and hard work
- being able to stand on one's own and yet be emotionally connected
- endless give and take
- the courage to express honest feelings
- the fortitude to negotiate differences of opinion and desires
- fully accepting oneself and the loved one, including differences in feelings, desires, and opinions
- resolving the inevitable misunderstandings and conflicts that arise.

Furthermore, to risk loving another exposes a person to the possibility of being hurt. Some believe it is simply safer not to care.

Shirley P. Glass, Ph.D., in *Not "Just Friends,"* quotes one man as saying, *"On a good day, when things are going well, I am committed to my wife. On a day when things are just okay, I am committed to my marriage. And on a day when things aren't so great, I satisfy myself by being committed to my commitment."*

Judith Wallerstein and Sandra Blakeslee, *The Good Marriage: How and Why It Lasts,* found that the wellbeing of the couple was regarded as being more important than the separate desires of either partner. Further research indicates that couples who were happily married for fifty years or more had a common vision about how they dreamed their life together would be.

*"(An affair) is a shallow relief that barely scratches the surface of authentic love, a commitment to a life partner who knows and*

*loves you despite disappointments. Real relationships have a way of rubbing our noses in the slime of life. It is within the alchemy of that authenticity that true love can be encountered."*

—Dr. Jay Kent-Ferraro, *Affair Love vs. Authentic Love*

## Love Alone is Not Enough: The Danger Signs

Even people in happy marriages are sometimes tempted to become involved with someone outside of the marriage. While rebuilding a relationship after infidelity is possible, the fallout leaves lasting imprints—on ourselves, our children, and our communities. It is far better to prevent an affair from ever happening.

Glass delineated three signs that can indicate to a person that they have crossed a marital boundary and may be dangerously close to having an affair.

- *Emotional intimacy*—Sharing deep personal thoughts and feelings with a person of the opposite sex. Talking about details of their marriage and any problems in that marriage. Saying things they wouldn't say if their spouse was there.

- *Sexual tension*—Feeling sexually attracted to another person, or imagining being with them in a romantic way.

- *Secrecy*—Leaving out details of their trip or their day because it includes spending time with the person they feel attracted to. Misleading the realities or lying to their spouse about this person.

## Protecting Your Marriage

Remain cognizant of the fact that love alone is not enough to protect a marriage. The assumption that it is, lays open territory for infidelity. Guidelines for protecting your marriage include:

- *Stand true to your commitment and your vow of fidelity.* Choose some way to remember and honor your commitment, each day.

- *Be aware of the danger zones.* The workplace and internet are the primary breeding grounds for infidelity.

  At the workplace, safety requires not spending time alone with a colleague or co-worker you may be attracted to. At work, or while traveling, socialize in groups and be cautious about drinking alcohol or using other mind-altering substances. Don't share the intimate details of your marriage with people at work. If you find yourself even thinking about doing or saying anything you would not do or say if your spouse was with you, you are heading into a danger zone.

Online relationships and emotional affairs that develop via email, chat rooms, or web based forums pose a major threat to marriages. Emotional affairs develop through sharing intimate thoughts or personal information, talking in detail about problems in your marriage, and/or keeping the relationship secret from your spouse. These violate the trust and honor that is a foundation of the marriage.

- *Discuss the boundaries and expectations of your relationship* in terms of fidelity—what is acceptable and what is not with a person of the opposite sex. Develop guidelines for how each of you will behave in different situations—for example not dining alone or consuming alcohol with someone you may be attracted to.

- *Be aware of and honest with yourself* with respect to your vulnerabilities to an affair—for example you may be more vulnerable if you are feeling angry with, resentful of or disconnected from your spouse; if either parent was unfaithful; or if you were abused as a child. Be aware of vulnerable periods such as pregnancy, the birth of a child, your child's teen years, when your children leave home, and mid-life or late-life crises.

- *Emotional transparency,* or in other words communicating your needs and feelings openly and honestly.

- *Choose your friends carefully,* and keep the company of those who respect and support your choice to be monogamous.

- *Review and revise agreements* as needed to meet the current stage of the relationship. Keep this conversation alive on at least an annual basis.

- *Make nurturing your marriage a priority.* This takes time and attention. Don't take your partner and marriage for granted.

Take a few minutes to read over this list again, and consider how well your marriage is protected from infidelity. Where are the strengths, and where are the weaknesses?

## Whole-Hearted Commitment

Considering what it takes to sustain a committed relationship—from giving yourself the deep love and acceptance you crave, to knowing what you want and need, setting personal boundaries, negotiating differences and resolving conflicts, balancing desires as individuals and as a couple, an awareness of your vulnerabilities and the "danger zones," and standing firm in your commitment—one might be tempted to say, *Oh, it's just too hard.*

Very few of us ever learned *any* of these skills at school, or even from our family. Few of us have learned them even as adults.

> *"If you dare ... if you have the willingness, guts, persistence and commitment both to developing yourself and investing in another human being in this thing called a 'Real Relationship,' then, and only then, do you have the right to expect 'true love.'"*

> —Dr. Jay Kent-Ferraro, Ph.D., *Affair Love vs. Authentic Love*

Or, in the words of Gay and Kathlyn Hendricks:

> *"Lasting relationships use whole-hearted commitment as a place to come home to and to steer the relationship. Commitment locates you on your relationship map so you can move from where you are to where you want to be. Recommitting when you mess up is the key, and recommitting to reveal your true self and your true feelings is the crux of it. For example, committing to reveal gains real traction when, in the moment of noticing that you're concealing anger, you take a breath, recommit to revealing, and share the experience of being angry. What doesn't work is concealing, noticing the concealing, blaming yourself for concealing, feeling like a failure, noticing that your partner conceals too and jumping on the blame merry-go-round."*

> —Gay and Kathlyn Hendricks, *Conscious Loving*

Yes, it takes time, but this is time invested in appreciating, supporting and enjoying each other. In the words of Jordan and Margaret Paul, co-authors of *Do I Have to Give Up Me to Be Loved By You?* it requires setting our intention on *"learning and loving"* rather than *"protecting and defending"* ourselves. When protecting and defending we are closed, unavailable, avoiding personal responsibility. In learning mode, we are curious, non-defensive, available, warm—vulnerable and open to exploring why we are feeling and behaving as we are. Suppressing our needs and our feelings and engaging in blame-games and power struggles take a huge toll on our energies. When instead the focus is on loving and learning, and on appreciating and supporting each other, a tremendous amount of energy is generated that serves both the individuals and the marriage.

When we dare to make a whole-hearted commitment to conscious loving, the benefits extend way beyond our marriage. Perhaps most immediate is that it supports our stepping into our own inner authority, authentic presence, and personal power. This strengthens all of our relationships, in every aspect of our life.

When the wellbeing of the relationship is primary, gratification isn't found in the egotistical pleasure of being right or winning the argument, but in alignment with the wellbeing of the relationship. It's about making decisions sourced in your commitment and connection with your partner, rather than from a place of control or coercion. It is then not a question of good behaviour versus narcissism, but recognizing what will ultimately support your wellbeing.

Chapter 8: *Choosing to Stay*, included the stories of couples who resolved to honor their vows and to rebuild a relationship that was richer, deeper, and more mature than before. In the following chapter, you will read stories of couples who chose to come apart—cleanly and caringly.

# CHAPTER 19

## Coming Apart, with Care and Compassion

The seeds for this chapter were planted when a friend commented on knowing a couple who had decided they had gotten what they came together for, and cleanly and caringly negotiated a coming apart. She said, *"I saw that someone had done that, and it could be done."* Her story—included in this chapter—inspired me to offer this possibility here, because I had heard from others that as a culture we *don't* know how to do this. Certainly, both culture and statistics carry weight. However, is it not true that an individual's consciousness and choice carries equal, if not more, weight in determining our options and decisions?

I wish I had more stories of couples who had come apart *"cleanly and caringly."* However, I hope that the few offered here will inspire others to do likewise. While these stories may not be complete or perfect examples of what is possible, they are far healthier than those we usually hear. They carry the potential to open doors—and hearts—to kinder ways of ending a relationship that has run its course.

The first is not an example of a couple mutually deciding to come apart, but is included here because it contains some interesting elements of such a possibility.

### SUZANNE: *"I learned ... how a really fine man can behave"*

*This was a man I felt deeply connected with on both a heart and soul level. We had been married for six years. For me, what happened came out of the blue, because there was no sign that he had lost his connection or commitment to me. I had helped him pack his case—he had even put a photo of me in it—to go to a yoga retreat where he was teaching. He fell in love with a woman he met in a taxi on the way to the retreat.*

*I didn't find out for a week. We had planned on going to Hawaii for my birthday—it was on the first night there that he told me. I went through this whole week in Hawaii with this man who'd fallen in love with another woman. He assured me had not slept with her and he was such an ethical person, I believed him—and I still think he told me the truth. I was in a state of shock the entire time. He was very solicitous, kind, and thoughtful. I went through such horrible and total inner turmoil. I wanted to know about it, I wanted a sense of what he saw in her, who she was ...*

*It had never occurred to me before that he would leave me; we were both such loyal people. I can see he was under enormous strain while we were together. My memories of being sexually abused as a child had surfaced. He had bought a punching bag for me, my rage was so immense, and he supported me through that. I had not been at all well, and my teen daughter of an earlier marriage had been very trying, and he was a very sensitive soul. I could understand why he chose to be in an easier relationship.*

*I was obsessed with knowing more about her. A lot of people tell their partner all about this other person, but John was very careful not to answer my questions about her. He told me repeatedly that it wasn't going to help me to know about her, that I was a wonderful person, and he didn't want to cause me more pain. I know that to hear about her would have been like rubbing salt into the wound. I would have compared her to me and come up lacking, but I was obsessed about her. He listened and listened to my distress and questioning and anger. He kept reminding me how much our relationship had meant to him, and that he hadn't been on the look out for another, and that he was deeply sad because of the pain it caused me. He took full responsibility.*

*Because I was in another overseas and it was in the nineties, before cell phones, I had no one to reach out to. I found some comfort in nature. But it was a nightmare, a nightmare. I tried practicing all I had learned over the years—focusing on my breath, connecting with my heart and staying in my body. It was very difficult to stay in the present. I kept popping into future things. What would become of me; what would I do now; what was wrong with me now; what was wrong with me then? It was very, very hard staying in the present. I was so full of fear and self-pity, of self-judgment. I couldn't stop comparing myself to who she might be. My self-esteem hit rock bottom. It was very difficult. It wasn't until I was back on the mainland that I could start connecting with others and reaching out. I was totally engulfed, drowning in self-pity and sorrow.*

*I had planned to go to a meditation retreat for ten days after we returned from Hawaii. He insisted I go. He felt it would be good for me, and he promised he would not sleep with her while I was away.*

*The meditation teacher quickly learned what was going on with me. He was so good. He insisted that I leave the meditation hall whenever I started to feel grief or rage. That I should go and sit under a tree and just be present to my feelings ... that I should pound the earth and do whatever I needed to do because that was part of my work.*

*This was twenty-three years ago, and yet I still vividly remember the big tree I sat under with my back up against it. It was very, very comforting to be there and to cry and cry and cry and to feel safe. The meditation teacher, though my age, felt like the good father my own father hadn't been. He told me I could talk to him at any time and just knowing that helped.*

*Sitting under that tree, time felt like it was forever. But the bell would ring—time for walking meditation, or time for silent preparation of meal, or time for sitting—it was a highly structured environment and this was very good. I think this can be a really good time for a woman to go to something like this— some kind of workshop or retreat space that connects her with her body and feelings.*

*At this time I felt not so much rage—I had been angry in Hawaii—but mostly incredible sorrow. It also brought up all the other losses in my life. I thought I could never stop crying. Really plunging into that well, it feels bottomless. The feminine side of the psyche, in joy and in sorrow, has no bounds—it's bottomless. It's wonderful when you are happy or in love but when in grief, it's frightening how sad you feel because there's no earth underneath you. This is why being in nature is so helpful, to feel the earth under you—or if in the city, to find a building with a waterfall, or gaze at the clouds.*

*When I returned, John made it clear he was going to move in with her, and he moved out into his VW van in the driveway. He insisted he first paint the house inside to get it ready for a housemate, and that he go to grief therapy for me, with me. He wanted to end this relationship in a conscious way. This is the most honorable thing anyone has ever done for me.*

*We had five sessions with a relationship counselor doing grief work. Even when we weren't in session, he would stay with me when I got really upset. I would scream at him, and he would take it. I think he felt he needed to—it was his to take. He knew he could not take the pain away, but he could be there for it. I learned a really profound lesson from all this, in terms of how a really fine man can behave. Wasn't it amazing?*

*It was another two and a half months before he left, and six or seven months of grieving after that before I started to find my feet again. He couldn't keep from sleeping with her while I was on retreat. But he was truthful about it, and he apologized, and that helped a great deal. Not everyone is up for that.*

*You can tell the way people end the relationship is how they were in the relationship. Some people behave badly, and are immature. Then that's the way they end a relationship. I was lucky to have someone I could go through that trial with, someone who was willing to take responsibility for what he had done and at same time keep his integrity, which in his case was to be with another woman.*

Suzanne's partner accepted responsibility for the energy he felt for the other woman, rather than allowing himself to be swept away by impulsive ways of acting. He recognized that his partner was going to be deeply hurt by his decision to enter a relationship with this other person. His willingness and initiative to enter counseling, to be fully present to the depth and breadth of Suzanne's anger and anguish at his decision to end the relationship, was not only an acceptance of responsibility but also a sincere expression of his caring.

In these ways he showed respect and honored the relationship they had shared over the years. This is true to the degree that Suzanne can say that she is thankful for the gift of learning *"how a really fine man can behave."* This, even after he slept with his lover. For Suzanne, his acknowledgement and apology was sufficient, and presumably in the counseling they did together this was in some way addressed. One could otherwise question to what degree, in accepting his apology with such gratitude, she was "taking crumbs."

That said, and without in any way diminishing Suzanne's experience of his doing *"the most honorable thing anyone has ever done,"* let us, for our own inquiry, pull this apart a little further. As I said, this isn't a perfect example of a coming apart, but illustrates some valuable points.

The fact is her partner made a unilateral decision to end the relationship. He closed the door to any form of counseling that would have determined whether or not there was anything to be retrieved from their relationship. At this point, there was likely little to be gained from demanding or urging him to keep that door open. Suzanne, in retrospect, saw that the strains on their marriage had likely become too much to him. Emotionally, he was already out the door.

Yes, Suzanne's partner was solicitous even to the point of supporting her through her anger and grief. Yes, this is huge. But it is far better when a person has the integrity and maturity to honor their commitment, even when they don't feel like it. To do this requires directly addressing the disillusionments and dilemmas that arise in any committed relationship, reviewing and revising expectations to meet what's currently needed, and supporting each other's highest potential and happiness.

Suzanne's partner did not step up to meet her as his wife and as someone worthy of such a mutual enquiry. This would have required exploring all possible options together, and only then, if no resolution is forthcoming, respectfully dissolving the relationship. To use an affair as the reason to exit, falls far short of the mark. That said, his willingness to honor the relationship to the degree he did, offered Suzanne a new and hopeful window into what could be expected of a man.

On another note: At the retreat, her meditation teacher was unusual in his honoring of the emotions and the feminine. By telling Suzanne to go out by the trees and allow the grief to move through her, rather than sit in meditation and observe the breath, he supported her in being present and surrendering to the impulses of her physical and emotional body. This is an element of honoring the feminine principle that is denied in so many patriarchal religions. This denial is so much a part of the air we breathe that even today, many women who have developed a good deal of self-awareness do not recognize that they are viewing the world and communicating with words and a language that has been passed to them through a male system.

The combination of nature and a structured and supportive healing environment, where she could deeply engage with her feelings while knowing that she was being cared for in body, mind, and spirit, offered Suzanne a wonderful space for setting out on that journey home to herself. Another woman may need more contact with known others, and familiar surroundings. Whatever it is, it is vital she do what she can to get these needs met to the degree possible.

## SONIA: *"I was proud of us"*

*My partner and I had talked at length about how to make it work between the two of us. He was aware of his constant criticism and general negativity, but felt powerless to change it. I felt drained by it. I felt increasingly drawn to spending more time with a guy I met at church choir, and it came to the point where I knew that I wanted out of the relationship with Jim. I told him I wanted to explore being in an intimate relationship this other man whom I had been seeing each weekend at choir.*

*Things had been getting increasingly strained between Jim and I. I told him I wanted out because I felt so inadequate and could see no way I could fill his neediness. I felt awful. I would have hated to be on the receiving end of being "left for someone else." Rejection was the last thing Jim needed, and I didn't want to publicly embarrass him, but I knew it was time. I told him I needed to be in a relationship where I could feel good about myself, and I couldn't do that as long as I felt I was continually failing in meeting his needs. I said I was leaving. He knew that I had been attracted to this other man, but I don't think he expected this.*

*We agreed to mark the end of our relationship with a ceremony to make it easier to release each other. I prepared some questions for us to consider, and we agreed to share our responses in the ceremony. We made a point of taking personal responsibility in our language so there was no blame. For example, rather than saying, "I couldn't take your constant criticism, unreasonable demands, and general negativity any longer," I would have said, "I learned that I have trouble staying true to myself when I'm in a challenging environment. I observed that my self-esteem was going downhill and I wanted to take measures to raise it up higher again. I was starting to develop the destructive belief that, 'I can't do anything right,' so I'm leaving the relationship to create an environment in which I like myself more and don't feel like a failure."*

*At the time of the ceremony, we sat in front of the fireplace and lit a candle. We began by sharing appreciations we had of each other. Then we each spoke of what we had learned, that we were taking with us. We shared the benefits we had enjoyed by being with the other. We shared life lessons we had learned from the other. For me, it was about telling the truth even if it's difficult. We then shared a wish we had for the other.*

*We also shared gifts. We had previously blended elements of rings we already owned to create two new rings. He filed off the portion from his gold ring that had come from mine, letting the gold dust fall on some lavender paper. I still have the packet of gold dust. I just looked at it and it says: "Sonia, this gold from your ring to mine I now return. From a round ball to powdery dust that can fly through the air coalescing again where it will. Love, Jim."*

*Finally, we shared practical requests. Here we discussed how to "split the sheets," how we would act in public together, and what we would tell other people since we lived in the same town and both worked in the same office.*

*How did I feel about doing this? I felt great satisfaction. I was proud of us, our maturity. I believe my partner was pleased too. We went on to work together very amicably for many years.*

*Many years later, I apologized for being so abrupt in my communication about my decision to leave. He told me that I had nothing to apologize for, and how much he appreciated the way I left. He said that it was the cleanest break he'd ever known of. He said that his agonizing and crying over my ending the relationship had little to do with my leaving and more to do with his own chronic depression—something he had struggled on and off with for years—and unhappiness. My leaving still caused pain, but he was clear that he understood it was not my intention to hurt him. He even said it was a model of how to do a healthy breakup and he really admired me.*

*I was shocked, though very pleased, at his perception. I assume it was because of the clear communication and honesty in the moment about what was happening. Though there had been a long-standing attraction between myself and this other man, there was no secret affair, or long-term deception.*

*Interestingly enough, when another partner and I later separated, I again suggested—well, insisted—that we do a closure ceremony. In the ceremony we burned photos of ourselves together, ticket stubs, small goofy gifts—all the memorabilia from our time together. (I kept a beautiful coat he gave me and one piece of jewelry that I really liked. I still have both of them today.) I felt terrific, liberated, proud. A week or so later, however, he told me he had hated every minute of it, wished he'd never agreed to it, and was really pissed about not having any photos left. I was really surprised. A factor in his upset may have been that he was hoping the relationship wasn't over—and the ceremony forced him to face that it was. I think part of my feeling good about it was that I knew I didn't want to get back together and the ceremony helped me set a completion point. When he told me of his anger about it, I felt sorry that I'd overpowered him in some way.*

*Given this experience, it is important to make sure both people want to mark the ending. In the event that one does not, the other could do a closure ceremony alone or with friends.*

Sonia had come to a place where she recognized that enough was enough. She and her partner had talked at length about how to make it work, to no avail. Aware that she was increasingly attracted to another man, she followed through to bring the best possible completion to her current relationship before entering a sexual relationship with this other man. Even while her empathy enabled her to feel awful about what this would mean for her partner, she was clear she needed to be true to herself—and that this included a caring and respectful coming apart.

Ritual is a time-honored means of completing cycles. It is a means of naming and honoring what has been and is no longer; what is called for in the present moment; and with clear conscience declaring the intention to move forward.

The seating before the fireplace and the lighting of the candle are time-honored practices for creating a shared sacred space of integrity and goodwill. Sharing appreciations, naming the lessons learned, and offering their wishes for the other are all avenues through which each partner can feel heard and seen.

Sonia designed this ceremony all the way through to the very practical decisions on how to divide up the material assets so each could walk away with clarity and self-respect. They had not only done their very best to bring this relationship to completion, but also now had an understanding of how to proceed from there—for example, making an agreement about what to tell other people.

In many ways, this offers one model of how to come apart cleanly and caringly—although what needs to be recognized here is the maturity and communication skills of this couple. It can be very easy—and unconscious—for a sharing such as this to be colored with subtle words and residues of blame, resentment, projection and condescending platitudes. When each person is able to bring deep heart, and clear intention to such a ceremony, this can bring the best possible completion to the cycle of their time as a couple.

The ability to create and to sit in this space together, to agree to *"taking personal responsibility in our language so there was no blame,"* is no small thing. When either partner is unsure of their ability to hold this space, if they recognize that there is such a depth of emotional chaos washing through them that might interfere with their ability to do this, it will be important to seek counsel on how to come to a place of clarity and acceptance of what is to be, before entering a ceremony. It can be helpful to have a skilled third person facilitate such a ceremony.

A person who lacks the courage, compassion, and integrity to see a relationship through to a caring and clean resolution, will find the easiest way out of a relationship is to "fall in love" with someone else. We can see in the stories above, and those that follow, what it can look like to choose otherwise.

### SONIA: *"Together, we decided to end this"*

*I knew of a couple who had decided that they had gotten what they came together for, and cleanly and caringly negotiated a coming apart. I saw that someone had done that, and it could be done. They still liked each other as people—and that remains true to this day. In their coming apart, there was a real emphasis on mutuality—so there was no blaming or shaming on either side. They came to a place where they could truly say, "Together, we decided to end this."*

*There will always be someone who initiates the closure, but where there is a skillful and compassionate sharing as to how to do this, and a sincere respect for each other, the communication can bring them to see that splitting is supportive for both partners. This means that no one has to be the persecutor and no one the victim. If either or both then later partner with someone else, it opens the door to an easier integration into each other's families—which is especially important when children are involved. Of course it's much, much harder to do any of this after there has been a breach of trust.*

*I learned from this couple that when you can be so self-aware and honest with yourself that you know when a relationship is over, and when you can communicate to your partner that it's over before entering into another relationship, then you don't need to enter an affair in order to challenge or end a relationship. When you cleanly end one relationship before entering another, you start the new relationship cleanly. You don't have to find rationalizations to justify in your mind having this affair, nor to convince people you just had to do what you did. You don't need to build a case to prove to yourself or others that you were right in doing what you did, you don't have to start thinking about how you deserve better, you don't have to make the other person out to be a horrible person or not good enough for you.*

*As I understand it, Buddhists see the purpose of life as being to end suffering, and so the Buddhist precepts have to do with not intentionally harming another. Some of the precepts have to do with avoiding misbehavior in sexual relationships—the key here being to not hurt another. Betrayal will inevitably harm another. There is an awareness that if you hurt someone else, you are hurting yourself. There is no guarantee that cleanly ending one relationship before entering another will prevent suffering, because the other person will almost surely be hurt—but at least avoiding an affair can minimize the hurt.*

Sonia had seen a relationship could be ended mutually, with care and respect. She had allowed this to make an impression on her, so that she carried the knowing that she, too, could do this. This requires a great deal of maturity. It requires a woman know what is true for her, know when *enough is enough*, know how to make and to renegotiate agreements—or at the very least, know that she needs to seek counsel with another, so as to come to a place of clarity with respect to what is needed.

The assets this accords the woman herself, her partner, and their children—and the seeds they sow for others to also know that, if need be, they too can cleanly and caringly negotiate a coming apart—are countless. Care, compassion, and respect are human qualities that a woman has a right and a responsibility to expect and request, both of others and of herself.

While Sonia says that *"this means that no one has to be the persecutor and no one the victim,"* the truth is that no one ever *has* to be the persecutor, nor the victim. However, the programming to fall into these roles is so strong in our culture that the tendency to do so in the ravage of the aftermath of infidelity is almost overwhelming. Even to be aware that one is caught in the drama of victim or persecutor, and that other choices are possible, is in itself huge.

As Sonia states, the process is so, so much easier and more supportive of both people when a person chooses to cleanly end a relationship. There is no need for the unfaithful partner to find rationalizations to justify having had an affair, nor to convince people he just "had to do" what he did.

These patterns of rationalization and justification are endemic to the roles of victim and persecutor, and sidestepped when the intention that holds the coming apart is clean.

Buddhist precepts offer general guiding principles, while in no way taking away a person's responsibility to make appropriate choices. It is never a matter of blindly applying a rule. Buddhism does have a strong sexual ethic, but not a repressive one. The main point of this ethic is the importance of non-harming in any area of life where one can do damage by acting violently, manipulatively, or deceitfully. Sexual misconduct leads to suffering. In his article *Buddhist Sexual Ethics*, Winton Higgins defines responsible sexual conduct as conduct based on loving kindness, generosity, honesty, and mental and emotional clarity.

When a person has an understanding of the concept held by many spiritual teachings that *"what goes around comes around,"* and when people recognize that ultimately they hurt not only their partner but also themselves, it minimizes actions of disrespect or revenge. While these perspectives may be very difficult to put into practice after infidelity, they are the foundations of what is needed to bridge the chasm that emerges between a couple, or at the very least to bring solace to the devastation that inevitably follows on the heels of any betrayal.

It takes tremendous courage and determination to face all those aspects of the self that have allowed one to willfully hurt another—most especially someone they have professed to love. In doing so, a person may discover they not only come to a place of deep compassion for their partner, but also for themself. They are carried into the heart of our shared humanity.

# CHAPTER 20

## *It All Starts Right Now*

*"There is nothing easy about becoming conscious. My own life was much easier before I knew about the deeper meaning of choice, the power of choice that accompanies taking responsibility … Once you know better, however, you can't get away with kidding yourself for long."*

—Caroline Myss, *The Anatomy of Spirit*

## The Power of Choice

### GAIL:

*He told me that he "could not control the timing of his heart." And yes, the big buzz is to "follow our bliss," but is this to be done at the expense of kindness, compassion and integrity in our relationships with others?*

*A friend reminded me of a popular quote from the Abraham teachings: "You can't go wrong if you follow your aliveness." Abraham responded to a question about how to reconcile binge eating and his teaching, "Nothing is more important than that I feel good." Someone was asking, "If I did what 'feels good,' I would eat a bag of Oreo cookies three times a day. Is that what it means to 'follow your bliss'?" Abraham clarified that "what feels good" refers to actions taken when one is aligned with Source. There is more to consider than a temporary energy spike like a drug fix or an act of infidelity. The overall concept of feeling good includes an appreciation of our interdependence, and integrity within the larger circle of life.*

Gail's partner justified his infidelity on the grounds that he was *"following his heart."* In Chapter 12: *Bad Girls—Looking for Love In All the Wrong Places*, Hannah spoke of her *"deep, primal longing for real intimacy,"* and how she felt the absence of this in her marriage is what gave her permission to sexually partner with another man.

### SHIRLEY:

*I would see friends cheating, sleeping with others' spouses, see the pain and drama. What occurred to me was that if you left one person because you found someone better for the moment, why wouldn't you keep on with that pattern and thus never really solve the problems at hand? I saw several relationships break up, the unfaithful partner get together with the lover, and then they would break up. It made no sense to me that cheating was a way to solve any problems in a relationship. If someone cheated once, why would they stop?*

When a relationship is not working, the solution is never to take the problem outside of the relationship. Any kind of clean resolution or healing needs to be addressed within the relationship, and perhaps with the help and support of a therapist—not in a sexual relationship with someone else.

The more we appreciate and understand the very substance of our interdependence within the larger circle of life, the more accountable we become for acting and speaking with kindness, respect and integrity—and the more difficult it becomes not to relate to others in these ways. Surely respect, empathy, and compassion are not only fundamental principles that make a society work; they are also the inevitable expression of an authentic awareness of our interdependence.

### GRACE:

*Compassion for a significant other in distress, especially when due to our own selfish actions, is a mark of our humanity. Surely indifference to or absence of presence to another's pain, especially someone close to us, indicates false growth—no matter how happy one purports to be! Indifference is a product of what you termed "numbed instincts."*

To the degree that we truly comprehend our interdependence, we naturally and spontaneously extend respect and loving kindness to others while remaining true to ourselves. If we feel magnetized to an out-of-bounds or illicit other, we do not act impulsively on that urge.

> *"Concern and regard for others, and human affection, are extremely important factors for our happiness … One's individual behavior can contribute to the making of a happier family and community."*
>
> —The Dalai Lama quoted in *Right Here With You: Bringing Mindful Awareness into Our Relationships,* edited by Andrea Miller

Meanwhile, the unfaithful partner may claim, *"I cannot plan or time any matters of my heart."* Firstly, is this truly a matter of heart? In true heart, would a person willfully act in a way that would hurt or harm another? Secondly, as mature adults, are we not called to consider the repercussions of our actions on others? Yes, the power of that surge of sexual energy cannot be underestimated—but knowing that every feeling, every impulse, does not need to be acted on … at what cost does a person follow that desire? At what cost to one's own sense of self-worth and integrity, and at what cost to others?

### HANNAH:

*Our society promotes these illicit encounters … the clandestine, the exciting, the secretive … the soap operas, the movies. Our society promotes and condones and wants to have these illicit encounters happen. Put all that together—the opportunities, the primal longing, the media and social condoning—and we have a majorly seductive force.*

The media and social condoning of illicit relationships is a phenomenal factor in perpetuating the epidemic of infidelity, but being more aware of the damage infidelity inflicts empowers us to make more responsible, informed and compassionate choices.

### KRISTI:

*People need to realize the damage done by the choices we make … by our taking the quick fix solution to buoy up the ego or mask the pain. Infidelity is never the answer. It will mask the pain only momentarily, and leave you with a host of side effects. The damage is real and it takes its toll on us. Until we teach that to our kids instead of making extramarital relationships look pretty and sexy like in the movies, we're in trouble. We need more movies that reveal the aftermath ...*

*In a culture driven by quick fix instant gratifications, it's so easy to think the grass is greener over there. It's so easy to be attracted to someone else; to be seduced by someone else's coming on to us. We can all have that experience at any time, because it's a chemical reaction and it changes our perspective so quickly—but it is so wrong to use that to act in a way that will bring long-term damage to others. We need to learn to go within, to a place where we can provide ourselves with those things we are looking to the other for: our sense of ego, of self-worth, of self-esteem.*

## Aware and Awake

Once we recognize not only the negligent cultural endorsement of infidelity, but also the seductive power of that deep, primal longing and the consequences and reverberations of acting impulsively on this longing with anyone in a committed relationship, what is a woman's responsibility to herself, her children, her community, and the Sisterhood?

At what cost do we trivialize, dismiss, or deny the repercussions of the choice to betray another woman, whether through sexually seducing or engaging with another woman's partner, or through colluding—verbally or in our silence—with any act of betrayal?

Illicit sexual encounters are perpetuated by our not wanting to get involved, wanting to remain "neutral," and choosing to be silent. Every act of betrayal between women engenders a deep wounding that continues to reverberate within and through the Sisterhood. No matter how subtle the violation may be, choosing to remain silent perpetuates, normalizes, and legitimizes the infidelity—and the anguish, trauma and mistrust that are the fallout of infidelity.

> *"We come to realize we are responsible for everything we do, say or think, responsible in fact for ourselves, everyone and everything else, and the entire universe."*
>
> —Sogyal Rinpoche, *The Tibetan Book of Living and Dying*

While it may appear that one woman breaking the silence, one woman choosing to no longer remain neutral, one woman standing up to support another, one woman trusting that another will not betray her will not change anything in the collective, is this really so? A woman's witnessed *or* unseen acts of courage will deeply affect and alter something, not only in herself but in her children and in the lives of those around her. Even those actions that are not witnessed? Yes, because as a result of those actions a woman will experience herself differently, hold herself differently—she will *be* different. These perhaps subtle but significant changes inevitably ripple out, touching and inspiring courage in others, and ultimately impact the greater collective.

Women who are socially, culturally, or soulfully conscious may find they are called to deal with a collective rage at the injustice that seeps up through them. It is not healthy for these women to suppress, rationalize, or spiritualize away their anger. It is natural to have strong reactions to disrespect, threat, and injury. It is important to recognize these reactions as a messenger, a teacher, and to inquire deeply into the source of these reactions and what is being asked of them. It is healthy to demand accountability and change in whatever form emerges—initiating dialogue, confronting the infidel, writing a song or a book.

Today, quantum science tells us what the ancients and mystics and indigenous cultures—and every woman in the depths of her being—have always known. We are intricately connected, and every shift in consciousness, however small, reverberates throughout this larger web of life. At some point, our seemingly insignificant choices not to perpetuate infidelity reach a momentum where their impact causes the consciousness of the whole collective to jump exponentially to a wholly different level.

That said, as we have seen, a woman's potential to bring about change is most effective when her focus is not on changing her partner, not on what she believes is to be changed "out there," but on what she is being asked to change within herself—in her own relationship with herself. It is these changes within the very substance of her being that will set in motion the reverberations that ultimately bring about those changes she longs to see in the world.

## How Does a Woman Remain Aware and Awake?

### REBECCA:

*To hold that place of awareness and strength in me can be so challenging ... when I talked with other women and heard in their voices the strength they have come to through life, through betrayals ... it really helped build that place of strength in me. My conversations with women about these issues is what keeps me awake.*

**MAGGIE:**

*When a woman witnesses and acknowledges me for having been especially discerning, or sticking to my guns about something, or in someway empowering myself ... that in turn strengthens that place in me—and in her, too. So each other's good company is so very important, especially through those dark nights of the soul—and betrayal is that, if anything.*

**SUZANNE:**

*In a society that is constantly bombarding us with messages that we don't need to experience discomfort; that there is a drug for this and a pill for that; that betrayal is a spectator sport and infidelity is "the name of the game," we are set up to be numb to the betrayals around us and to be overwhelmed when betrayed ... What we don't want is betrayal and then, on top of that, the trauma that was never dealt with. You can see it as you walk through the street: people who have never recovered. You can see it on their face, in their posturing. It needn't be that way. We really are our brothers' and sisters' keepers ... we really are obliged to put out our hand to someone who is in that state of shock or trauma because it could be us, just as easily.*

## A Higher Ground?

Abraham Maslow, one of the fathers of modern psychology, is known even today for his hierarchy of needs, in which he identified self-actualization as the highest human experience. In his later years he revised this, recognizing not self-actualization but self-transcendence, or living for a purpose higher than self, as the highest human experience.

**MAGGIE:**

*My intuition is that when fidelity is taken care of on an individual level, then the ways we hurt and abuse and betray each other on the collective level will start to untangle. Some of us are starting to recognize that our experience of the world starts right here, inside ourselves. With that awakening, the covenant to self starts to dawn.*

*If we take the book or arc of civilization and look at the way we betray each other—our children, poor people, homeless people, other nations, the indigenous people and all those other people we are busy betraying—it all comes down to the way we have ultimately lost our sense of self or have no relationship with self.*

It is true that a growing number of people are espousing an awareness of the importance of the covenant to self, and that our connections with others are key to our personal and planetary wellbeing. However, the naked truth of our integrity with this awareness is revealed in our day-to-day actions, not in our words or our rhetoric. What matters is not how many global causes a person supports, nor how many books they have written on global issues, nor how many followers a person has in their ashram or on Facebook. It is in our actions—how we relate to and care for those in our home and everyday lives—that the rubber meets the road. It is in the immediacy of our personal lives that our proclamations for a better world acquire real life meaning.

Can it be that through this unrelenting epidemic of infidelity we are being invited to choose a "higher ground"? Invited to awaken to both our own numbed instincts and the numbed instincts of the collective toward what is surely a massive breach of trust, a glaring absence of care and respect? Are we being asked to hold ourselves, and each other, accountable for our words and actions?

Can it be that this "higher ground" is not simply a moral stand but an imminently practical one, when we consider the repercussions on not only the individuals directly involved, but also our families, and our communities? Can this higher ground be sourced or cultivated in a deep appreciation—at a cognitive if not embodied level—of our profound connection to each other in the web of life? This entreaty to a higher ground can be found in an abundance of age old and age new teachings, expressed in the Buddhist precept, *"Do nothing to bring undue suffering on another;"* the Pagan ethic, *"Do what you will but harm none;"* the Christian commandment, *"Do unto your neighbor as you would have your neighbor do unto you;"* and the new physics research that everything is connected to everything else, everywhere.

> *"Buddhism teaches that a craving for things outside ourselves causes an unhappy and pointless search for security. It teaches me to stop following every impulse. Whether you call it Buddhism or another religion, self-discipline, that's important ... self-discipline with awareness of consequences."*
>
> —The Dalai Lama, commenting on Tiger Woods' *Infidelity: Is It Always Wrong?* Published: The Washington Independent, Feb 22, 2010

Many of us are immersed in a contemporary spiritual subculture that sees the reason for working on spiritual growth as being so that we can live wealthier, happier, and more fulfilled lives as individuals. "Enlightened teachers" of this subculture of spiritual materialism have mushroomed over the past decade, and those enlightened teachers who teach, as did Jesus Christ and Buddha, that genuine evolution moves us beyond ego, are not easy to find.

Meanwhile, quantum physics verifies that in both tangible and mysterious ways, we are participating in something far greater than our individual and possibly even our collective body. Our lives are not simply our own to do with as we please—our every choice either contributes to or hinders the evolution of the whole. Humanity's evolution out of egoic self-interest requires our willingness to rise above a purely self-referential viewpoint and to act in alignment with the greatest evolutionary good, rather than securing our own happiness.

On some level, from the perspective of the larger context in which infidelity is occurring, it can be said that all that appears to be so terrible is because it *needs* to be so terrible. This is what is needed to wake us up to proclaim *Enough. No more.* Just as we look at children on the battlefield, children at the point of fire, children carrying weapons of war … slowly, slowly something in us begins to change. Eventually, when we have seen enough of it, we will recognize the deeper meaning of choice that accompanies taking responsibility. From that point onwards, whenever we find ourselves faced with such a decision—whether to perpetuate the horror of war, or trauma of infidelity, or any such violation of another human being—we will choose differently.

Author and teacher Thich Nhat Hanh speaks of *"Peace in yourself, peace in the world."* He reminds us that whenever we aren't kind or compassionate to another person, as will happen because we're human, the beautiful thing about this is that we can always begin again.

## MOVING FORWARD

Thank you for joining me—and the other women in this book—on this journey to make good of this momentous experience of infidelity in our lives.

I hope that you have found insights, encouragement, and strength in these pages. And most especially, I hope that you have been supported in deepening your connection to your own inner authority, authentic presence, and personal power. Know that every step you take in this direction is not for yourself alone, but also for your children and your children's children. Every shift in consciousness inevitably ripples out to touch everyone and everything around you.

I would love to hear, directly, how this book has impacted you on your journey. You can email me at meryn@afterhisaffairbook.com.

You can also email me to schedule a fifteen-minute complimentary call to explore how I might further support you with counseling or with an akashic reading. These sessions can broaden your perspective, deepen your understanding, and offer guidance and insights that are unique to your situation.

Please let others know about this book. Since it is such an important issue for so many of us, this book will lend itself well to book discussions and book clubs. Request a copy for your library. A review will be greatly appreciated.

With appreciation,

Meryn

# BIBLIOGRAPHY

Selected books cited in text:

Brown, Brené. *Daring Greatly: How the Courage to Be Vulnerable Transforms the Way We Live, Love, Parent and Lead.* Gotham Books, 2012

Cherlin, Andrew J. *The Marriage-Go-Round: The State of Marriage and the Family in America Today.* Random House, 2010

Chödrön, Pema. *The Places That Scare You: A Guide to Fearlessness in Difficult Times.* Shambhala Publications, 2007

Druckerman, Pamela. *Lust in Translation: Infidelity from Tokyo to Tennessee.* Penguin Books, 2008

Glass, Shirley P. *Not "Just Friends": Protect Your Relationship from Infidelity and Heal the Trauma of Betrayal.* The Free Press, 2003

Hendricks, Gay and Kathlyn. *Conscious Loving: The Journey to Co-Commitment.* Bantam, 1992

Johnson, Sue. *Hold Me Tight: Seven Conversations for a Lifetime of Love.* Little Brown, 2009

Jordan, Paul and Margaret. *Do I Have to Give Up Me to Be Loved by You?* Hazelden, 2002

Kent-Ferraro, Jay. *Affair Love vs. Authentic Love*

Levine, Stephen. *Healing Into Life and Death.* Anchor Pubs, 1989

Levine, Stephen. *Turning Toward the Mystery.* Harper One, 2002

Miller, Andrea. *Right Here With You: Bringing Mindful Awareness into Our Relationships.* Shambala, 2011

Myss, Caroline. *The Anatomy of Spirit.* Bantam Books, 1998

Nogales, Ana L. *Parents Who Cheat: How Children and Adults are Affected When Their Parents Are Unfaithful.* Health Communications, 2009

Ortman, Dennis Ph.D. *Transcending Post-Infidelity Stress Disorder.* Celestial Arts, 2011

Rinpoche, Sogyal. *The Tibetan Book of Living and Dying.* Harper San Francisco, 2012

Spring, Janis Abrahm. *After the Affair: Healing the Pain and Rebuilding Trust When a Partner Has Been Unfaithful.* William Morrow, 2012

Trungpa, Chogyam. *The Sacred Path of the Warrior.* Shambala Pubs, 1984

Wallerstein JS, Lewis, JM, and Blakeslee, S. *The Unexpected Legacy of Divorce: A 25-Year Landmark Study.* Hyperion, 2001

Wosick, Kassia. *Sex, Love, and Fidelity: A Study of Contemporary Romantic Relationships.* Cambria Press, 2012

# ABOUT THE AUTHOR

Meryn Callander was born in Portland, Australia, in 1952. She graduated from Monash University, Melbourne, with degrees in both economics and social work. At 25, she quit her position working with children in crisis, feeling she was doing little but applying Band-Aids to gaping wounds. Searching for that illusive something more, she headed to Europe, and then the U.S.

It was there she met John W. Travis, M.D., known to many as the founding father of wellness. Their marriage and professional partnership spanned almost three decades, during which time they pushed the leading edges of wellness—going well beyond the popular focus on nutrition and physical fitness, into the mental and emotional, interpersonal and spiritual dimensions of wellbeing. They co-authored several pioneering books on wellness, and facilitated seminars and retreats in the U.S. and internationally.

In 1993, Meryn became a mother. After decades of working in adult wellness, she gleaned a whole new appreciation of how profoundly our early years impact the wellbeing of the adults we become. In 1999 she co-founded, and served for several years as president of, the Alliance for Transforming the Lives of Children. The Alliance emerged from a core group of interdisciplinary experts dedicated to supporting caregivers, professionals, and policymakers in practicing the art and science of nurturing children.

*Why Dads Leave: Insights and Resources for When Partners Become Parents* (whydadsleave.com) grew out of their journey through the early years of parenting. While John stayed well beyond the challenges of those early years, their experiences compelled her to identify the dynamics underlying the epidemic of men leaving their families—physically or emotionally—soon after the birth of a child, and how couples can grow together rather than apart. The book offers insights and practical ways of preventing the devastating impact of this dynamic.

Her latest book, *After His Affair: Women Rising from the Ashes of Infidelity* is a reflection of her concern at the escalating rates of infidelity and the devastation that is left in its wake. How can we, as women, make good of our heartbreak? And how might we avoid—or heal from—the trauma of infidelity?

Meryn is a counselor, spiritual intuitive, and akashic reader.

# GRATITUDES

Gratitude extends first and foremost to my 21-year-old daughter, Siena Ariel. In a beautifully and skillfully orchestrated series of graceful moves, Siena went from reading the initial manuscript to becoming editor, proofer, interior designer, cover designer, website designer—and doing what was needed to get the manuscript in digital form to the printer, to Amazon, and even Kindle. It was far beyond what I—and I think she—ever imagined. Not only did I have the gift of her self-sourced expertise in all these areas, but also the pleasure and pride of collaborating with her on a book that is dear to both our hearts. This is a young woman who exemplifies one who emerges from deep disappointment—even devastation—with a deeply sourced strength and courage, and pure heart.

I must follow with the two women who are godmothers to my daughter, and have stood with me as needed, over the past three decades. These women were gifted to me on arrival in California, in 1977. This was the same night I met my husband-to-be, father of Siena. These women became my most immediate and enduring family in the U.S.—and through my return to Australia. Firstly, Bobbie Burdett, who recently, and with the courage and finesse that exemplified her living, passed over to the other side. She was an enduring voice of encouragement and support in the writing of this book. And Joy Holloway—forever a steady pillar of strength, inspiration, and Light. Joy forged her way through the very first rough draft of this book with the repeated exclamation, *"This book must be written."* Not an easy task—stumbling through rambling sentences and poor grammar—for a literary buff.

In addition, I have been blessed on my journey through the inevitable twists and turns, trials and tribulations of life with a phenomenal circle of women—each their own unique blend of wild, witty, courageous, creative, kind, and compassionate; and each generous in their love for me, and in their support for this book: Suzanne Arms, Ruth Burnell, Kristi Cowles, Pam Leo, Marilyn Milos, Cheryl Radetsky, Gaye Raymond, Lisa Reagan, and Kelly Wendorf. The fact that much of the time we are separated by many miles, and even oceans, speaks to the reach of the energy of the heart. Phone and Skype lines are an added bonus.

My gratitude extends also to those women who at some time and in some way over the several years of my writing this book, offered support, caring, encouragement, and resources: Lizi Beadman, Leslie Campbell, Jill Cheeks, Louise de Dassell, Jackie Dee, Grace Gawler, Evelyn Grewal, Kristin Griffey, Kim Griffith, Meg Hanshaw, Amelia Johnson, Meg Jordan, Julia Karas, Cathy Lanigan, Melissa Lord, Kate Luchetta, Kate Lynch, Pamela McDonald, Pat Meyer-Peterson, Elly Taylor, and Rachel Zinman-Jeanes.

And for those "real men" who similarly supported me at crucial time—each in their own time, and their own way—most especially Kent Peterson, and also Phillip Cornell and Jed Diamond.

Siena, too, would want to extend gratitude to our animals—Rosie and Jemma—who both comforted us and brought us such joy. While we have had to part with these magnificent creatures in recent years, they parted from us with such courage and dignity, and remain ever alive and loving in our hearts.

I also give thanks to my siblings, Berry and David and Del. And to my parents Bonnie and Wilbur, both passed over, for their still ever present love. And to the oceans and birds of Byron Shire, N.S.W., Australia; and the deep heart of Bali.

Finally and forever, deep gratitude to the Source that inspired, and drove to completion, my journey with this book.